Mortgage Loan Originator License Exam Prep

All-in-One Review and Testing to Pass the NMLS SAFE MLO Exam

First Edition

Stephen Mettling
Ellen Barski
Ryan Mettling

Performance Programs Company
6810 190th Street East
Bradenton, Florida 34211
www.performanceprogramscompany.com

Material in this book is not intended to represent legal advice and should not be so construed. Readers should consult legal counsel for advice regarding points of law.

© 2024 by Performance Programs Company
6810 190th Street East, Bradenton, FL 34211
info@performanceprogramscompany.com
www.performanceprogramscompany.com

ISBN 978-1955919807

Contents

Introduction

Welcome licensee candidates and future MLO professionals!

We know you have worked hard just to get here – you have completed or nearly completed your pre-license curricula, and now all you have to do is pass the license exam. But, admittedly, easier said than done. That is where we at Performance Programs Company come in. We know the exam can be tough, and very nerve-wracking to prepare for. That's why we created aur *Mortgage Loan Originator License Exam Prep (MOLEP)* the way we did. Since we have been developing and publishing real estate curriculum programs and products for forty years, we know how all this works – or fails to work. And let us assure you – you have made the right decision acquiring this publication to prepare for your MLO exam. Our content and organization streamline and reinforce the learning process.

As you will see, the MOLEP is comprehensive in that it contains both key content review and testing practice. The text review specifically follows the MLO National Test outline as promulgated by NMLS testing officials. This outline sets the standard for content coverage, test section weighting, and, essentially, what is on the MLO test.

A word about the MOLEP's organization. Consistent with the promulgated NMLS license examination outline, the main sections of the exam prep cover:

> Federal Mortgage Related Laws
> General Mortgage Knowledge
> Mortgage Loan Origination Activities
> Ethics
> Uniform State Content

Following each major section is a chapter-end quiz to test your mastery of the subject material. This is further reinforced by explanations in the Answer Key to each chapter quiz. Exam candidates should also note that all content to our exam prep is tersely presented in bullet point lists. We make every effort to present only the essential material that you need to learn the test outline subjects.

Finally, our MOLEP challenges candidates to take and pass two 100-item practice tests covering the entire test outline. Again, each practice test comes with an answer key and explanation.

Taken as a whole, if you learn the content in our exam prep resource, we know you will pass the MLO license examination. Testing officials went into great detail outlining what would be presented in the MLO license exam. And we went to great lengths to explain all this content in our publication.

So, at this point, it's all up to you. There's a lot of material to be learned in our text's 100 some-odd pages. And it will take some real concentration and hard work to prepare for this examination. There are no guarantees of passing, and don't be fooled by those who would say otherwise. But we are also very confident that, with focused studying and preparation, you will be successful! So good luck!

About the authors

Stephen Mettling. For over fifty years, Stephen Mettling has been actively engaged in real estate education. Beginning with Dearborn Publishing in 1972, then called Real Estate Education Company, Mr. Mettling managed the company's textbook division and author acquisitions. Subsequently he built up the company's real estate school division which eventually became the country's largest real estate, insurance and securities school network in the country. In 1978, Mr. Mettling founded Performance Programs Company, a custom training program publishing and development company specializing in commercial, industrial, and corporate real estate. Over time, Performance Programs Company narrowed its focus to real estate textbook and exam prep publishing. Currently the Company's texts and prelicense resources are used in hundreds of schools in over 48 states. Mr. Mettling has authored over 100 textbooks, real estate prelicense programs and exam prep manuals.

Ellen Barski. Ellen Barski has enjoyed a career as a writer, editor, and content developer for close to 30 years, the last eight of which have been in real estate-related education. She has written and developed pre-license, post-license, test prep, and continuing education courses in multiple states. Ellen takes great pride in empowering aspiring and seasoned professionals alike, guiding them towards achieving their career goals with confidence and expertise.

Ryan Mettling. As President and publisher of Performance Programs Company, Ryan Mettling is an accomplished online curriculum designer, author and textbook developer specializing in real estate, license training, and exam prep manuals. To date, Ryan has managed the development and all revision work for our 65-title product line involving author recruitment, product design, executive management, production, printing and marketing. Mr. Mettling graduated Valedictorian from the University of Central Florida's College of Business Administration in 2012.

MLO Essential Key Point Review

Section I: Federal Mortgage Related Laws

- ➢ **Real Estate Settlement Procedures Act (RESPA)**

- ➢ **Equal Credit Opportunity Act (ECOA)**

- ➢ **Truth in Lending Act (TILA); Regulation Z**

- ➢ **TILA-RESPA Integrated Disclosure Rule (TRID)**

- ➢ **Other Federal Laws and Guidelines**

    - **Home Mortgage Disclosure Act**

    - **Fair Credit Reporting Act**

    - **FTC Red Flags Rule**

    - **Bank Secrecy Act/ Anti-Money Laundering**

    - **Gramm-Leach-Billey Act**

    - **Mortgage Acts and Practices; Advertising (Reg N)**

    - **Electronic Signatures (E-SIGN Act)**

    - **USA Patriot Act**

    - **Homeowners Protection Act**

    - **Dodd-Frank Act**

- ➢ **Regulatory Authority**

    - **Consumer Financial Protection Bureau**

    - **Department of Housing and Urban Development**

Real Estate Settlement Procedures Act (RESPA)

➢ **RESPA legislation**

- federal statute enacted in 1974; enforced and regulated by Consumer Financial Protection Bureau (CFPB)
- Regulation X: rules for RESPA compliance

➢ **Purposes of RESPA**

- requires advance disclosure of financing costs to consumer
- enables consumers to make informed decisions on financing alternatives, housing affordability
- prohibits / minimizes unlawful or unethical business practices, e.g., kickbacks, referral fees, undisclosed compensation, etc.

➢ **Definition of a mortgage broker**

- "a person that renders origination services and serves as an intermediary between a borrower and a lender in a transaction"
    - under RESPA, mortgage brokers are required to disclose fees and costs to borrower

➢ **RESPA-applicable loan types**

- RESPA applies to federally related mortgage loans secured by 1- to 4-unit residential property, including loans:
    - insured or guaranteed by federal government (FHA, VA, USDA)
    - made by federally regulated lenders, or whose deposits are federally insured, or who loan more than $1,000,000 per year
    - intended to be sold to Fannie Mae or Freddie Mac
- includes home purchase, home improvement loans, refinances
- home equity loans, home equity lines of credit, reverse mortgages
- approved loan assumptions

➢ **RESPA prohibitions**

- RESPA **prohibitions** include:
    - receiving or giving any sort of compensation (e.g., kickback, fee split, unearned fee) for a referral in a mortgage transaction without any actual service having been performed
    - requiring buyers to use a particular settlement company as a condition of sale
    - mandating excessive escrow account obligations for borrowers
- lenders may only require an escrow account per government loan program stipulation
    - required monthly escrow deposits for borrowers cannot exceed 1/12 of annual estimated payment for taxes, insurance, and other impounds plus a cushion, which cannot exceed 1/6 (or about two months) of total amount of items paid out of escrow account each year

- *example*: annual escrow needed to pay taxes, insurance, etc. = $1,200, therefore
  - borrower's monthly escrow payment cannot exceed $100/month
  - escrow cushion cannot be more than $200 (1/6, i.e., two months, of annual payments)

➢ **RESPA** loan **exemptions**
  - business, commercial, or agricultural loans
  - loans for vacant lots
  - loans for 25 acres or more
  - temporary loans (e.g., construction loans)
  - secondary market transactions
  - assumptions that <u>do not</u> require lender approval
  - loan conversions

➢ **Settlement services requiring RESPA compliance**
  - providers must comply with RESPA requirements when rendering services in connection with a transaction, including:
    - loan origination of a federally related mortgage loan -- services include loan document preparation, loan processing, credit reporting, underwriting, and funding
    - mortgage brokerage services such as counseling, arranging a loan between borrower and lender, assisting with communications between borrower and lender
    - real estate agent or broker services
    - escrow account management
    - title services, searches, abstracts, surveys, commitments, title insurance policies
    - attorney's services related to real estate transaction
    - appraisals
    - mortgage insurance; hazard, flood, casualty insurance; home and other warranties
    - property tax related services
    - settlement document preparation; document notarization and recordation

➢ **Required borrower information on application (Regulation X)**
  - basic required information for a loan application includes:
    - borrower's name
    - Social Security number for credit report
    - property address
    - property's estimated value
    - borrower's monthly income
    - desired loan amount

➢ **Foreclosure processes**
  - lenders' **first notice of default** can only be sent when:
    - borrower is 120 days delinquent on payments, OR
    - borrower violated a due-on-sale clause, OR
    - another lienholder began foreclosure action

- **pre-foreclosure period**: borrower may submit a loss mitigation application for lender review to evaluate whether borrower qualifies for any foreclosure alternative

- three foreclosure types: **judicial foreclosure** (a court action / proceeding); **non-judicial foreclosure** with no court action but **with public notice** or document recording requirement, but no court action; and **non-judicial foreclosure with no court proceeding** and no public notice or document recording requirement

- **short sale**: agreement in lieu of foreclosure between lender and borrower in which property is sold for less than principal balance; if no sale results, title is conveyed to lender and property becomes an REO (real estate owned) asset of the lender

> **RESPA disclosure requirements**

- **three disclosure documents** given to borrowers within three business days of receiving or preparing a loan application with basic required information (borrower's name, Social Security number, monthly income, desired loan amount, property address, and property's estimated value):

  o **Loan Estimate**: details estimated interest rates, monthly payments, and total closing costs

  o **Mortgage Servicing Disclosure Statement**: informs borrower of lender's intent to service loan or transfrer it to another lender

  o CFPB's **Home Loan Toolkit** booklet: required for home purchase loans only

- other RESPA-required disclosures:

  o **Affiliated Business Arrangement Disclosure**: used when lender has an arrangement with another service provider involved in transaction (insurance company, title company, etc.); disclosure provided within three business days of application whenever lender requires borrowers to use a specific affiliate

  o **Closing Disclosure**: finalizes loan terms, closing costs, and other fees; provided to borrower at least three business days before closing

  o **Servicing Transfer Statement**: notifies borrower that lender is transferring loan servicing rights to another entity; provided 15 or fewer days before transfer occurs

- Other RESPA escrow-related regulations

  o **initial escrow statement for borrower**: itemized accounting of all escrow items to be paid from account in the first year; provided at closing or within 45 days of opening escrow account

  o **annual escrow statement**: reviews past year's escrow account activity; details how funds were used; projects coming year's expenses; notes any changes to monthly payment

- o **escrow shortage**
    - if escrow balance is less than one month's escrow payment, lender can require borrower to repay it within 30 days

    - if more than one month's escrow payment, borrower can repay over 12+ months

- o **escrow surplus**: if $50 or more, surplus must be returned to borrower within 30 days of discovery

Equal Credit Opportunity Act (ECOA) (Reg B)

➤ **Purpose; primary thrust of ECOA**

- prohibits discriminatory practices in granting or denying credit
- applies to applicants as well as any co-signers

➤ **Protected classes.** The following classes of people are specifically protected by the anti-discrimination provisions of ECOA:

- race
- religion
- nationality
- ethnicity
- sex
- marital status
- age (party must have capacity to enter into a legally binding contract)
- those who receive public assistance benefits

➤ **Three types of discrimination**

- **overt**: explicit or obvious discrimination

- **disparate treatment**: treating members of a protected class differently from other classes

- **disparate impact**: a policy or practice appears nondiscriminatory but affects members of a protected class negatively in disproportionate numbers; illegal even when unintentional

➤ **Loan denial criteria.** The following are legitimate, non-discriminatory rationales for denying credit to an applicant:

- insufficient income
- poor credit history, lack of credit history, poor credit score
- high debt-to-income ratio
- inadequate collateral for a secured loan, e.g., property has insufficient value
- unstable employment or lack of employment history
- immigration status, but only as it relates to ability to repay loan

- ➢ **Regulation B, notice of adverse action**

  - federal regulation instituted to protect applicants from discrimination in credit process
  - **adverse action**: negative action related to credit application denial or alteration, e.g., refusing to grant credit as requested in application (loan amount or terms)
  - Reg B notice requirements for adverse action apply to completed credit applications, incomplete applications, existing credit accounts
  - action notice requirements include

    - notice of action taken provided to borrower within 30 days
    - must include: reason, creditor name and address, credit information, credit reporting agency (when credit history is the basis), ECOA notice of discrimination prohibition

- ➢ **Application denial—required disclosures upon denial**

  - reason for denial or statement informing applicant of right to request reason for denial
  - specific reasons for denial, e.g., employment history, income, credit score, etc.
  - negative credit report details
  - right to receive a copy of lender's property appraisal, if applicable, e.g., unfavorable value of collateral property
  - reasons for less favorable terms, if lender offers any

- ➢ **Information required on credit application**

  - includes questions regarding creditworthiness

    - when not all information is submitted, lender may send notice of incompleteness within 30 days of incomplete application receipt, including submission deadline
    - when deadline passes with no applicant response, incomplete application will be closed

  - includes race, gender, and ethnicity questions

    - applicants do not have to answer
    - lenders check box "Did not wish to furnish"

- ➢ **Acceptable income for loan review**

  - income includes part-time work compensation, alimony, Social Security payments, public assistance, pensions, etc.

  - applicants are not required to list alimony, child support, or other maintenance as income

- ➢ **Creditworthiness**

  - ECOA does not specify explicit credit analysis guidelines.

  - permitted analysis methods include creditor judgment, credit scoring, etc.

- **prohibited considerations**: family status, lack of telephone listing, excluding part-time income

---

Truth in Lending Act (TILA) (Reg Z)

➤ **Purpose of TILA**

- ensures consumers receive clear, understandable information about costs and terms of loans before they enter into a credit agreement

- promotes informed use of consumer credit, e.g., household, family, or personal purposes

- requires disclosure of terms and costs; includes interest rates, amount financed, total payments, and payment schedule disclosures

➤ **Loans covered under TILA**

- **personal use loans with a minimum of four installment payments**: residential mortgage loans, home equity loans, home equity lines of credit, credit cards, personal loans, auto loans, retail installment sales, short-term loans, e.g., payday loans

- does <u>not</u> apply to commercial or business loans

➤ **Definitions**

- **APR, or annual percentage rate:** total cost to borrower for borrowing principal amount; includes interest rates and any other finance-related costs such as points, broker fees, and loan closing costs; **does NOT include appraisal, credit reporting, or inspection costs**

- **finance charge**: any fee, paid directly or indirectly, to obtain credit

- **dwelling**: residential structure consisting of one, two, three, or four dwelling units

- **residential mortgage loan**: a secured loan, i.e., backed by property itself as collateral, to finance purchase or refinance of a residential property

➤ **Notice of right to rescind**

- **right to rescind**: a consumer protection that gives borrowers the right to cancel a loan transaction within a specific time period, typically three business days; without penalty or obligation; only pertains to refinancing loans and home equity loans

- **notice requirements**: after closing, lender must provide borrower with TILA-required disclosures and two copies of a notice explaining right to rescind. Notice includes:

  o Statement of the Right to Rescind

13

- o specific instructions on how to exercise right to rescind

  - o explanation of what happens if borrower exercises this right

  - **three business day rule**: three-day rescission period starts the day after all lending conditions are met, i.e., the loan closes, the rescission notice is delivered, and all TILA disclosures are received

➢ **Seller contributions to buyer**

- seller contributions may be used for closing costs, pre-paid expenses, or discount points; they may NOT be used for down payments
- limits apply depending on loan type:

  - o conventional loan, primary resident:
    - ▪ less than 10% down: 3% max
    - ▪ 10-25% down: 6% max
    - ▪ 25% down or more: 9% max
  - o conventional, investment property: 2% max
  - o FHA and USDA loans: 6% max
  - o VA loan: 4% of sales price plus reasonable and customary loan costs

➢ **HOEPA; high-cost mortgages**

- Home Ownership and Equity Protection Act (HOEPA): 1994 amendment to TILA; enforced by CFPB
- applies to high-cost mortgages, i.e., high APRs, high points and fees:

  - o first mortgage with APR exceeding Average Prime Offer Rate (APOR) by 6.5 points or more
  - o second mortgage with APR exceeding APOR by 8.5 points or more
  - o total closing costs, fees, and points exceed 5% of total loan amount threshold adjusted annually for inflation
  - o total closing costs, fees, and points exceed either 8% of loan amount less than annual set amount OR dollar amount adjusted annually, whichever is less

- relevant to certain transactions besides high-cost mortgages, e.g., refinances and home equity loans with same lender as original loan; open-end credit plans and reverse mortgages; loans secured by borrower's primary residence

➢ **Higher-priced mortgages**

- loans secured by borrower's primary residence and APR exceeds APOR by at least:

  - o 1.5 percentage points for first mortgages
  - o 3.5 percentage points for subsequent mortgages

- does not apply to HELOCs, construction loans, reverse mortgages, bridge loans of fewer than 12 months, manufactured home loans

➢ **Mortgage Loan Originator (MLO) compensation**

- applies to compensation for activities such as:

  - o taking an application
  - o working with consumer to obtain or apply for residential mortgage credit

- offering, obtaining, or negotiating consumer credit for another person
- representing or advertising that the MLO does any of above activities

- **permitted** compensation types/terms include:
  - salary or set hourly wages
  - fixed percentage of loan amount; cannot vary with loan terms
  - flat fee per transaction; does not vary based on loan amount or other terms
  - bonuses and profit-sharing plans, retirement plans; cannot be tied to specific loan terms
  - amount based on percentage of applications that close successfully
  - payment for tasks not specifically related to loan origination

- **prohibited** compensation includes compensation based on:
  - interest rate or other loan terms
  - steering borrowers to loans with higher interest rates, prepayment penalties, or less favorable terms, OR to affiliated businesses
  - volume, e.g., total number of loans originated or total loan volume produced
  - loan or loan pool profitability
  - splitting fees with parties other than loan originators

TILA RESPA Integrated Disclosure Rule (TRID) "Know Before You Owe"

➤ **Purpose of TRID**

- simplifies and streamlines mortgage process for both lenders and borrowers

- enhances consumer understanding of mortgage loan terms

- standardizes required disclosures to help reduce confusion arising from different lender forms. Key standardizations include

  - **the Loan Estimate**: clearly states loan terms and estimated fees

  - **the Closing Disclosure**: provides actual closing costs; can vary from Loan Estimate

- helps borrowers make better informed decisions when choosing a lender/product

- provides clearer guidelines for lenders on what information needs to be disclosed and when

➤ **Loans covered**

- TRID is primarily focused on residential mortgage loans, including

  - fixed rate and adjustable rate mortgages

  - FHA, VA, and USDA loans

- loans not impacted by TRID:
    - reverse mortgages
    - HELOCs (home equity line of credit)
    - loans secured by a residence that is not attached to real property (e.g., a mobile home)
    - loans made by an entity that lends five or fewer mortgages annually

➢ **The Loan Estimate: facts; required information; charges/fees**

- designed to help borrowers understand key features, costs, and risks of a mortgage before they commit

- form details include:
    - **loan terms**: best estimate of loan amount, interest rate, monthly payment, any prepayment penalty or balloon payment
    - **projected payments**: payment calculation for principal, interest, mortgage insurance, and estimated escrow
    - **closing costs**: estimate of total closing costs and amount of cash needed to close, including calculations
    - **comparisons**: information that helps borrower one loan's costs with other loans, including total payments over five years, principal paid in five years, and Annual Percentage Rate (APR)
    - **other considerations**: important aspects like appraisal requirements, homeowner's insurance requirements, late payment fees, refinancing options, and whether loan is assumable

- Disclosed charges and fees include:
    - loan costs: origination charges, services you cannot shop for, and services you can shop for

        - services that cannot be shopped for: appraisal fee, credit report fee, and flood determination fee; generally set by lender and non-negotiable

        - services that can be shopped: inspection fees, title service fees, and survey fees

    - estimated property taxes, government recording fees, insurance costs, and other prepaids

    - initial escrow costs

➢ **Definition of loan consummation**

- point at which borrower becomes contractually obligated to lender on loan

- refers to borrower's agreement to loan terms

- **not** the same as closing, or settlement, which includes completion of all transactions involved in the conveyance, including transfer of property ownership

- ➤ **Special information booklet**

  - part of TRID's required disclosures along with Loan Estimate; aka settlement costs booklet

  - helps familiarize borrowers with homebuying and mortgage process

  - covers information such as: home buying steps, mortgage process, fees, and disclosures

- ➤ **Closing Disclosure**

  - breaks down final loan costs and terms
  - includes:
    - o final interest rate, APR, and total cost of loan
    - o monthly payment
    - o closing costs and cash to close
    - o total interest paid over life of loan
    - o late payment penalties, any prepayment penalty, negative amortization
    - o loan assumption permission, if any

- ➤ **Disclosure timing**

  - **Loan Estimate**: provided to borrower no more than 3 days after lender receives borrower's loan application and no fewer than 7 days prior to loan consummation

  - **revised Loan Estimates** must be provided within 3 days of new or altered information and no fewer than 4 days prior to consummation

  - **Closing Disclosure**: provided 3 days before loan consummation, not including Sundays and federal holidays

- ➤ **MLO actions if TRID disclosure is incomplete**

  - once discovered, missing items on Loan Estimate must be requested immediately
  - borrower must provide requested information immediately

- ➤ **"Change of circumstances"**

  - situations under TRID in which a lender can issue a revised Loan Estimate, including:
    - o extraordinary events beyond anyone involved in transaction's control, e.g., a natural disaster that requires another appraisal
    - o changed consumer requests, e.g., larger loan amount, different loan products, etc.
    - o information lender relied on to render a decision has changed, e.g., borrower's employment
    - o changes based on borrower's locking in an interest rate that was previously floating, e.g., altered fees
    - o new information relevant to loan's terms or costs is discovered after LE is issued

o borrower does not express an intent to proceed with loan within 10 business days after LE is delivered

- lenders may revise only those charges affected by changed circumstances

- original LE for data will no longer apply unless lender issues a revised LE in which settlement costs are reduced

- revised LE must be mailed or provided to borrower within 3 business days after lender learns of changed circumstances

- revised LEs cannot be received by borrowers on the same day or after they receive Closing Disclosure; instead, lender must revise CD and not LE

➤ **Information that must be provided to consumers upon request**

- consumer-requested changes that alter LE require disclosure of results and impact on revised LE

➤ **Borrower's right of rescission**

- borrower may cancel a refinance or home equity loan "no questions asked" within a period of 3 business days after closing

- does NOT apply to home purchase loans

➤ **Annual escrow statement**

- purpose: apprises borrowers of differences between estimates for property taxes and insurance and actual amounts paid monthly
- annual escrow account reassessments determine if escrow amounts should be increased or decreased, based on actual expenditures
- annual escrow statement alerts borrowers to necessary changes for coming year

Other Federal Laws and Guidelines

➤ **Home Mortgage Disclosure Act (HMDA)**

- **purpose**: to ensure fair and equitable access to housing finance and to combat discriminatory lending practices such as redlining; adopted in 1975

    o **redlining**: arbitrarily denying mortgage loan applications in certain geographical areas without considering an applicant's qualifications

- HMDA requires mortgage lenders to collect, report, and publicly disclose housing-related lending activity data, including:

    o home acquisition loans, home improvement loans, and refinances
    o loan applications that do not result in origination, were denied, or withdrawn
    o applicants' race, ethnicity, sex, income, assets, loan type and amount, etc.

- **Answering demographic questions**: under HMDA, eliciting demographic data helps to ensure fair lending compliance and identifies potential discrimination patterns, however applicants have right to not answer personal demographic questions

➤ **Fair Credit Reporting Act (FCRA) / Fair and Accurate Credit Transactions Act (FACTA)**

- **purpose of the Acts**: ensure accuracy, fairness, and privacy in collecting, sharing, and using consumer credit information to make lending decisions

- FCRA and FACTA provisions limit lenders to requesting credit information for loan applicants who have authorized such a request

- requires lenders to notify applicants in writing when taking an adverse action based on credit report information
  - **adverse action as relates to FCRA**: an unfavorable decision against an applicant based in whole or part on credit information
  - notice must include reporting credit bureau's name, address, and toll-free phone number
  - adverse information to remain on consumer credit report for 7 years only; chapter 7 bankruptcies for 10 years from filing date

- other permitted purposes for accessing a consumer's credit report include employment purposes, insurance underwriting, other legitimate business need, e.g., court orders, investor considerations, assessing a business partnership risk, etc.

- requires credit bureaus to issue individual credit reports for free every 12 months, upon request

- provides for placing three types of fraud alerts on consumer credit files to help guard against identity theft and fraud:
  - one-call (initial): for individuals who believe they may be a victim of fraud or identity theft; lasts for 1 year and can be renewed
  - extended: for victims of actual identity theft who have a police report or a Federal Trade Commission Identity Theft Report; lasts for 7 years
  - active duty: for military personnel on active duty; lasts for one year but can be renewed
  - creditors required to clear fraud alerts before extending credit

- enables consumer to place a credit freeze on their credit reports, making reports inaccessible to lenders unless consumer lifts freeze; protects against fraud and identity theft

➤ **FTC Red Flags Rule**

- part of FACTA; designed to combat identity theft; applies to financial institutions and creditors; requires a written identity theft prevention program be implemented
- programs to include procedures to identify "red flags" in everyday operations, i.e., signs of identity theft, such as:
  - discrepancies in account or credit report information
  - alerts, notifications, and warnings from a credit bureau
  - unusual account activity

- o suspicious documents or personally identifying information
- o fraud alerts on a consumer report
- o attempted use of suspicious account application documents
- programs also to include appropriate actions to address red flags
- two types of covered accounts:
  - o accounts primarily for personal, family, or household purposes that involve multiple payments or transactions, e.g., credit card accounts, mortgage loans, vehicle loans, checking/savings accounts, or utilities accounts
  - o any other account that poses a reasonably foreseeable risk of identity theft, e.g., small business accounts, sole proprietorship accounts, or single transaction accounts

➤ Bank Secrecy Act/Anti-Money Laundering (BSA/AML)

- purpose: established to detect, report, and prevent money laundering and other financial crimes
- requires financial institutions to keep detailed records and file reports such as Currency Transaction Report (CTR) for transactions exceeding $10,000
- mandates due diligence for financial institutions, e.g., Know Your Customer processes to verify clients' identity and assess potential risks of illegal intentions
- Suspicious Activity Reports (SARs): filed with Financial Crimes Enforcement Network when institutions suspect suspicious activity that might indicate money laundering, fraud, terrorist funding, tax evasion, or other criminal activities
- SARs alert authorities about activity that may require an investigation, such as:
  - o suspicious activity: unusual transaction patterns, sudden and unexplained influx of funds, transactions structured to evade reporting requirements, etc.
  - o typical thresholds:
    - ▪ insider abuse: any amount
    - ▪ transactions with a suspect: $5,000 or more
    - ▪ transactions without a suspect: $25,000 or more
    - ▪ suspicious activity that indicates money laundering: $5,000 or more
  - o institutions can file for lower amounts if activity is deemed suspicious
- timing to file: no more than 30 days after initial detection
- retention: financial institutions to keep reports and documentation for 5 years
- privacy: institutions may not alert individuals being investigated

➤ Gramm-Leach-Billey Act

- purpose: protects consumers' personal financial information; requires financial institutions to explain how they will share and protect such information

- requires financial institutions to provide customers with a written privacy notice when customer relationship is established and annually thereafter

- privacy notice explains:
  - o what personally identifiable information is collected about the customer
  - o where this information is shared
  - o how it is used
  - o how it is protected
  - o opt-out options

- privacy notice may be sent electronically when specifically requested by consumers in writing

- financial institutions required to develop, implement, and maintain comprehensive information security programs to protect customer information

- **National Do-Not-Call Registry purpose**: protects consumers from unwanted phone solicitations
    - limits telemarketing calls
    - consumers may join list online for free
    - telemarketers required to check list at least once every 31 days

    - exemptions include:
        - charities and non-profits
        - surveys or political polls
        - business with an existing relationship with a customer (18-month call window)

    - consumers may file complaints with FTC

    - potential penalties for telemarketers in violation: up to $16,000 per incident

- **Mortgage Acts and Practices—Advertising (Reg N)**
    - part of FTC's rules established to govern mortgage advertising through any medium, such as print, online, broadcast, direct mail, etc.

    - prohibits misrepresentations about terms of any mortgage credit product, including:
        - mortgage fee type and amounts
        - loan amount, payments, or terms
        - taxes and insurance
        - mortgage type
        - interest rate details
        - loan approval details

    - requires clear, concise, specific wording in ads related to APR, repayment terms, down payment amounts

    - ads related to any sort of credit required to include terms that are easily available to public

    - **triggering terms** require additional disclosure details and include: down payments, number of payments, loan term, finance charges, such as:
        - specific down payment amounts or percentages
        - actual repayments terms, i.e., specific number of payments or repayment period
        - use of term "annual percentage rate" and whether that rate may increase
        - amount of any finance charge

    - non-triggering terms: general statements or descriptions about mortgage loans that do not include specific financial details

➢ **Electronic Signatures (E-SIGN ACT)**

- purpose: gives electronic signatures same legal standing as traditional handwritten signatures; enacted in 2000
- ensures legal effect and enforceability of electronic contracts and electronic signatures
- applies to transactions in interstate and foreign commerce
- requires consumers' explicit consent to use electronic records and signatures
- requires electronic records to reflect the agreement correctly and be properly stored and retrievable so they are readily accessible to all parties involved
- exceptions: electronic signatures not valid with wills, divorce documents, and certain court documents

➢ **USA PATRIOT ACT**

- acronym for "Uniting and Strengthening America by Providing Appropriate Tools Required to Intercept and Obstruct Terrorism Act"
- a significant legislative response to terrorist attacks of September 11, 2001
- purpose: introduced measures to enhance national security and prevent future terrorist activities
- broad and complex, encompassing numerous provisions to enhance due diligence across various areas of law and policy:
  - expands governmental authority to monitor phone and email communications, collect bank and credit reporting records, and track activity of suspected terrorists through more lenient search warrant requirements
  - makes it easier to detain and deport immigrants suspected of terrorism-related acts
  - includes significant measures to prevent and prosecute international money laundering and financing of terrorism
  - breaks down barriers between intelligence and law enforcement agencies, allowing them to share information more freely
  - ramps up requirements for financial institutions to prevent, detect, and report money laundering activities

  - requires financial institutions to verify customers' identity, understand their customers' businesses, and report any suspicious activity via:
    - implementing a customer identification program to collect name, date of birth, address, and identification number (e.g., Social Security number) and verify details
    - performing additional scrutiny for certain customers, e.g., digging deeper into customer's background, understanding transaction's purpose, and closely monitoring account activity
    - filing a Suspicious Activity Report (SAR) when dubious activity is suspected
    - maintaining verification process and transaction records for five years

- necessitates regular training for MLOs and other staff in financial institutions to be up to date on latest requirements and compliance procedures

➢ **Homeowners Protection Act**

- **purpose: protect homebuyers from excessive private mortgage insurance (PMI) charges**, ensuring they do not pay PMI longer than necessary; enacted 1998

- addresses PMI cancellation conditions

- **PMI**: typically required by lenders when a homebuyer makes a down payment of less than 20% of home's purchase price

- key provisions include:
  - automatic termination: PMI automatically terminated when mortgage balance reaches 78% of home's original value, as long as payments are current
  - borrower-requested termination: can be done when mortgage balance falls to 80% of home's original value
  - lenders' initial disclosure: provide to borrowers PMI details, e.g., cost, cancellation policies, and borrower's rights
  - annual disclosure: statement sent to borrowers detailing rights to cancel and requirements for cancellation

> **Dodd-Frank Wall Street Reform and Consumer Protection Act (Dodd-Frank Act)**
  - enacted in July 2010 in response to 2008 financial crisis
  - most comprehensive changes to financial regulation since Great Depression
  - established Consumer Financial Protection Bureau (CFPB); responsible for:
    - protecting consumers in financial sector
    - overseeing financial products and services
    - ensuring banks, lenders, and other financial institutions treat consumers fairly

  - created Financial Stability Oversight Council (FSOC)
    - identify risks to nation's financial stability
    - promote market discipline
    - respond to emerging risks to national financial system's stability

  - instituted Volcker Rule: restricts banks from making certain kinds of speculative investments that do not benefit their customers; protects consumers from banks taking on too much risk

  - provided greater incentives and protections for whistleblowers who report securities law violations to Securities and Exchange Commission (SEC)

  - introduced new mortgage lending standards and processes to avoid risky lending practices that contributed to housing bubble and crash in 2008, such as:
    - ability-to-repay requirements, e.g., setting minimum underwriting requirements for residential mortgages, except HELOCs, reverse mortgages, temporary financing, timeshare loans, etc.
      - requires lenders to use verified and documented information to determine whether a consumer has a reasonable ability to repay a loan as well as taxes, insurance, and assessments
      - gives borrowers **private right of action**, i.e., they can sue creditors when they realize they cannot afford their loan *and* they feel creditor did not properly determine their ability to repay
    - a standard for **qualified mortgages**, i.e., standards that mortgages must meet to be considered safer and easier for consumers to understand

- less risky for both lender and borrower
- designed to reduce likelihood of default
  - o new disclosure requirements

- **Dodd Frank set rules for MLO compensation to eliminate incentives for MLOs to steer borrowers into higher-cost or riskier loans;** prohibits compensation based on terms of loan

- **steering**: when an MLO or lending institution directs a borrower to a certain loan product to increase compensation even though that loan is "not in the consumer's interest"

- **limiting pre-payment penalties**
  - o may not last more than 3 years on a residential mortgage
  - o cannot exceed 2% of outstanding balance if loan paid off in first 2 years, OR 1% if loan paid off in third year
  - o prohibited on ARMs, high-cost mortgage loans, and higher priced mortgage loans

- increased regulatory oversight and standards for large banks and financial institutions, e.g., higher capital requirements, enhanced risk management standards, and more rigorous supervision

- requires large financial companies to develop plans in case of financial distress

- establishes an orderly process for liquidating financial companies that pose a significant risk to the United States' financial stability

Regulatory Authority

➢ **Consumer Financial Protection Bureau (CFPB)**

- **purpose: protects consumers** in the financial sector via revised provisions in mortgage products

- **regulates and supervises banks**, credit unions, and other financial companies, including mortgage lenders, servicers, and brokers

- creates and enforces rules that govern the mortgage industry to **protect consumers from unfair, deceptive, or abusive practices**

- ensures financial entities comply with federal consumer financial laws

- provides a **platform for consumers to file complaints** about issues they encounter with financial products

- works to **educate consumers** about their rights and financial products

- **offers consumers resources** including guides, calculators, and other tools to help consumers understand mortgage terms, choose best options, and avoid unfair practices

- enforces laws and regulations by investigating companies, conducting examinations, and taking **legal action for violations of consumer financial laws**

- collects and publishes data on consumer financial products and services, including mortgages

- works in conjunction with other federal and state agencies to ensure cohesive regulatory environment

- **Department of Housing and Urban Development (HUD)**
  - established in 1965 as a cabinet-level federal agency to address housing issues, particularly in context of urban renewal and development

  - oversees aspects of housing market and mortgage lending, with a strong focus on **fair practices and affordable housing**

  - goals: increase homeownership and access to affordable housing, rid housing industry of discrimination, and support community development

  - **Federal Housing Authority**, an agency within HUD: primary role is to insure mortgages made by approved lenders, which:
    - protects lenders against losses in case a borrower defaults on a mortgage
    - enables more Americans, especially first-time homebuyers and those with lower incomes, to access home financing
    - insures mortgages for buyers who might not qualify for conventional loans (lower down payments or less-than-perfect credit scores)
    - expands homeownership opportunities for a significant portion of population

  - sets **standards for residential construction** and underwriting, and ensures compliance with federal housing laws

  - enforces Fair Housing Act: **prohibits discrimination in housing** and mortgage lending based on race, color, religion, sex, national origin, disability, or family status by:
    - investigating complaints
    - conducting compliance reviews
    - taking action against violators

  - administers programs for **housing rehabilitation**; supports low-income individuals with housing assistance

  - provides grants to **support housing and services for the homeless**; assists in rebuilding communities affected by natural disasters

Section I Quiz: Federal Mortgage-Related Laws

1.1   Which entity enforces and regulates the Real Estate Settlement Procedures Act (RESPA)?

     a. Federal Housing Administration (FHA)
     b. Consumer Financial Protection Bureau (CFPB)
     c. Federal Trade Commission (FTC)
     d. Department of Housing and Urban Development (HUD)

1.2   Which of these identifies the rules for RESPA compliance?

     a. Regulation Z
     b. Regulation B
     c. Regulation X
     d. Regulation A

1.3   Which of the following is a primary purpose of RESPA?

     a. Requires advance disclosure of financing costs to consumers
     b. Sets non-discrimination rules and regulations
     c. Promotes consumer education regarding available loan products
     d. Protects consumers' right of rescission

1.4   Which of the following describes a mortgage broker?

     a. A lender's employee who services a loan for a borrower
     b. An agent of the buyer who helps that buyer decide on the best loan option
     c. A financial institution or entity that underwrites a loan and provides funds to a borrower
     d. An individual other than a lender's employee who acts as a go-between for a borrower and a lender

1.5   Per RESPA, which of the following is a feature of a federally related mortgage loan?

     a. Non-conforming
     b. Insured or guaranteed by the federal government
     c. Will not be sold to Fannie Mae or Freddie Mac
     d. Made by a lender that loans more than $500,000 annually

1.6   Borrower Stan's estimated annual escrow amount for taxes and insurance is $2,436. That means his monthly escrow payment, excluding any funds for a cushion, cannot exceed

     a. $100.
     b. $203.
     c. $243.60.
     d. $406.

1.7   RESPA's requirements would apply to which of the following loans?

     a. A loan to purchase a 10-unit apartment building
     b. A loan to purchase a retail property
     c. A loan to purchase unimproved vacant land
     d. A loan to purchase a residential duplex

1.8 Assuming all RESPA conditions are met, which one of the following scenarios illustrates a legal compensation arrangement related to a mortgage transaction?

    a. A title company charges a homebuyer a fee of $1,000 for title services related to a home purchase, and then splits this fee, giving $300 to the referring loan officer at a mortgage bank.
    b. A real estate agent refers a client to a specific mortgage broker, and the mortgage broker offers the agent $500 as a referral fee.
    c. A mortgage broker offers $200 as a "thank you" payment to any real estate agent who refers clients to the broker.
    d. A lender pays its loan officer employees a bonus for closing a certain number of transactions per year.

1.9 Which scenario depicts a specific RESPA violation?

    a. A settlement company splits a percentage of its fees with its employees.
    b. A neighborhood developer requires all homebuyers to use her family's settlement company to close escrow.
    c. A loan officer responds in writing to a consumer's qualified written request 10 days after he receives the request.
    d. A settlement company sends a $50 check to thank a real estate agent for a referral. The agent then voids the check and returns it to the settlement company.

1.10 Borrower Maria's annual taxes and insurance expenses total $6,042. What is the maximum amount a lender can require for a cushion in her escrow account?

    a. $503.50
    b. $1,007
    c. $1,510.50
    d. $6,042

1.11 Which of the following is a permissible reason to deny a loan application?

    a. Part-time job
    b. Public assistance benefits
    c. High debt-to-income ratio
    d. Familial status

1.12 What is the primary purpose of the Equal Credit Opportunity Act (ECOA)?

    a. Ensures equal access to credit for all loan applicants
    b. Prohibits creditors from discriminatory practices when granting credit
    c. Specifies credit analysis practices for lenders
    d. Codifies the specific language used on loan applications

1.13 Single father Martin is applying for a home loan. Which of the following information is he *not* required to provide on his application?

    a. Names and ages of his children
    b. Alimony he receives
    c. His race
    d. His work history

1.14 Moneybags Mortgages rejected Susan's loan application because the property serving as collateral for the loan is overvalued. Under these circumstances, which of the following should be included in the notice of adverse action that Moneybags will send to Susan?

   a. Information on Susan's right to receive a copy of the lender's appraisal
   b. Susan's negative credit report details
   c. Comments on Susan's employment history
   d. Details on Susan's rights to appeal the lender's rejection

1.15 Which of the following statements about the Equal Credit Opportunity Act (ECOA) is true?

   a. ECOA specifies strict credit analysis guidelines lenders must follow when assessing applicants' creditworthiness.
   b. Loan applicants are required to report all income they receive, including public assistance, alimony, child support, part-time work, etc.
   c. Marital status is not considered a protected class under ECOA.
   d. Creditors may consider applicants' immigration status, but only as it relates to the ability to repay the loan.

1.16 _____ is explicit or obvious discriminatory behavior or action.

   a. Overt discrimination
   b. Disparate treatment
   c. Disparate impact
   d. Covert bias

1.17 Which of the following is one purpose of the Truth in Lending Act (TILA)?

   a. Requires disclosure of loans' terms and costs
   b. Promotes the informed use of commercial and consumer credit
   c. Ensures fair and equitable access to housing finance
   d. Ensures accuracy, fairness, and privacy for consumer credit information

1.18 Which of the following statements is true regarding loans covered under TILA?

   a. Only residential mortgage loans fall under TILA's regulations.
   b. TILA applies to personal use loans with a minimum of four installment payments.
   c. TILA regulations are relevant to all types of loans.
   d. Business and commercial loans must adhere to TILA mandates.

1.19 The annual percentage rate (APR) for a loan is the total cost for borrowing the principal amount. It includes several different costs and fees, such as _____.

   a. a credit reporting fee
   b. an appraisal fee
   c. inspection costs
   d. the interest rate

1.20 TILA addresses MLO compensation, such as permitted and prohibited compensation types and terms. _____ is an example of permitted compensation.

   a. An amount based on a loan's profitability
   b. Earnings based on interest rates
   c. A fixed percentage of the loan amount
   d. Fee splitting with other involved parties

1.21 Which of the following MLO compensation types does TILA expressly prohibit?

  a. A percentage of applications that close successfully
  b. Bonuses and profit-sharing plans not tied to specific loan terms
  c. A flat fee per transaction
  d. Splitting fees with parties other than loan originators

1.22 The TILA RESPA Integrated Disclosure Rule (TRID) primarily focuses on residential mortgage loans, which includes

  a. reverse mortgages.
  b. FHA, VA, and USDA loans.
  c. home equity lines of credit.
  d. mobile home loans.

1.23 One of TRID's purposes was to standardize required disclosures to help reduce consumers' confusion arising from different lender forms. Which TRID-related form was designed to help borrowers understand the key features, costs, and risks of a mortgage before they commit?

  a. Closing Disclosure
  b. Borrower's Right to Rescind Notice
  c. Loan Estimate
  d. Good Faith Estimate

1.24 The Closing Disclosure details information such as _____.

  a. the total interest that will be paid over the life of the loan
  b. appraisal requirements for the loan
  c. projected payments, such as estimated escrow
  d. loan comparison information, such as total payments over five years

1.25 The Loan Estimate discloses costs and fees for services that borrowers cannot shop for, which includes costs for

  a. inspections.
  b. credit reports.
  c. surveys.
  d. title-related services.

1.26 When must lenders provide a Loan Estimate to borrowers?

  a. At least 10 days prior to closing
  b. Three days before loan consummation, not including Sundays and federal holidays
  c. Between three and seven days after the lender receives the borrower's loan application
  d. No more than three days after lender receives borrower's loan application and no fewer than seven days prior to loan consummation

1.27 TRID allows lenders to issue a revised Loan Estimate under "change of circumstances." Which of the following situations would generally fall under this permission?

  a. The borrower requests a larger loan amount.
  b. The rate lock expires and the rates go up.
  c. The borrower fails to provide required documentation in a timely manner.
  d. The lender miscalculates fees in the initial Loan Estimate.

1.28 Per TRID, which of the following statements is true regarding a borrower's right of rescission?

a. Once closing has occurred, borrowers may not rescind any housing-related loan.
b. Borrowers are permitted to cancel any housing-related loan within seven business days after closing.
c. Borrowers may rescind home purchase loans and refinances up to three days after closing, but home equity loans are exempt from the right of rescission.
d. Borrowers are permitted to cancel a home equity loan "no questions asked" within three business days after closing.

1.29 Which of the following descriptions matches the purpose of the Home Mortgage Disclosure Act (MMDA) of 1975?

a. Ensures accuracy, fairness, and privacy in collecting, sharing, and using consumer credit information to make lending decisions
b. Mandates programs designed to detect, report, and prevent money laundering and other financial crimes
c. Helps to ensure fair and equitable access to housing finance and to combat discriminatory lending practices
d. Protects consumers' personal financial information and requires financial institutions to explain how they will share and protect such information

1.30 Which of these scenarios would be a red flag to an MLO, per the FTC Red Flags rule?

a. An applicant's credit report shows multiple hard inquiries from other mortgage lenders, car dealerships, banks, and utilities. The applicant has just moved across country.
b. An applicant's address history on the application shows frequent changes and is inconsistent with information on the credit report.
c. An applicant provides a well-documented source of income and a stable employment history but opts for a loan amount significantly lower than their qualification limit.
d. An applicant insists on communicating only via email and refuses to provide a phone number. They have provided all required documents and identification.

1.31 Financial institutions are required to file SARs with the Financial Crimes Enforcement Network when they detect certain types of suspicious activities. Which of the following activities would most likely seem to indicate legal, business-as-usual activity?

a. Consistent contributions to an investment portfolio
b. Regular but unexplained withdrawals just under $10,000
c. Rapid movement of funds without a clear business reason
d. Complex layers of transactions involving multiple parties

1.32 The _____ protects consumers' personal financial information and requires financial institutions to explain how they will share and protect such information.

a. Gramm-Leach-Billey Act
b. Mortgage Acts and Practices—Advertising (Reg N)
c. Homeowners Protection Act
d. Dodd-Frank Act

1.33 The Mortgage Acts and Practices—Advertising (Reg N) is part of the FTC's rules established to govern mortgage advertising through any medium. Which of the following details would be considered a triggering term in an ad that would require additional disclosures when mentioned?

a. Services related to credit counseling
b. Flexible repayment options
c. Actual repayments terms
d. Non-specific statements about savings

1.34 Which of the following is a provision of the USA PATRIOT ACT?

a. Expanding the government's authority to collect bank and credit reporting records
b. Prohibiting misrepresentations regarding the terms of any mortgage credit product
c. Requiring financial institutions to provide customers with a written privacy notice when a relationship is established
d. Requiring financial institutions to file a Currency Transaction Report (CTR) for transactions exceeding $10,000

1.35 According to the E-SIGN Act, how should MLOs handle the retention of electronic records?

a. Electronic records must be converted to paper and stored physically.
b. Electronic records must be accessible to all parties involved for the legally required retention period.
c. Electronic records do not need to be retained if a paper copy exists.
d. There are no specific requirements for electronic record retention.

1.36 What is the main purpose of the Homeowners Protection Act of 1998?

a. To protect homebuyers from excessive private mortgage insurance (PMI) charges
b. To respond to emerging risks to national financial system's stability
c. To ramp up the requirements for financial institutions to report money laundering activities
d. To prohibit misrepresentations regarding the terms of any mortgage credit product

1.37 Which of the following is one provision the Dodd-Frank Act established to avoid risky lending practices that contributed to the 2008 housing crash?

a. Automatic termination guidelines for PMI
b. Identity verification programs
c. National do-not-call registry
d. Ability to repay requirements for borrowers

1.38 The _____ protects consumers in the financial sector, regulates and supervises banks, credit unions, and other financial companies, including the mortgage industry.

a. Department of Housing and Urban Development (HUD)
b. Consumer Financial Protection Bureau (CFPB)
c. Truth in Lending Act (TILA)
d. Federal Trade Commission

1.39 What is one of HUD's main purposes?

a. Helping to ensure fair and equitable access to housing finance and to combat discriminatory lending practices
b. Ensuring accuracy, fairness, and privacy in collecting, sharing, and using consumer credit information to make lending decisions
c. Overseeing aspects of housing and mortgage lending, with a strong focus on fair practices and affordable housing
d. Promoting the informed use of consumer credit, e.g., household, family, or personal purposes

1.40 MLO Stan will not underwrite loans for applicants buying homes in the west part of town, no matter what their qualifications are. What is this practice called?

a. Puffing
b. Steering
c. Blockbusting
d. Redlining

1.41 Dodd-Frank prohibits MLOs or lending institutions from directing borrowers to a certain loan product in order to increase compensation, even though that loan product is not in the consumer's interest. What is this practice called?

a. Puffing
b. Steering
c. Blockbusting
d. Redlining

1.42 The Dodd-Frank Act gives borrowers _____, meaning they can sue creditors when they realize they cannot afford their loan and they feel creditor did not properly determine their ability to repay.

a. private right of action
b. triggering terms
c. red flags
d. adverse action

Section II: General Mortgage Knowledge

➢ **Qualified and Non-Qualified Mortgage Programs**

- **Mortgage market overview**
- **Qualified mortgages**
- **Conventional / Conforming loans**
- **Government Loans**
- **Conventional nonconforming Loans**

➢ **Mortgage Loan Products**

- **Fixed-rate loans**
- **Adjustable loans**
- **Purchase money second mortgages**
- **Interest-only loans**
- **Balloon mortgage**
- **Reverse mortgage**
- **Home Equity Line of Credit (HELOC)**
- **Construction loans**

➢ **Terms Used in the Mortgage Industry**

- **Loan terms**
- **Disclosure terms**
- **Financial terms**
- **General terms**

Qualified and Non-Qualified Mortgage Programs

➢ **Mortgage market overview**

- **primary mortgage market: where loans are originated**, i.e., borrowers and lenders work directly together to create new mortgages
- **secondary mortgage market: where existing mortgages are bought and sold** via mortgage-backed securities (MBS); no direct interaction with borrowers

  o secondary market provides liquidity to primary market lenders to fund more mortgage loans
  o lessens interest rate risk for lenders; enables portfolio diversification
  o promotes industry standards for credit requirements, loan types, and loan documents
  o major secondary market players: **Fannie Mae, Freddie Mac, Ginnie Mae, Federal Home Loan Bank System**, private investors

- Fannie Mae (Federal National Mortgage Association)
  - **purpose**: buys loans from primary market lenders in order to provide local banks with federal money for home mortgages

  - created by Congress in 1938 during the Great Depression

  - **government-sponsored enterprise (GSE)**: financial service corporation Congress created to enhance credit flow, particularly in housing sector; privately held but supported by federal government

  - Fannie Mae buys mortgages from primary market lenders, e.g., commercial banks, savings and loans, mortgage companies, etc.

  - Fannie Mae converts then bundles loans into mortgage-backed securities, which are then sold to investors

  - guarantees investors will receive timely principal and interest payments of mortgage-backed securities (MBS), even if original borrower defaults

  - investors include:
    - individuals
    - pension funds
    - state governments
    - investment management funds
    - foreign government entities

  - FNMA sets underwriting standards for mortgages it is willing to purchase; these standards impact industry-wide underwriting practices for other lenders

  - FNMA sets loan limits on mortgages it will buy; loan limits are adjusted annually

  - formal lender approval process: ensures lenders meet specific criteria to establish annual contract with Fannie Mae, e.g., capital, profitability, experience, underwriting standards, licensing, technology, insurance, legal compliance, etc.

- Freddie Mac (Federal Home Loan Mortgage Corporation)
  - **purpose**: expands secondary mortgage market; originally created by Congress in 1970 to provide a market for mortgages originated by savings and loans

  - operates in secondary market as a second GSE; competes with Fannie Mae

  - similar to Fannie Mae: buys mortgages, bundles them into mortgage-backed securities, sells to investors
    - guarantees investors receive timely principal and interest payments from MBS, even if original borrower defaults

- sets underwriting standards for mortgages it purchases; like Fannie Mae, Freddie Mac lending standards impact industry-wide underwriting practices

- sets loan limits on mortgages it will buy; adjusted annually

- Freddie Mac utilizes a formal lender approval process

- Ginnie Mae (Government National Mortgage Association)
  - **purpose: issues government guarantees** on bond pools of government-backed loans, e.g., FHA, VA, and USDA loans

  - Ginnie Mae is a government-owned corporation; part of HUD

- Federal Home Loan Bank System (FHLB)
  - **purpose:** provides stable, low-cost funding to financial institutions for home mortgage and economic development loans; created in 1932 during the Great Depression
  - designed to bolster lending in local communities
  - consists of 11 regional Federal Home Loan Banks (FHLBs), with 8,000+ financial institution members across the country
  - membership is voluntary; includes banks, credit unions, insurance companies, and community development financial institutions.
  - governance: each FHLB is privately capitalized, cooperatively owned corporation; members are owners and customers
  - channel resources into housing finance and community development projects in their geographic areas
  - supports smaller financial institutions; promotes financial system's diversity and stability

- Private investors
  - individuals, corporations, financial institutions, hedge funds, insurance companies, etc., **that invest in mortgage-backed securities** (MBS) and other mortgage-related financial products; non-governmental entities

  - investment products: MBS (agency and non-agency), collateralized mortgage obligations (CMOs), real estate mortgage investment conduits (REMICs)

  - **agency MBS**: issued by government-sponsored enterprises (GSEs); typically consist of **conforming loans**; tend to be lower risk, lower yield
    - conforming loan: mortgage that adheres to underwriting guidelines set by Fannie Mae and Freddie Mac, or Ginnie Mae government-insured loan

  - **non-agency MBS**: issued by private financial institutions, e.g., investment banks, mortgage companies, other non-government entities; often include non-conforming loans, typically higher risk, higher yield
    - non-conforming loan: jumbo loans, subprime mortgages, Alt-A mortgages, etc.

➢ **Qualified mortgages (QMs)**

- **definition of qualified mortgage (QM)**: a mortgage that meets certain CFPB standards, ensuring that lenders make loans that borrowers have ability to repay

- qualified mortgages are essentially a tool to ensure responsible lending and borrowing, thereby promoting financial stability in mortgage market

- enacted as part of Dodd-Frank in 2014; included in a broader set of financial reforms introduced by Dodd-Frank Act in 2010

- key features and requirements of QMs include:

    o limits on points and fees charged to borrowers

        ▪ 3% of total loan amount for a loan greater than or equal to $100,000
        ▪ $3,000 for a loan greater than or equal to 60,000 but less than $100,000
        ▪ 5% of total loan amount for a loan greater than or equal to $20,000 but less than $60,000
        ▪ $1,000 for a loan greater than or equal to $12,500 but less than $20,000
        ▪ 8% of total loan amount for a loan less than $12,500

    o risky loan features not allowed, including:

        ▪ negative amortization
        ▪ interest-only payments
        ▪ balloon payments
        ▪ terms that exceed 30 years

    o parties involved in lending process **must make a reasonable and good-faith determination of borrower's ability to repay loan**: including verifying borrower's income, assets, debts, and credit history

    o **debt-to-income (DTI) cap**: borrower's DTI ratio typically should not exceed 43%, i.e., total monthly debt payments, including mortgage, should not be more than 43% of monthly pre-tax income

- QM underwriting standards protect consumers from predatory lending practices and from obtaining loans they cannot afford

- protects lenders against borrower lawsuits, particularly a "safe harbor" in proving compliance with ability-to-repay rules

- QM standards influence how lenders assess borrower's eligibility and loan terms

- exempt loans include:

    o open-end credit plans
    o timeshare plans
    o reverse mortgages
    o bridge loans
    o short duration construction loans
    o consumer credit transaction secured by vacant land

- different categories of QMs
  - **general QMs**: loans that adhere to basic QM requirements

  - **temporary QMs**: created to provide transition period when QM rules were established under Dodd-Frank; ensured continued access to credit while mortgage industry adapted to new QM standards

  - **small lender QMs**: designed for smaller lenders who might not be able to meet all standard QM requirements
    - must have less than $2 billion in assets and originate fewer than 2,000 QMs per year
    - allows more flexibility in determining a borrower's DTI ratio

  - **balloon-payment QMs**: allow balloon payments at end of loan term; normally not permitted for QMs
    - only available to small creditors operating in rural or underserved areas

- ➤ **Conventional / conforming loans**
  - **conventional loan**: any loan the federal government does <u>not</u> insure or guarantee

  - **conforming loan**: any loan that meets Fannie Mae/Freddie Mac standards and follows their guidelines

  - like the QM, **conforming loan standards ensure loans are stable and relatively low risk;** more attractive for investors in secondary mortgage market

  - **Fannie Mae/Freddie Mac conforming loan standards** include:
    - **loan limits**: current (2023) baseline loan limit for single-unit properties is $726,200 in most areas; can be as high as $1,089,300 in high-cost areas; limits adjusted annually based on changes in average U.S. home price

    - **credit score requirements**: generally at least 620; higher credit score help with better interest rates and loan terms

    - **down payment**: generally 5% minimum; down payment of less than 20% usually requires private mortgage insurance (PMI) until borrower has 20% equity

    - **debt-to-income ratio (DTI)**: ratio of borrower's total monthly debt payments to their monthly income; most conforming loans require DTI of 43% or less

    - **loan-to-value ratio (LTV)**: ratio of loan amount to property's appraised value
      - higher LTV means riskier loan
      - conforming loans typically have maximum LTV limits, depending on loan program and borrower qualifications

- o **documentation**: borrower proof of income, employment, assets, and debts required, e.g., W-2 statements, tax returns, bank statements, credit reports

- o **property appraisal**: ensures appraised value meets or exceeds loan amount; ensures lender can recover loan amount if borrower defaults

- o **property type**: primary residences, second homes, and investment properties permitted; different standards and requirements apply for each type

- o **underwriting guidelines**: requires automated underwriting systems like Fannie Mae's Desktop Underwriter (DU) or Freddie Mac's Loan Product Advisor (LPA) to assess borrower eligibility

- o **other requirements**: may be additional requirements regarding borrower's bankruptcy or foreclosure history, and guidelines for self-employed borrowers

- **seller concession limits**:
  - o primary or secondary home:
    - less than 10% down: concessions capped at 3% of purchase price
    - 10% - 25% down: 6% cap.
    - 25% or more: 9% cap
  - o investment properties: usually capped at 2% no matter down payment amount

- **Loan-Level Price Adjustments** (LLPAs)
  - o risk-based fees Fannie and Freddie assess on lenders; often passed on to borrowers
  - o determined by factors that influence loan's perceived risk, such as:
    - lower credit scores
    - higher LTV ratios
    - property type, e.g., single-family home, multi-unit, investment property, etc.
    - loan purpose, e.g., purchase, rate/term refinance, cash-out refinance, etc.
    - loan features, e.g., interest-only payments or loan term longer than 30 years
  - o help Fannie Mae and Freddie Mac manage risks of buying and guaranteeing mortgages; aim to offset potential losses from defaults

  - o can either be paid up front at closing, incorporated into loan's interest rate, or a blend of both approaches

  - o can significantly influence loan cost, especially for borrowers with lower credit scores or high LTV loans

  - o Fannie Mae and Freddie Mac both publish LLPA matrices detailing fees based on risk factors; used by lenders to calculate loan fees

  - o LLPAs do <u>not</u> apply to government loans

- **low down payment programs**: *HomeReady* (Fannie Mae) and *HomePossible* (Freddie Mac); first-time homebuyers and low to moderate income buyers

  o reduced down payment of 3% (97% LTV)

  o permits grants and second mortgages to cover down payment and closing costs

  o borrower incomes cannot be more than 80% of American Median Income

    ▪ example: 2022 median income was $74,580; 80% of that is $59,664

➢ **Government loans**

  • **Federal Housing Administration (FHA) loans**

    o loans insured to protect lenders against borrower default

    o require two types of mortgage insurance: upfront mortgage insurance premium (UFMIP) and annual mortgage insurance premium (MIP)

      ▪ UFMIP: one-time fee; calculated by multiplying loan amount by a certain factor, currently 1.75% of loan amount; can be paid at closing or financed into mortgage

      ▪ MIP: ongoing cost, paid monthly; calculated by multiplying base loan amount by a certain factor and then dividing by 12

    o offered by variety of FHA-approved financial entities, e.g., banks, credit unions, mortgage companies, and online lenders

    o designed to help lower-income and first-time homebuyers purchase homes

      ▪ low down payments: typically as low as 3.5% of purchase price
      ▪ more lenient credit requirements than conventional loans

    o **loan limits**: typically set at a percentage of Federal Housing Finance Agency's conforming loan limits; vary based on local residential prices in each county; can change annually

    o **property requirements**: homes required to meet HUD's minimum property requirements (MPR), i.e., certain safety, security, and soundness standards

      ▪ issues with structural integrity, safety, or sanitation render property ineligible for FHA loan
      ▪ appraisals to be performed by FHA-approved appraiser

    o various property types:

      ▪ **must be owner-occupied** one- to four-unit residence, e.g., single-family, multifamily, manufactured homes, etc.

      ▪ **borrowers must occupy residence within 60 days after closing**; continued occupancy for minimum one year

- **LTV limits**: maximum LTV of 96.5% on purchases (3.5% down); 97.75% on rate/term refinances; 80% on cash-out refinances

- **assumable**: a future buyer permitted to take over an FHA loan under original terms, subject to loan servicer approval and HUD credit guidelines

  - **novation**: new borrower replaces original borrower, who is released from any liability; new borrower takes over all future payments and loan obligations
  - **simple assumption**: new borrower takes over payments, but original borrower remains liable if new borrower defaults

- refinancing options, such as streamline, cash-out, rate-and-term, rehab loan, simple, reverse mortgage

- **qualifying ratios**: percentage of monthly gross income going toward housing costs (front-end ratio) cannot exceed 31%; percentage of monthly gross income for all monthly debts including housing (back-end ratio) cannot exceed 43%

- anti-flipping provisions:

  - property ineligible for FHA loan if potential buyer contracts to buy property within 90 days of seller acquiring said property i.e., buyer must hold purchased property for 90 days before selling via FHA loan

  - 90-day rule: if potential buyer contracts to buy home within 90 days of previous sale, FHA will not insure mortgage

  - resale between 91-180 days: if property is being resold within 91 to 180 days after previous sale, and new selling price is more than 100% of price seller paid, lender is required to obtain a second appraisal to ensure increased price is justified by actual improvements or market conditions

  - lender/seller pays for required second appraisal

- **U.S. Department of Veterans Affairs (VA) loans**

  - designed for veterans, service members, and families to finance owner-occupied homes

  - VA guarantees loans, which reduces risk for lenders; such as banks, thrifts, and mortgage companies

  - often do not require a down payment

  - do not require borrowers to pay private mortgage insurance, even with down payment

  - typically lower interest rates than conventional loans

  - limited closing costs lenders can charge

  - no prepayment penalty

- assumable, as long as new borrower meets VA and lender criteria

- assistance offered to borrowers experiencing financial hardship to help avoid foreclosure

- **loan eligibility** depends on duration and type of service; veterans, active-duty service members, National Guard members, reservists, and certain surviving spouses generally eligible

  - requires a funding fee of about 1.4% to 3.6% of loan amount; lower with down payment and higher for subsequent VA loan benefit uses; often rolled into loan amount

  - helps fund VA loan program

  - depends on factors like borrower's military service and whether it is a first-time or subsequent use of VA loan

  - certain veterans and family members exempt from funding fee; e.g., Purple Heart recipients, veterans with service-connected disability, spouses of service members who died as result of service, spouses of prisoners of war

- **Certificate of Eligibility (COE)** required to prove veteran, service member, or surviving spouse is eligible

- no VA-set loan limits and no required down payment for borrowers with full entitlement

- loan limits apply for borrowers with partial entitlement; limits vary based on county and conforming loan limits set by Federal Housing Finance Agency

- borrowers required to have stable income that is sufficient to cover monthly expenses plus new mortgage payment

- **benchmark DTI of 41% or lower**

- specific residual income (amount left over each month after major expenses are paid) applies; adheres to family size and regional cost of living guidelines; subtract income taxes and monthly debts from gross income to get residual income to be used for food, gas, and other living expenses

- no VA-set minimum credit score requirement; lenders set their own criteria: generally at least 620

- minimum property requirements (MPRs): home must meet VA MPRs for safety, structural soundness, sanitation, and specific standards for systems

- **loans apply to primary residences**; borrower must intend to occupy property within reasonable period after closing, e.g., within 60 days

- loan types: purchase loans, interest rate reduction refinance loan (IRRRL) / VA streamline refinance, and cash-out refinance

- o **Certificate of Reasonable Value (CRV) /VA appraisal**: required to assess home's value and ensure it meets MPRs; performed by VA-approved appraiser

- **United States Department of Agriculture (USDA) loans**
  - o only available in eligible areas, typically rural areas or towns of fewer than 35,000 people
  - o no down payment required
  - o lower insurance rates
  - o often lower interest rates
  - o two types: USDA guaranteed loans and USDA direct loans

  - o **USDA guaranteed loans** – key characteristics:
    - made by private lenders but guaranteed by USDA

    - available to low- and moderate-income borrowers, i.e., household income no greater than 115% of area's median income; for parties who have trouble locating affordable conventional credit

    - minimum credit score of 640 generally expected; lower scores may be approved based on other compensating factors

    - **limited to owner-occupied, single-family homes** (no multi units)

    - **USDA guarantee fees apply**: upfront fee (can be financed) is 1% of loan amount; and annual fee (spread over monthly payments) is 0.35%

    - maximum LTV: 100% when upfront fee is fully paid; 101% when upfront fee is financed

    - DTIs: front-end 29; back-end 41

  - o **USDA direct loans**
    - issued by USDA for low- and very-low-income applicants; income thresholds vary by region

    - income limits typically below 50% to 80% of area's median income

    - applicant's demonstrated ability to repay loan

    - do not require a down payment

    - subsidized interest rates; can be as low as 1%, depending on borrower's income and subsidy applied

    - payment assistance subsidy that reduces mortgage payment for a short time; amount of assistance based on adjusted family income

    - can have repayment terms of up to 33 years, and 38 years for very low-income applicants who cannot afford 33-year term

➢ **Conventional / non-conforming loans**

- **conventional loans**: private mortgages with flexible terms; **not backed by any government agency**; divided into two categories: conforming (discussed above) and non-conforming

- **conventional non-conforming loans**: conventional, but do <u>not</u> follow Fannie Mae or Freddie Mac rules; key characteristics include:

  o may exceed FHFA loan limits, allowing borrowers to access higher loan amounts

  o tend to command higher down payments and interest rates

  o can work with lower credit scores

  o may have more stringent requirements depending on lender

- **jumbo loans**
  o useful for high-value properties, especially in markets where housing prices exceed national average
  o loan limits exceed FHFA's maximum limits for conforming loans, i.e., $726,200 for most of U.S. in 2023; higher in areas with more expensive real estate markets
  o stricter qualification criteria
  o excellent credit usually required, higher than conforming loans; 700+ credit score is common, varies by lender
  o typically involve larger down payments, such as 20% or more; varies by lender
  o stringent DTI requirements necessary to indicate borrowers can manage debts along with larger mortgage
  o competitive interest rates but may be slightly higher due to lenders' increased risk with larger loan amounts
  o more rigorous documentation and income verification processes often required
  o more detailed property appraisals may be necessary
  o no government backing, so lenders enjoy more freedom to set own criteria

- **Alt-A (Alternative A-paper) loans**
  o considered non-conforming due to lender's increased risk because borrower cannot meet underwriting standards for conforming loan, generally related to documentation requirements

  o suitable for borrowers with diverse financial backgrounds and needs, e.g., lower credit scores, higher DTIs, less conventional documentation

  o offer more flexibility with borrower credit scores, income, and asset levels

  o considered riskier than prime (A-paper) mortgages but less risky than subprime loans

- often associated with limited documentation; utilize alternative methods for income verification, e.g., bank statements instead of tax returns

- suitable for individuals with non-traditional income sources or limited credit history, etc.

- higher interest rates, closing costs

- short- to medium-term financing option for borrowers planning a future refinance into a standard mortgage

- **cannot be bought or sold**

- **subprime loans**
  - designed for borrowers with poor credit scores or other financial challenges making them a higher risk for lenders

  - generally higher interest rates than traditional loans to compensate for lender's risk of borrower default

  - borrower characteristics include:
    - credit score lower than 660
    - history of late payments
    - foreclosure / bankruptcy
    - DTI of 50% of more

  - applicable regulatory changes to protect borrowers from taking on more debt than they can afford

- *Guidance on Non-Traditional Mortgage Product Risk*
  - set of guidelines and principles established primarily for lending institutions; issued 2006

  - addresses risks associated with non-traditional mortgage products, including features like:
    - interest-only payments
    - negative amortization
    - balloon payment
    - payment-option ARMs
  - risk management recommendations include:
    - **responsible underwriting standards**, e.g., assessing borrower's ability to repay loan considering potential increases in payment obligations

    - **clear, comprehensive information to consumers**, such as explaining potential risks and future payment increases at time of loan selection and monthly thereafter

    - **regular reviews and audits to ensure compliance** with all applicable laws and regulations

- **sound underwriting practices** at all times

- **non-qualified mortgages**
  - a type of home loan that does not adhere to Dodd-Frank and CFPB strict lending requirements, i.e., regulations introduced to ensure borrowers can repay loans

  - non-qualified mortgage beneficial for individuals with income or credit history that does not fit stringent standard mortgage loan program guidelines

  - DTIs above 43%, alternative documentation for income often apply

  - may include features such as interest-only payment period, negative amortization, balloon payments, or terms longer than 30 years

  - often have higher interest rates and upfront fees; more expensive long term

  - less regulatory protection for borrowers

  - application process typically more lenient; less documentation required

  - offered by fewer lenders due to higher risk

Mortgage Loan Products

➤ **Fixed-rate mortgages**

- **interest rate stays same** over life of loan; does not change with market fluctuations

- **monthly principal and interest payments remain same** from first payment to last

- form of insurance against rising interest rates, ensuring housing costs remain unaffected by market changes

- can feature 15, 20, or 30 year loan terms; shorter terms have higher monthly payments; longer terms have higher total interest paid

- suitable for borrowers who plan to stay in homes for a long time

- refinance can be an opportunity if interest rates drop significantly

➤ **Adjustable-rate mortgages (ARMs)**

- **interest rate changes over time**, typically in relation to an index rate, after initial fixed-rate period (often 3, 5, 7, or 10 years)

- **often start with lower interest rates** compared to fixed-rate; attractive for borrowers planning to sell or refinance before rate adjusts

- **usually a cap on how much rate can change** at each adjustment period and over life of loan

- **rate adjustment depends on index** the loan is tied to and loan's specific terms; monthly payments can be unpredictable

- often **chosen by borrowers who expect income to rise**, plan to move in a few years, or anticipate dropping interest rates

- **can be riskier** if rates rise or borrower's plans change

- can be refinanced

- can incur "payment shock": when interest rates rise significantly and monthly payments increase greatly

➢ **Purchase money second mortgages (PMMs)**

- secondary-priority loan – or junior loan - taken out during a home purchase to help finance purchase

- often used to cover part of purchase price that first mortgage does not cover
  - first mortgage typically covers majority of home price, and purchase money second mortgage makes up difference
  - **example**: buyer wants to avoid PMI, so buyer chooses an 80-10-10 arrangement in which first mortgage covers 80% of home's value, second mortgage covers 10%, and buyer puts down 10%

- interest rate on a purchase money second mortgage is generally higher than that of first mortgage because it is considered riskier and has a secondary lien priority, meaning that it can only be collected after the senior lien has been paid off

- loan terms can vary, with some PMMs being short-term loans with or without a balloon, or amortized over longer period

- borrower makes separate payments on both first and second mortgage

- lender of first mortgage gets paid off first in event of foreclosure

- advantages:
  - ability to buy a home without a full 20% down payment and without paying PMI
  - potential tax advantages: interest on both first and second mortgages may be tax-deductible

- risks:
  - more borrower debt
  - two mortgage payments
  - could owe more than house is worth if house's value decreases

- requires good credit and a stable income to offset lender risk

46

➢ **Interest-only loans**

- borrower pays only the interest on loan for set period, usually first few years (generally 5-10 years)

- during interest-only period, principal payments are postponed:
    - principal balance remains unchanged
    - monthly payments are lower initially but can increase significantly once interest-only period ends

- after interest-only period, loan typically converts to standard amortizing loan; payments include both principal and interest; results in a monthly payment increase

- often for borrowers who anticipate a higher future income, plan to sell property before interest-only period ends, or intend to refinance

- also used with investment properties where cash flow is key consideration

- risks:
    - potential for significantly higher payments once interest-only period ends
    - can be challenging to manage increased payments or refinance loan if property value does not increase or borrower's income does not grow as expected

- benefits: lower initial payments can free up cash for other investments, home improvements, or managing irregular income streams

- availability can vary with market conditions, and qualifying for them might be more stringent

➢ **Balloon mortgages**

- **short-term loan with large final payment**: 5- to 7-year loan term with final "balloon" payment covering remaining principal balance

- offers lower initial payments than fixed-rate mortgage; often calculated as if loan had longer term

- interest rates can vary; can be higher to cover lender's risk

- amortization: schedule is longer than actual loan term;
    - example: balloon mortgage with a 5-year term is amortized over 30 years
        - monthly payments are calculated as if loan would take 30 years to pay off
        - at end of 5-year term, remaining principal balance is due in one large "balloon" payment

- option for borrowers who plan to refinance, sell, or pay off loan with cash by the time balloon payment is due

- **strategy often used by people expecting to be in stronger financial position in the future or those who anticipate moving within loan term**

- **risks: inability to pay balloon payment when it is due**

- less common than fixed-rate or adjustable-rate mortgages; sometimes used in commercial real estate or in specific situations where borrower has strong plan for paying balloon payment

➢ **Reverse mortgages**

- specifically designed for seniors, i.e., aged 62 and older

- **allows homeowners to convert part of home's equity into cash without having to sell** home or take on additional debt; essentially borrowing from their home's equity

- amount available to borrow depends on several factors, including home's current market value, homeowner's age, and interest rates

- lender makes payments to owners against accumulated home equity

- **homeowner can choose to receive payments as lump sum, line of credit, or regular monthly installments**

- interest and fees apply; can have higher upfront costs compared to other loan types, including origination fees, insurance, and closing costs; typically financed as part of loan

- all fees deferred until specific trigger event occurs, usually when borrower sells home, moves out permanently, or dies

- **when borrower moves out of home or dies, home is usually sold, and sales proceeds used to repay loan**, including principal and accrued interest

- no risk of borrower defaulting on loan due to non-payment

- equity in home decreases over life of reverse mortgage; proportionately lowers amount heirs will inherit

- borrower or heirs never owe more than home is worth due to non-recourse feature of federally-insured reverse mortgages

- financial counseling with HUD-approved counselor usually required to ensure borrowers fully understand reverse mortgage implications

➢ **Home equity lines of credit (HELOCs)**

- **line of credit that allows homeowners to borrow against equity in their home**

- revolving line of credit; secured by borrower's home as collateral

- borrowers approved for maximum loan amount and can borrow as much as they need up to that limit

- **only pay interest on amount actually borrowed**

- typically have two phases: a draw period and a repayment period
  - draw period: borrow funds, and perhaps only have to pay interest
  - repayment period: paying back both principal and interest; begins when draw period ends

- interest rates usually variable; can fluctuate over time based on market conditions

- often used for home improvements, debt consolidation, emergency funds, educational expenses; etc.; flexible option

➤ **Construction loans**

- used to finance a new build or major renovation, home or other real property

- usually short-term loans, e.g., a year or so, to complete construction; borrower thereafter refinances to more traditional mortgage

- often more complex and riskier than standard mortgages

- stringent underwriting standards include:
  - borrower's credit history, income stability, and debt-to-income ratio
  - construction project feasibility, detailed construction plan, budget, timelines, and builder / contractor qualifications, financial stability, credibility, etc.
  - appraisal to ensure loan amount aligns with property's projected market value
  - may also involve interest reserves to cover interest payments during construction and contingency funds for unforeseen expenses

- after construction loan approval, funds typically disbursed to builder in stages, or "draws," as construction reaches specific milestones; each stage requires inspection and approval

- borrowers often make interest-only payments calculated on disbursed funds, not on entire loan amount

- generally require higher interest rates; may require larger down payments, e.g., 20-25%

- loans convert to traditional mortgage after construction is complete; aka "construction-to-permanent" loan

Terms Used in the Mortgage Industry

➤ **Loan terms**

- **subordinate loan**: type of loan ranked below primary loan in terms of claim on property assets in event of default; subordinate loan creditors are paid *after* primary or senior debt holders; subordinate loans are higher risk, thus have typically higher interest rates

- **escrow account**: third-party account that holds funds until transaction conditions are fulfilled; often holds buyer's earnest money or funds for property taxes and homeowner's insurance

- **lien**: legal claim or right against a property; often used as security for a debt in which property acts as collateral against amount owed; when debt is not paid, lien holder can seize property; common types include mortgage liens, tax liens, and mechanic's liens

- **tolerance**: limit on how much final closing costs can exceed estimates provided in Loan Estimate form; set by the Real Estate Settlement Procedures Act (RESPA); cost categories are zero tolerance, 10% cumulative tolerance, and no or unlimited tolerance, and each has specific rules on cost increases

- **rate lock agreement**: lender's promise to hold certain interest rate and specific number of points for a buyer for specified period while loan application processes; protects borrower from rate fluctuations during loan application process

- **table funding**: mortgage broker originates and processes a loan but a third party (e.g., a wholesale lender) provides funds loan at closing table

➤ **Disclosure terms**

- **annual percentage rate (APR)**: broad measure of a loan's total cost; represents annual cost of funds over loan term; **includes interest rate, broker fees, finance charges, discount points, and some closing costs, etc.;** expressed as a percentage

- **yield spread premium**: compensation a mortgage broker or loan officer receives for originating a loan with interest rate higher than lender's par rate, i.e., rate at which lender would not pay a rebate or charge a fee; profit broker makes for selling a higher-than-par-rate loan

- **federal mortgage loan**: loans guaranteed or insured by the federal government; includes FHA loans, VA loans, and USDA loans

- **servicing transfer**: occurs when a company handling and processing a loan (servicer) transfers this responsibility to another company; requires borrower notification and details such as new servicer's name and contact details; does not affect borrower or other payment terms

- **lender credit: funds lender provides to help cover borrower's closing costs,** typically in exchange for higher interest rate; reduces amount of cash borrower needs at closing but typically results in higher costs over loan life

➢ **Financial terms**

- **positive amortization: loan balance decreases over time as payments are made**; typical in standard loan repayment plans where monthly payments cover interest and a portion of principal

- **negative amortization: when monthly payments are not large enough to cover interest due on a loan**; unpaid interest is added to principal balance, so total amount of **debt increases** over time

- **discount points**: fees borrower pays directly to lender at closing in exchange for reduced interest rate; one point equals 1% of loan amount; helps lower monthly mortgage payments

- **2-1 buydown**: financing technique that reduces mortgage interest rate in a stepped fashion during loan's initial years, then reverts to standard rate for remaining term; e.g., 2% reduction in first year and 1% in second year ; buydown fee can be paid by borrower, home seller, or builder as incentive to purchase

- **LTV ratio**: compares loan amount to property's value; calculated by dividing loan amount by property's appraised value or purchase price, whichever is lower; used to assess lender's risk; higher LTV ratio is riskier

- **DTI ratio**: measures borrower's monthly debt load compared to gross monthly income; used to assess borrower's ability to manage monthly payments and repay debts

- **housing ratio**: indicates what portion of income is used to pay housing costs, including mortgage payments, insurance, property taxes, and homeowner's association fees; aka front-end ratio

- **accrued interest**: interest on a loan or mortgage that has accumulated over time but has not yet been paid; for mortgages, it is interest that has accrued each month in between payments

- **finance charge**: total cost of borrowing, including interest, origination fee, discount points, mortgage insurance, lender charges, etc.; represents entire loan cost to borrower

- **settlement**: conclusion of a real estate transaction; property's title transfers from seller to buyer, and all necessary payments and paperwork are completed

➢ **General terms**

- **loan subordination**: a lender agrees to position their loan claim below another lender's claim in terms of priority for debt repayment in event of default; most often relevant when refinancing a first mortgage and holder of second mortgage allows their loan to remain in secondary position

- **conveyance**: act of transferring ownership of a property from one party to another; typically done through legal document such as deed

- **primary market**: where borrowers and mortgage originators come together to negotiate terms and create a mortgage loan

- **secondary market**: where loans that originated in primary market are sold to investors; including Fannie Mae and Freddie Mac which buy mortgages and package them into securities

- **third-party provider**: company or individual that provides services to lenders or borrowers in the course of originating, processing, or closing a mortgage loan; includes appraisers, title companies, credit reporting agencies, and attorneys

- **assumable loans**: mortgage loans that can be transferred from seller to buyer where buyer takes over mortgage payments, often benefiting from existing interest rates that may be lower than current market rates

- **mortgage banker:** an individual or business entity that originates, sells, and services mortgage loans; typically using his, her or its own funds for financing

- **mortgage broker**: acts as an intermediary who brokers mortgage loans on behalf of individuals or businesses; mortgage brokers do not fund loans themselves but find lenders for borrowers

- **commercial bank**: type of financial institution that provides services such as accepting deposits, providing business loans, offering basic investment products and often offering mortgage loans

- **thrift**: financial institution that primarily accepts savings deposits and makes mortgage and other loans; aka savings and loan associations

- **floating rate (adjustable rate)**: interest rate that changes over life of loan; typically tied to index like the prime rate

- **prepaids**: expenses related to mortgage that are paid in advance; often include property taxes, homeowners insurance, and interest that will accrue between closing date and date of first mortgage payment

Section II Quiz: General Mortgage Knowledge

2.1   Which of the following statements relates to the primary mortgage market?

    a. Liquidity is provided to lenders so they can fund more mortgage loans.
    b. Borrowers and lenders work directly together to create new mortgages.
    c. Industry standards for credit requirements, loan types, and loan documents are set.
    d. Existing mortgages are bought and sold via mortgage-backed securities.

2.2   Which of the following is one purpose of the secondary mortgage market?

    a. Provides liquidity to mortgage-backed securities
    b. Originates loans
    c. Enables portfolio diversification; augments liquidity to primary market
    d. Eliminates all risk for lenders

2.3   _____ is a financial service corporation created by Congress to enhance credit flow, particularly in the housing sector.

    a. The Federal Housing Authority (FHA)
    b. The Federal Home Loan Bank System (FHLB)
    c. A government-sponsored enterprise (GSE)
    d. An agency mortgage-backed security (MBS)

2.4   Which statement is true of Fannie Mae?

    a. It creates mortgages on the primary market and sells them to commercial banks.
    b. It buys loans from loan pools and provides them directly to borrowers.
    c. It provides stable, low-cost funding to financial institutions for economic development loans.
    d. It guarantees investors will receive timely principal and interest payments of MBS, even if original borrower defaults.

2.5   A _____ adheres to underwriting guidelines set by Fannie Mae and Freddie Mac.

    a. non-conforming loan
    b. conforming loan
    c. conventional loan
    d. mortgage-backed security

2.6   Which of these statements about conforming loans and conventional loans is true?

    a. All conventional loans are conforming loans.
    b. All conforming loans are conventional loans.
    c. All conventional loans are insured or guaranteed by government agencies.
    d. All conforming loans are insured or guaranteed by government agencies.

2.7   _____ are considered to be non-conforming.

    a. FHA loans
    b. Conventional loans
    c. Jumbo loans
    d. Second home loans

2.8   A mortgage that meets certain CFPB standards, ensuring that lenders make loans that borrowers
       have ability to repay, is considered to be a

       a. qualified mortgage.
       b. conforming mortgage.
       c. conventional mortgage.
       d. non-conforming mortgage.

2.9   Which of the following loan features would be permitted for a qualified mortgage?

       a. Loan principal that increases over time
       b. Balloon payment at the end of the loan term
       c. Negative amortization
       d. Limits on points and fees charged to borrowers

2.10   A _____ is any loan the federal government does not insure or guarantee.

       a. conforming loan
       b. qualified mortgage
       c. conventional loan
       d. non-conforming loan

2.11   A key benefit of conforming loan standards is that that they

       a. are designed to help lower-income and first-time homebuyers purchase homes.
       b. require loans to be assumable on subsequent sales.
       c. are useful for high-value properties.
       d. ensure loans are stable and relatively low risk.

2.12   Which of the following is a Fannie Mae/Freddie Mac key conforming loan standard?

       a. Required down payment of 20% or greater
       b. DTI of 50 % or less
       c. Primary residences, second homes, and investment properties permitted
       d. High LTV maximum compared to other loans

2.13   Which of the following loans could fall under the category of a qualified mortgage, assuming it
       meets CFPB standards?

       a. Reverse mortgage
       b. Bridge loan
       c. VA loan
       d. Three-month construction to permanent loan

2.14   Certain factors influence a mortgage loan's perceived risk, such as

       a. its purpose.
       b. the property's neighborhood.
       c. the borrower's race.
       d. the previous owners.

2.15   Which of the following statements about FHA loans is true?

       a. They are offered by the FHA directly.
       b. They require an upfront funding fee.
       c. They offer low down payments.
       d. They have the most stringent credit requirements.

2.16 For which property could a buyer use an FHA loan to fund the purchase?

a. A triplex, with one unit owner occupied
b. A 10-unit apartment building, with one unit owner occupied
c. A vacation home
d. A manufactured home park of 100 lots

2.17 Alex is assuming Cameron's FHA loan. Alex will take over all future payments and loan obligations, and Cameron will be released from any liability. What type of loan assumption does this arrangement describe?

a. Assignment
b. Basic assumption
c. Simple assumption
d. Novation

2.18 Investor Tracy bought a property that needed some TLC for $125,000. She spent six weeks renovating it extensively, and then listed it for $260,000. First-time buyer Cliff, who is using an FHA loan, contracted with Tracy to buy the house. Which of the following statements is true about this specific scenario?

a. The FHA will require that Cliff's lender obtain two appraisals to ensure Tracy's list price is justified.
b. The FHA will not insure the mortgage, so Cliff cannot use an FHA loan to buy it.
c. Cliff will have to pay a larger down payment than the FHA typically requires.
d. Cliff will have no problem using an FHA loan because the house has been renovated and is considered a low risk.

2.19 _____ is a type of mortgage insurance that is ongoing over the life of the loan.

a. UFMIP
b. PMI
c. MIP
d. VA funding fee

2.20 Which if these is true of the VA loan program's funding fee?

a. It helps fund programs for disabled veterans.
b. It is not dependent on factors surrounding the borrower's military service.
c. It is required for all VA loan users.
d. It is often rolled into the loan amount.

2.21 MLO Duane is discussing the loan process with Manuel, a Navy veteran. How would he describe the purpose of the CRV?

a. "The CRV is primarily used to determine your eligibility for a VA loan based on your service record."
b. "The CRV is required to assess the home's value and ensure it meets VA-specified minimum property requirements for safety and condition."
c. "The CRV provides a government-backed guarantee for the total loan amount, regardless of the property's value."
d. "The CRV is designed to assess your creditworthiness and ability to repay the loan."

2.22　U.S. Department of Veterans Affairs (VA) loans _____.

    a.　are designed for veterans to purchase residential property
    b.　offer assistance to borrowers to help avoid foreclosure
    c.　are fully assumable by buyers who meet the lender's criteria
    d.　require a small down payment

2.23　Both USDA guaranteed loan programs and direct loan programs are

    a.　only available to borrowers with very low income.
    b.　made by private lenders but guaranteed by the USDA.
    c.　subject to a 1% or more down payment.
    d.　accessible to borrowers in certain eligible geographic areas.

2.24　Non-conforming loans are

    a.　conventional loans that do not adhere to Fannie Mae or Freddie Mac rules.
    b.　jumbo loans with no government backing.
    c.　conventional loans that can be sold in the secondary market.
    d.　government loans that are insured but can be guaranteed.

2.25　Jumbo loans are a good option for

    a.　a first-time homebuyer with a $60,000 down payment.
    b.　a buyer looking for a loan that exceeds the FHFA's maximum limits.
    c.　a buyer who cannot meet conforming loans' underwriting standards.
    d.　a buyer with a poor credit history.

2.26　The *Guidance on Non-Traditional Mortgage Product Risk* addresses risks associated with non-traditional mortgage products, such as _____.

    a.　negative amortization
    b.　jumbo loans
    c.　seller concession limits
    d.　simple assumption

2.27　Non-qualified mortgages do not adhere to Dodd-Frank and CFPB strict lending requirements, i.e., regulations introduced to ensure borrowers can repay loans. Which of the following can be associated with a non-qualified mortgage?

    a.　DTI below 43%
    b.　Alternative documentation for income
    c.　Stringent regulatory protection for borrowers
    d.　Rigorous application process

2.28　Which mortgage loan products acts as a form of insurance for borrowers against rising interest rates?

    a.　ARM
    b.　Balloon mortgage
    c.　Fixed-rate mortgage
    d.　Reverse mortgage

2.29　A(n) _____ is a secondary loan taken out at the same time as the primary mortgage to help finance the purchase.

    a.　adjustable-rate mortgage
    b.　reverse mortgage
    c.　purchase money second mortgage
    d.　balloon mortgage

2.30   With an interest-only loan, what generally happens once the interest-only period ends?

a. The borrower makes one balloon payment to pay off the loan.
b. The loan typically converts to a standard amortizing loan.
c. The borrower takes out a second mortgage to cover principal payments not paid during the interest-only period.
d. The loan converts to a jumbo loan.

2.31   Which of the following is a definitive feature of a balloon mortgage?

a. The home's equity converts into cash without having to sell the home.
b. It finances a new build or major renovation.
c. Its interest rate changes over time.
d. It is a short-term loan with a large final payment.

2.32   Which of the following is true about reverse mortgages?

a. Two phases are involved: a draw period and a repayment period.
b. The home's equity decreases over the life of the mortgage.
c. Lenders generally utilize alternative documentation for income qualification.
d. All fees are paid up front.

2.33   For which type of loan are funds disbursed in stages, or draws?

a. Jumbo loan
b. Interest-only loan
c. Construction loan
d. Adjustable-rate loan

2.34   For FHA loans, the percentage of a borrower's monthly gross income going toward housing costs (front-end ratio) cannot exceed _____.

a. 30%
b. 31%
c. 41%
d. 43%

2.35   John is applying for an FHA loan. His gross monthly income is $4,000. According to FHA guidelines, what is the maximum monthly mortgage payment John qualifies for?

a. $1,200
b. $1,240
c. $1,640
d. $1,720

Section III: Mortgage Loan Origination Activities

➢ **Application Information and Requirements**

- **Borrower application**
- **Verification**
- **Suitability of Products and Programs**
- **Accuracy (tolerances)**
- **Originator's Disclosures**
- **Loan Estimate Timing**

➢ **Qualification: Processing and Underwriting**

- **Borrower analysis**
- **Appraisals**
- **Title report**
- **Insurances: hazard, flood, mortgage**

➢ **Closing**

- **Settlement agent**
- **Explanation of fees**
- **Explanation of documents**
- **Funding**

➢ **Financial Calculations Used in Mortgage Lending**

- **Period interest**
- **PITI payments**
- **Mortgage insurance**
- **Downpayments**
- **Debt-to-income ratio**
- **Buydowns**
- **Closing costs; prepaid items; prorations**
- **ARM indexed rates**

Application Information and Requirements

- ➢ **Loan origination process overview**

  - **pre-qualification phase**

    - ○ initial stage: borrower provides financial information to a lender
    - ○ lender assesses information to estimate mortgage amount for which borrower may qualify
    - ○ generally non-binding; serves as preliminary assessment of borrower's financial capability

  - **loan application**

    - ○ borrower completes formal mortgage application, often referred to as form 1003
    - ○ application requires detailed information about borrower's employment, income, assets, liabilities, and a property description

  - **application processing**

    - ○ lender processes application by verifying information borrower provided
    - ○ includes confirming borrower's employment status, income levels, credit history, and property value via appraisal

  - **underwriting process**

    - ○ underwriter evaluates application to determine risk involved in lending to borrower
    - ○ involves thorough review of borrower's creditworthiness and property value
    - ○ ensures application meets regulatory and lender-specific criteria

  - **credit decision**

    - ○ underwriter either approves, suspends (needs additional information), or denies application
    - ○ **decision based on underwriter's assessment of borrower's likelihood of borrower repaying loan _and_ property's value as collateral**

  - **closing**

    - ○ closing process begins upon loan approval
    - ○ involves preparing and signing legal documents that finalize mortgage agreement
    - ○ borrower and lender sign:

      - ▪ **mortgage note** -- outlines terms of the loan
      - ▪ **mortgage or deed of trust** -- serves as security for loan

  - **post-closing**

    - ○ after closing, lender may retain loan or sell it on secondary mortgage market
    - ○ borrower starts making regular mortgage payments as per agreed terms
    - ○ lender is responsible for managing loan, including collecting payments and managing escrow accounts

➢ **Borrower application**

- industry standard form: the **Uniform Residential Loan Application** (URLA); aka the 1003, Fannie Mae's form number for the application

- also known as **Freddie Mac's Form 65**

- recent redesign (2021): streamlined format, improved organization, updated terminology, improved accessibility, enhanced data collection, compliance with regulatory changes, Uniform Data Set (UDS), which standardizes data collection across industry

- generally completed twice: on initial application and at closing

- components include:

  o **borrower information**
    - name and alternate name, if applicable
    - Social Security number, birthdate, and citizenship
    - type of credit desired
    - marital status and dependents
    - contact information, addresses
    - employment history, income, any additional employment / income information, previous employment details if current is less than 2 years
    - assets, liabilities, real estate owned (if applicable)
    - loan and property information, other mortgages, any rental income on desired property, any gifts or grants to help with loan
    - declarations: specific questions about property, funding, past financial history, and personal finances, e.g., co-signs, outstanding judgments, defaults, foreclosures, bankruptcy, etc.
    - acknowledgements and agreements, signatures
    - military service
    - demographic data
    - loan originator information: completed by MLO

  o **lender loan information**
    - property and loan information, including transaction details
    - title details: how estate will be held and why type (sole ownership, tenancy in common, etc.)
    - mortgage details
    - borrower qualification specifics, including minimum funds needed

  o **additional borrower**: used when more than one individual is applying for the mortgage
    - requested information mirrors information required for primary buyer

  o **unmarried addendum**: may be used only when borrower selected "Unmarried" in Section 1

  o continuation sheet: used when more space is needed to complete URLA

- accepting applications
  - minimum details required for lender to receive application includes:
    - borrower's name
    - borrower's income
    - borrower's Social Security number
    - property address
    - property's estimated value
    - borrower's desired loan amount

- MLO's offering / negotiating loan terms
  - presenting loan offer to borrower for acceptance; could also require:
    - further information verification
    - conditional statements within offer
    - tasks performed by other individuals to complete the loan process
  - responding to borrower requests for different terms, e.g., lower rate or fewer points
  - presenting revised offer to borrower

- managing information
  - MLO is responsible for ensuring applications are completed accurately and thoroughly
  - tasks include ensuring these items are provided:
    - all documents
    - minimum information
    - appropriate disclosures
  - analyzing information for inconsistencies
  - verifying information is correct

- permissible questions: emphasis on questions that qualify applicant's ability to repay loan. including:
  - income
  - credit history
  - assets
  - liabilities
  - employment
  - ethnicity, to avoid discrimination
  - legal history

61

- **gift donors** for applicants using financial gift to cover mortgage costs: per Fannie Mae, donors must be related to applicant by blood, marriage, adoption, or legal guardianship
  - gift permissions and restrictions
    - conventional loan, 20% down: gift may cover all costs
    - conventional loan, less than 20% down: restrictions on how much gift may cover; varies by loan type
    - FHA / VA loans, credit score of 620 or greater: gift may cover all costs regardless of down payment amount
    - FHA / VA loans, credit score less than 620: borrower responsible for 3.5% of down payment

- ➢ **Verification**
  - **authorization forms**: certain borrower-supplied information must be verified by third parties listed on application; forms to use for verification include:
    - **VOD**: confirms availability and source of funds borrower intends to use for down payment, closing costs, or reserves
      - typically includes information about borrower's account balances and recent transactions
      - seasoned money often preferred, meaning funds have been in the account for more than 60 days; helps prove borrower is not borrowing other funds improperly for down payment
      - MLOs contact borrower's bank or financial institution to obtain VOD

    - **VOE**: confirms a borrower's current and past employment history, income, and job stability
      - may involve collecting pay stubs, W-2 forms, and tax returns to cross-verify income details borrower provided
      - most lenders require income to be verifiable over previous 2 years; often take two-year average of income for qualification purposes
      - MLOs typically contact borrower's current and, if applicable, previous employers directly or use third-party verification services to obtain information

- ➢ **Suitability of products and programs**
  - MLO must understand **borrower's goals** to match borrower with suitable loan product; actions include:
    - inquiring about **loan purpose**, e.g., home purchase, existing mortgage refinance, home equity access for other financial needs

    - learning applicant's **homeownership objectives**: plans to stay in home long term or plans to sell or refinance within a few years

  - **borrower's timelines**, including:
    - purchase timing: may have urgent need, e.g., job relocation, or a more flexible timeline

- retirement or other future plans; may impact loan product decision
- refinancing plans for future
- other financial goals, such as paying off mortgage early or leveraging property for investment purposes
- life events: can influence timeline for homeownership decisions and financial situations
- selling plans: related to job changes, downsizing, or other life circumstances

- **match risk tolerance with loan product**; how comfortable is borrower with:
  - potential fluctuations in interest rates, monthly payments, overall loan terms
  - various risk factors of different mortgage products, e.g., interest rate variability, potential for payment increases, long-term financial implications
  - risk vs. reward: weigh potential benefits of lower initial interest rates against risks of future rate adjustments

➤ **Accuracy (tolerances)**

- three types of tolerance thresholds established by TRID; designed to ensure transparency and protect borrowers from unexpected changes in loan terms and costs

- **zero tolerance**: applies to fees that **must remain the same** from initial Loan Estimate (LE) to final Closing Disclosure (CD), including:
  - fees paid to lender or loan originator, e.g., origination charges
  - fees for services provided by lender's / MLO's affiliates
  - transfer taxes

- **10% cumulative tolerance**: applies to fees that can increase by up to 10% in total from initial LE to final CD, including:
  - recording fees
  - fees paid to third-party service providers not affiliated with lender
  - charges for services borrower selects but are on lender's list of preferred providers

- **no or unlimited tolerance**: applies to fees that can change from LE to final CD without restrictions, including:
  - fees for services lender does not require
  - fees paid to third-party service providers chosen by borrower and not on lender's list
  - fees for services where borrower shops for providers and chooses one that is not on the lender's list.
  - fees for optional services, such as owner's title insurance (unless required by lender)

➤ **MLO disclosures**

- **purpose**: certain disclosures required by federal law to ensure transparency and inform borrowers about terms, costs, and risks associated with mortgage loans

- **Loan Estímate (LE)**
  - ○ **TILA requirement to complete**
  - ○ **initial LE**: standardized form; includes key loan terms, estimated closing costs
    - ▪ helps borrowers understand loan terms, e.g., interest rate, monthly payments, and any potential changes over time
    - ▪ outlines estimated closing costs, so borrowers can compare offers from different lenders
    - ▪ must be provided to borrowers within <u>3 business days</u> of completed loan application
  - ○ **revised LE**: may be necessary if specific circumstances change during application process, e.g., loan amount or interest rate changes, tolerance corrections exceed the limits, or changes to other factors that affect loan terms or costs
    - ▪ must be provided within <u>3 business days</u> of receiving new information that triggers revision
    - ▪ applicant must receive revised LE at least 4 business days before closing
  - ○ **LE expires 10 days after it is issued to borrower if borrower does not provide a notice of intent to proceed**

- **Mortgage Loan Servicing Disclosure** (RESPA requirement)
  - ○ outlines whether lender intends to service loan or transfer it to another entity for servicing
  - ○ must be provided to borrowers within <u>3 business days</u> of completed loan application

- **CFPB Home Loan Toolkit** (TILA and RESPA reference)
  - ○ for purchase transactions only
  - ○ **assists borrowers in understanding mortgage loan process**
  - ○ **provides borrowers with information about their rights and responsibilities,** as well as various stages of obtaining a mortgage, including:
    - ▪ loan application process
    - ▪ loan estimates and closing disclosures
    - ▪ interest rates and mortgage terms
    - ▪ loan offer comparisons
    - ▪ credit reports and credit scores
  - ○ must be provided to borrowers within <u>3 business days</u> of completed loan application

- **Prospective settlement service providers** (TILA requirement)
  - ○ written list of prospective settlement service providers involved in closing process, e.g., title insurance companies, settlement agents

- o disclosure informs borrowers about options for essential services related to mortgage transaction

- o borrowers are <u>not</u> required to select a service provider from the list; they may choose their own with no penalty or liability for discrimination

- o service provider list must be provided to borrowers within <u>3 business days</u> of completed loan application

- **Affiliated Business Arrangement Disclosure**, (RESPA requirement)
  - o **must disclose any interests that settlement service providers may have in affiliated businesses such as title insurance, mortgage insurance, real estate brokerage, or other services related to transaction**

  - o typically addresses:
    - affiliated business arrangement, including ownership interests or financial ties
    - estimated charges or fees associated with the services provided by the affiliated business

  - o borrower may shop for settlement services and is <u>not</u> obligated to use affiliated business services

  - o must be provided to borrowers at or before time of loan application

  - o failure to disclose affiliated relationship can result in penalties and legal consequences for involved lenders and settlement service providers

- **Consumer Handbook on Adjustable-Rate Mortgages**, aka CHARM booklet (TILA requirement)
  - o informs borrowers about adjustable-rate mortgages and helps them make informed decisions when considering or choosing an ARM

  - o ensures borrowers are aware of potential risks and benefits

  - o topics include:
    - differences between ARMs and fixed-rate mortgages
    - interest rate adjustments and payment changes
    - interest rate indexes and margins used to calculate ARM rates
    - rate caps, payment caps, and negative amortization
    - budgeting and financial planning to prepare for ARM payment adjustments

  - o must be provided to borrowers within <u>3 business days</u> of completed loan application

65

- **Adjustable-Rate Mortgage Disclosure** (TILA requirement)

  - only required when ARM is involved

  - comprehensive explanation of ARM's key characteristics, how they work, and potential changes that may occur in interest rates and payments

  - highly specific to individual ARM loan that is offered to borrower; includes precise details about the loan's facts, including:

    - initial interest rate, as well as any introductory or teaser rates
    - interest rate index used for rate adjustments
    - the margin, which is added to the index to determine the new interest rate
    - interest rate caps, including initial adjustment caps, periodic adjustment caps, and lifetime caps
    - payment adjustment calculations, including impact on monthly payments
    - potential for negative amortization, i.e., when unpaid interest is added to loan balance
    - scenarios showing interest rate adjustment effects on monthly payments
    - borrower's responsibilities, including payment obligations

  - must be provided to borrowers within <u>3 business days</u> of completed ARM loan application

- **Homeownership Counseling Disclosure** (TILA requirement)

  - informs borrowers of right to seek homeownership counseling services

  - emphasizes importance of seeking advice and assistance from qualified housing counselors

- **Closing Disclosure** (TILA requirement)

  - **provides detailed breakdown of <u>final</u> loan terms and closing costs**

  - allows borrowers to review and compare final terms to those disclosed on LE to ensure consistency and accuracy

  - must be provided at least <u>3 business days</u> before scheduled closing date

  - significant changes to loan terms or Closing Disclosure after it has been initially provided to borrower may require a new three-day waiting period.

    Changes triggering a revision include:

    - APR increases by more than 1/8 of a percentage point for fixed-rate loans or 1/4 of a percentage point for variable-rate loans
    - borrower switches to different loan product
    - prepayment penalty is added to loan terms
    - loan term (e.g., the length of the loan) changes
    - increases in certain fees or costs beyond allowable tolerances

- **timing requirements**; the "3-7-3 Rule"
  - o simplification for disclosure timing requirements associated with TILA and the Mortgage Disclosure Improvement Act (MDIA) of 2008

  - o **The 1ˢᵗ "3":** lenders are generally required to **make initial disclosures** within 3 business days of receiving mortgage loan application. Disclosures include the aforementioned:
    - **Loan Estimate**
    - **Home Loan Toolkit**
    - **Homeownership Counseling Disclosure**
    - CHARM booklet, if applicable
    - ARM Disclosure, if applicable

  - o **The "7":** under MDIA, the **earliest a lender can close mortgage loan is on the seventh business day** after providing initial disclosures to borrower
    - Closing Disclosure can be sent during this period

  - o **The 2ⁿᵈ "3":** if significant changes are made to loan terms after initial disclosures have been provided, borrowers must receive redisclosures with updated terms, triggering another 3-day waiting period

  - o business day definition:
    - TILA/TRID requirements: any calendar day except Sundays and legal public holidays

    - RESPA requirements: any day when an institution's offices are open and carrying out all business functions

- **delivery method; timing of disclosure delivery**
  - o timing of when applicant is considered to have received disclosures is an important aspect of regulatory compliance in mortgage lending process

  - o choice of delivery methods for disclosures can impact when applicant is deemed to have received those disclosures

  - o mail delivery: disclosures such as LE and CD are deemed to be received on third business day after they are placed in the mail; aka the **mailbox rule**

  - o electronic delivery:
    - applicant must consent to electronic delivery prior to delivery
    - applicant must have access to electronic disclosures, e.g., via email or disclosures must be in a format that the applicant can retain and access later (e.g., PDF) secure website)
    - same 3-day rule for receipt as regular mail <u>unless</u> applicant sends lender a return receipt message

  - o fax delivery: deemed to be received day after successful transmission

  - o in-person delivery: deemed to be received on the date of face-to-face meeting.

Qualification: Processing and Underwriting

➢ **Borrower analysis**

- **verify and validate accuracy of application**

  ○ purpose: a thorough evaluation of borrower's financial creditworthiness determines whether the borrower qualifies for the requested mortgage loan

  ○ steps:

    ▪ **review loan application** information for completeness and accuracy

    ▪ prepare and **deliver initial disclosures** as required by law

    ▪ **conduct credit check**

    ▪ **submit file to underwriter for analysis**

- **assets**

  ○ identify assets available for down payment and monthly payment obligations, closing costs, escrow accounts

  ○ most common asset types include:

    ▪ bank accounts, money market accounts, CDs
    ▪ retirement accounts
    ▪ business accounts
    ▪ stocks and bonds
    ▪ real estate: investment, vacation, or sale of current residence
    ▪ sale of assets
    ▪ gift funds
    ▪ down payment assistance programs

  ○ two asset categories: **liquid** (aka current) assets can be easily converted to cash or cash equivalents; **fixed** (non-current) assets cannot be easily converted to cash or cash equivalents

  ○ lenders often consider seasoning of funds, i.e., whether funds have been in borrower's account(s) for any length of time

  ○ verify that funds reported on application are accurate and in order

- **liabilities**

  ○ like assets, lenders evaluate borrower's liabilities or financial obligations, which can impact ability to make mortgage payments

  ○ common liability types include:

    ▪ existing mortgages
    ▪ loans: auto, personal, student
    ▪ revolving accounts, e.g. credit cards

- child support / alimony
- legal judgments, tax liens, other outstanding debts

- **income**
  - income verification includes analysis of pay stubs, W-2s, and tax returns to assess stability and consistency; helps in determining borrower's ability to make monthly mortgage payments

  - income usually required to be verifiable over the past 2 years; sometimes 2-year average is used for variable income such as commissions, bonuses

  - income with expiration date (child support, alimony, long-term disability, etc.) must be likely to continue for 3 years after closing

  - acceptable income with proper documentation includes:
    - employment income: salary hourly, self-employed, side gigs
    - rental income
    - retirement income
    - investment income
    - alimony
    - bonus and commission income
    - non-taxable income: permanent disability payments, Social Security benefits, child support

    - unemployment compensation, if part of the regular annual work cycle, e.g. for a seasonal worker with normal down time (fishing, construction, farming); 2 years of tax returns required, with employment income and unemployment income each averaged; <u>cannot</u> be used as qualifying income when received due to layoff or termination

  - capital gains income requires 3 consecutive years of documentation and must appear on tax returns; year-to-date breakdown also required

  - non-taxable income, such as permanent disability payments, Social Security benefits, child support, etc.
    - can be subject to "grossing up": lender calculates what the tax would be and adds that amount to gross amount received
    - "gross up" factors are from 15% to 25%: non-taxable income multiplied by 115% to 125% to adjust

  - self-employed borrower: 2 years most recent tax returns; Form 1040, Schedule C for sole proprietors, or business tax returns for partnerships and corporations

  - employment gaps: may require letter of explanation
    - less than 6 months: can typically qualify with current job verification, as long as meets other criteria
    - more than 6 months: may need to be with full-time job for at least 6 months before qualifying

- **credit report**
  - purpose: used along with other financial information to assess borrower's creditworthiness and eligibility for mortgage loan

  - national credit reporting agencies (aka credit bureaus): Equifax, Experian, and TransUnion

  - credit scores, such as FICO score or VantageScore: derived from credit report information; provide numerical representation of borrower's creditworthiness and risk
    - range from 320 to 850, depending on agency
    - higher scores indicate low risk and thus better credit

  - crucial factors to determining credit score include:
    - paying bills on time; accounts for 35% of score
    - ratio of credit debt to credit limit; 30% of score
    - credit account ages: older credit accounts are considered more reliable information sources; 15% of score

    - credit type: revolving or installment "credit mix"; indicates borrower can manage different credit types responsibly (financial versatility); 10% of score

    - number of credit report inquiries: multiple recent credit inquiries is not advantageous for borrower; may suggest to creditors that borrower is actively seeking credit from several sources; 10% of score

  - **credit history**: detailed record of borrower's credit accounts, such as credit cards, loans, mortgages, and other lines of credit; includes information on account balances, payment history, and any derogatory marks
    - **derogatory remarks**: late payments, current delinquencies, collections, judgments, bad debt write-offs, foreclosures, bankruptcies

- **qualifying ratios** (housing, debt-to-income)
  - **purpose**: used to assess borrower's financial capacity and ability to manage mortgage payments responsibly

  - borrower must qualify on both housing ratio and DTI ratio

  - certain loan programs have specific qualifying ratio requirements that must be met for loan approval

  - helps determine appropriate loan amount for which a borrower qualifies

  - housing ratio, aka front-end ratio, top ratio
    - percentage of gross monthly income devoted to total monthly housing expense payment: PITI and any homeowners association fees; PITI: principal, interest, taxes, and insurance
    - generally, cannot exceed 28% to 31% of gross monthly income depending on loan type; can be higher with some lenders based on other

factors

- PITI <u>only</u> applies to applicant's primary residence, <u>not</u> any additional mortgage loans borrower is paying off

- benchmark ratio: a guideline that can be exceeded based on **compensating factors**, i.e., applicant's other positive characteristics, e.g., high credit score, substantial financial reserves

- **formula**:

  Housing Ratio = (PITI on Primary Residence) ÷ (Gross Monthly Income)

o debt-to-income ratio, aka back-end ratio, bottom ratio

- percentage of all monthly debt obligations; includes PITI, revolving debts, installment debts, alimony and / or child support

- does <u>not</u> include utilities, groceries / food, educational expenses other than student loans, childcare other than child support, medical insurance premiums, entertainment

- generally cannot exceed 33% to 43% of gross monthly income, depending on loan type; can be higher with some lenders based on other factors

- **formula**:

  DTI Ratio = (All Recurring Monthly Debt) ÷ (Gross Monthly Income)

- **loan-to-value ratio (LTV)**

  o purpose: measures relationship between mortgage loan amount and appraised value or purchase price of property securing the loan

  o helps ensure property's value supports requested loan amount

  o higher LTV suggests smaller down payment and potentially higher risk; borrower is requesting a larger percentage of property's value as a loan

  o lower LTV means borrower is making larger down payment; implies lower risk for lender; may result in lower interest rate

  o different mortgage loan programs may have specific LTV ratio requirements

  - government-backed loans e.g., FHA and VA loans, may allow for higher LTV ratios compared to conventional loans

  o LTV ratios exceeding 80% generally mean borrower must purchase PMI

  o **formula**:

  LTV Ratio = (Loan Amount) ÷ (Property Value)

- **ability to repay rules**
  - o federal regulations established by Consumer Financial Protection Bureau (CFPB) as part of Dodd-Frank Wall Street Reform and Consumer Protection Act

  - o purpose: ensure lenders make mortgage loans to borrowers who have ability to repay them; promote responsible lending practices; protect borrowers from mortgage loans they cannot afford

  - o required evaluations include:
    - income
    - employment status
    - assets
    - mortgage payment
    - property taxes, insurance, and other associated costs
    - monthly debt obligations
    - qualifying ratio limits
    - credit history

  - o MLOs must document and verify borrower's financial information, including income, employment, assets, and credit history

  - o alternative: lender presumed to be in compliance with ability to repay rules if the loan is a qualified mortgage (QM)

  - o lender protections under ATR rules:
    - **Safe Harbor**: for loans that meet all QM criteria, including the 43% DTI limit; strong legal protections; borrowers have limited ability to challenge lender's compliance with ATR rules

    - **Rebuttable Presumption**: for QM loans that exceed 43% DTI limit; still protected, but borrowers have more flexibility to challenge compliance in certain situations

  - o **prohibitions**: in general, balloon payments, negative amortization, no documentation loans, and interest-only loans longer then first five years

  - o do not apply to: HELOCs, reverse mortgages, timeshare loans, temporary financing, or loans for business purposes

- **tangible net benefit**
  - o financial advantages or benefits that borrower is expected to gain from refinancing existing mortgage loan into a new one

  - o financial advantage typically relates to reducing borrower's monthly payments, lowering interest rate, or achieving other cost savings

  - o several factors evaluated to determine if refinance offers net tangible benefit, including:
    - interest rate reduction: can result in reduced monthly mortgage payments and long-term interest savings

- monthly payment reduction more affordable for borrower
- shortening loan term: can lead to interest savings over life of loan
- switching from adjustable to fixed rate: transitioning to fixed-rate mortgage can provide stability and protection against interest rate fluctuations
- eliminating PMI: if borrower's equity has increased, refinancing to eliminate PMI can reduce monthly payments
- accessing home equity: can address other financial needs, such as home improvements or debt consolidation
- consolidating debt: combining high-interest debt into lower-interest mortgage can result in overall savings

    o **loan flipping, or churning**: refinancing borrowers <u>without a tangible net benefit</u> for borrower for purpose of generating fees and charges for lender; considered form of loan fraud

➢ **Automated Underwriting Systems (AUS)**

    o **Fannie Mae's Desktop Underwriter** (DU): lenders use to evaluate borrowers' creditworthiness and to determine whether loan meets Fannie Mae's eligibility and underwriting guidelines

- integrates with Form 1003's information, including credit history, income, assets, and liabilities
- streamlines underwriting process, reduces manual review, and provides lenders with consistency and efficiency in lending decisions
- generates risk assessment and provides recommended loan decision based on information provided
- provides recommendation on whether loan should be approved, referred to manual underwriting, or denied

    o Freddie Mac's Loan Product Advisor (LPA)

- similar to and serves same purpose as DU; used by lenders who work with Freddie Mac

    o DU and LPA provide automated recommendations; final lending decision may involve additional factors, e.g., lender-specific policies and risk assessment

    o systems periodically update to align with changing industry standards and regulations

➢ **Appraisals**

- purpose: determine property's fair market value to confirm it is worth the mortgage loan amount

- lender will not approve a loan amount that exceeds property's appraised value; ensures property can be sold to cover the loan debt in case of borrower default

- definitions:

    o **subject property**: property being appraised

- o **comparable sales** (comps): similar properties in same area and used as basis for comparison when determining a property's value

- o **comp adjustments**: changes made to value of comparable properties to make them more similar to subject property for accurate comparison

- approaches

  - o **sales comparison approach**: involves comparing subject property to similar recently sold properties; aka market data or market approach

    - select comparable sales: appraiser identifies recently sold properties (comps) similar to subject property in terms of location, size, condition, and features
    - adjustment factors: appraiser examines differences between subject property and comps, e.g., number of bedrooms, yard size, or recent renovations; assigns value adjustments to account for differences
    - comparison and adjustment: appraiser adjusts each comp's sales price based on factors, either adding or subtracting value to make comp more comparable to subject property
    - final value estimate: adjusted sale prices of the comps are used to estimate subject's fair market value

  - o **cost approach**: based on cost to rebuild or replace property; useful when appraising properties that are not frequently bought or sold, such as unique or specialized properties

    - **estimating replacement cost**: appraiser calculates cost to rebuild or replace subject property with a similar one, including construction costs, labor, materials, associated fees

    - accounting for depreciation: appraiser takes into account any depreciation as a reduction in property's value due to factors like wear and tear, age, or obsolescence; typically three types of obsolescence:

      - **physical depreciation**: damage or wear to property itself
      - **functional obsolescence**: issues related to property's layout or design
      - **external obsolescence**: factors off property, like changes in the neighborhood

    - **adding land value**: appraiser estimates value of underlying land typically determined separately from cost of structure; note: land cannot be depreciated, therefore the land value must be kept separately from improvement value, then added back in to complete the cost analysis

    - final value estimate: appraiser adds estimated land value to depreciated cost of structure, arriving at value estimate of property

  - o **income approach**: used for income-generating properties, estimating value based on potential rental income

    - used to determine the value of income-producing properties, e.g., hotels, apartments, or complex commercial buildings, by assessing income potential

- **estimating potential income**: appraiser estimates property's potential income, including rental income from all units, parking fees, vending machines, laundry, etc.

- **operating expenses**: appraiser subtracts property's operating expenses, including property taxes, insurance, maintenance costs, management fees, to calculate property's net operating income (NOI)

- **formula**:

    $NOI = (Estimated\ Potential\ Income - Operating\ Expenses)$

- **capitalization rate (cap rate)**: appraiser divides NOI by property's current market value or acquisition cost to determine cap rate, which represents expected rate of return an investor would require to invest in property

- value estimation: appraiser uses cap rate to estimate property's value; calculation provides property's value based on its income-generating potential

- **formula:**

    $Value = (NOI \div Cap\ Rate)$

- higher NOI and lower cap rate generally result in a higher property value

- appraisal rules, disclosure, and timing

  - Equal Credit Opportunity Act (ECOA) Valuations Rule: primarily focuses on how creditors handle property appraisals related to mortgage loan applications

  - required lender disclosure must be provided to borrower at time of application or within 3 business days of receiving application; disclosure notices include:

    - borrower has right to receive a copy of any appraisal or valuation developed in connection with their mortgage loan application
    - borrower must make request to receive appraisal in writing
    - borrower may waive right to receive appraisal copy; must be in writing

  - creditors must provide appraisal or valuation upon completion or 3 business days before closing, whichever is earlier

- independent appraisal requirement

  - purpose: ensure property appraisals are conducted without undue influence or bias

  - ECOA appraisal rules include:

    - lenders <u>cannot</u> pressure appraisers to provide specific value for property

- lenders must select independent appraisers with necessary qualifications and experience to perform reliable appraisals

- lenders <u>cannot</u> directly compensate appraisers <u>based on appraisal outcome</u>

- appraiser to conduct accurate and impartial evaluations leading to opinions of value

- additional information may be provided to appraiser for consideration if lender / borrower notices missing or incorrect information on appraisal report

➢ **Title reports, binders, and title insurance**

- **title report:** detailed history of the property's ownership and any associated legal issues

  - verifies current and previous ownership
  - ensures seller has legal right to transfer ownership to buyer
  - provides legal description of property, including precise property location and boundary identification
  - identifies any outstanding liens, mortgages, or encumbrances on the property
  - includes information about any easements or restrictions that may affect the use of the property

- **underwriting**: title report assessed as part of due diligence

  - significant title issues can impact loan approval or terms
  - problems must be resolved before transaction can proceed

- **obtaining reports**: buyer selects title company

  - professional title company: specializes in conducting title searches and providing comprehensive reports
  - attorney: particularly applicable in states requiring attorney closings
  - local county recorder's office
  - online title service: report can be ordered electronically

- **preliminary title report and commitment**

  - preliminary title report prepared by title company early in process, typically shortly after purchase agreement signed

  - **attorney / title company conducts thorough title search**

    - involves researching public records, deeds, mortgages, court records, other relevant documents
    - aims to trace history of ownership and identify any liens, encumbrances, or legal issues associated with property

- o **title search findings compiled them into preliminary title report**
  - includes details about the property's ownership history and legal descriptions
  - provides initial information about status of property's title
  - highlights any potential complications for transferring property, e.g., liens, encumbrances, easements, restrictions, unpaid tax bills, etc.

- o **title company issues commitment to provide title insurance**
  - commitment outlines terms and conditions under which title insurance policy will be issued at closing
  - includes: property details, current owner, title exceptions, requirements that must be met for policy to be issued, and cost of insurance
  - buyer / seller / agents / attorneys review title insurance commitment to ensure no unexpected title issues; any title exceptions or requirements listed must be resolved before closing
  - borrower pays for lender's title insurance policy; may opt to purchase their own policy too

- o **preliminary title report and commitment for title insurance provides assurance that property's title will be clear and marketable at closing**

- **timing of title report and commitment**
  - o must be obtained before closing
  - o title search and reporting typically takes 2 weeks, but can be longer depending on property

- **final title report / title insurance policy**
  - o final title report issued after any necessary issues are resolved and the transaction proceeds
  - o title insurance company issues title insurance policy: a binding agreement that provides ongoing protection
    - policy typically issued to lender as the insured party; buyer may also purchase a separate owner's policy
    - provides coverage and protection to insured parties against any covered title defects or issues that may arise in the future
    - remains in effect for as long as insured parties hold interest in property

- ➢ **Insurance: hazard, homeowners, flood, mortgage**
  - **purpose**: lenders typically require borrowers to have certain insurance policies as a condition of loan to protect lenders' financial interest in property
    - o in event of significant damage or loss to property, ensures lender's investment is protected
    - o if property is damaged or destroyed, insurance proceeds can be used to repair or rebuild the home, and this benefits both the homeowner and the lender
    - o often required to be paid from escrow accounts
    - o proof of insurance coverage required before loan can be finalized and property transaction can be completed; includes:
      - a copy of the insurance policy
      - proof of payment for the first year's premium

- o force-placed insurance: if required insurance is cancelled or not obtained, lender can insure property and force borrower to pay for it

- **hazard insurance**

  - o protects structure of home
  - o covers specific perils or hazards like fire, windstorm, theft, vandalism, etc.
  - o often included as a component of homeowners insurance

- **homeowners insurance**

  - o provides broader coverage than hazard insurance alone
  - o covers not only structure of home but also personal belongings, liability protection, and additional living expenses
  - o comprehensive protection for both property and homeowner

- **flood insurance**

  - o floods typically <u>not</u> covered by standard homeowners insurance policies
  - o specialized flood insurance coverage required based on several factors, including:
    - location and elevation
    - flood zone designation

  - o if actual structure is <u>not</u> located in Special Flood Hazard Areas (SFHA), no flood insurance required

  - o Federal Emergency Management Agency (FEMA)
    - designates areas as flood zones based on risk of flooding
    - range from high-risk zones (SFHAs) to moderate-to-low-risk zones
    - lenders most likely to require flood insurance for properties in high-risk flood zones

  - o National Flood Insurance Program (NFIP)
    - common source of flood insurance in participating communities
    - administered by FEMA

  - o private flood insurance
    - alternative to NFIP coverage
    - must meet specific requirements and offer comparable coverage to be approved by lender

  - o flood insurance must remain in effect over life of loan

- **Private Mortgage Insurance (PMI)**

  - o purpose: protects lender against losses when borrower defaults on conventional mortgage loan
  - o required when LTV for conventional loan is greater than 80%; can request to cancel PMI when borrower reaches 20% equity in home
  - o single-premium plan: borrower pays entire PMI premium upfront in lump sum at closing vs. ongoing monthly PMI payments

- can reduce monthly mortgage payments
        - may not be refundable if borrower refinances or sells home before reaching 20% equity
    - monthly premium plan: borrower pays mortgage insurance each month along with PITI payment; most common method
    - MI factor: numerical value or percentage of loan amount used to calculate annual PMI cost
        - based on LTV, credit score, loan type, and other risk-related issues
        - divided by 12 to determine monthly premium

Single-Premium Formula: Loan Amount x Factor

Monthly Premium Formula: (Loan Amount x Factor) ÷ 12

example: $365,000 loan, MI factor of 1.56% (.0156 as a decimal)

1. single premium: $365,000 x .0156 = $5,694
2. monthly premium: $5,694 ÷ 12 = $474.50

- government mortgage insurance (MIP)
    - purpose: promotes and facilitates homeownership by reducing financial risks faced by lenders and borrowers using FHA loans, which are insured by the Federal Housing Administration
    - paid over life of the loan
    - mandatory mortgage insurance premiums (MIP); consist of upfront premium and annual premium
        - upfront premium can be financed into loan
        - annual premium typically paid monthly

Closing

➤ **Settlement agent -- role, value, key tasks**

- **primary role**: facilitate and oversee the final steps of the home buying or selling process; acts on lender's behalf; aka closing agent, escrow agent

- exact party dictated by state laws and custom: could be title company, escrow company, attorney, or real estate broker

- **value of settlement agent**
    - serves as a neutral third party, ensuring all parties involved in transaction are treated fairly and that terms of agreement are met
    - settlement agents have deep understanding of real estate laws and conveyance-related regulations, which helps ensure that transaction complies with all legal requirements

- agents hold funds and documents in escrow to provide secure and trustworthy means of conducting financial aspects of transaction
- settlement agent works to resolve any issues or discrepancies that arise during closing process, keeps transaction on track

- key tasks include:
  - responsible for **coordinating and conducting closing process**, ensuring all necessary documents are prepared, reviewed, and signed by relevant parties

  - often acts as escrow agent, **holding important documents and funds** in secure and neutral account until all conditions of sale are met

  - reviews and approves any power of attorney (POA) if borrower cannot be present at closing

  - **may conduct or oversee title search** to ensure property's title is clear of any liens, encumbrances, or legal issues that could affect sale

  - **prepare key transaction documents** including settlement statement and deed and other legal documents required for transaction

  - **schedules and coordinates signing of documents** by buyer, seller, and any necessary third parties, such as lenders

  - **oversees closing meeting**, where documents are signed and funds are exchanged

  - **records deed and other necessary documents** with the appropriate government authorities

  - **provides parties with copies** of all relevant documents after closing

➢ **Explanation of fees: origination, discount points, closing costs, prepayment penalties**
- MLO responsible for educating borrower on fees associated with mortgage loan early in process

- **origination fees**: charges imposed by lender or mortgage broker for processing, underwriting, and originating loan; typically expressed as percentage of loan amount
  - cover cost of evaluating borrower's creditworthiness, processing loan application, and other administrative tasks
  - borrower has right to negotiate or compare this fee among different lenders
  - MLOs to clearly explain origination fee, its percentage, and total dollar amount to borrower

- **discount points**: optional fees paid upfront to lower interest rate on mortgage; each point typically costs 1% of loan amount
  - allow borrower to "buy down" interest rate, which can lead to lower monthly mortgage payments over life of loan
  - MLOs to help borrowers understand how paying discount points affects monthly payments and whether it makes financial sense based on plans to stay in home

80

- **closing costs**: collection of fees and charges associated with finalizing mortgage loan and transferring property ownership

  - can include fees for appraisal, title search, attorney fees, survey, home inspection, recording fees, mortgage insurance, title insurance, document preparation, etc.
  - MLO to provide estimate of expected closing costs early in the process, often in form of Loan Estimate (LE) to help borrower budget for home purchase

- **prepayment penalties**: charges some lenders imposed if borrower pays off mortgage loan before a specified period, typically within first few years

  - designed to protect lenders from lost interest income in case borrowers refinance or pay off the loan early
  - MLOs to inform borrower if loan includes prepayment penalty, and explain associated terms and conditions
  - borrowers should be aware of any potential penalties for paying off loan ahead of schedule
  - common method is to charge a percentage of the remaining loan balance as a penalty; e.g., prepayment penalty of 2% of outstanding loan balance if borrower pays off loan within penalty period of first three years

➢ **Explanation of documents**

- **promissory note**: legally binding contract between borrower and lender outlining **borrower's promise to repay loan** amount to lender under specific terms and conditions; key characteristics include:

  - lists loan details, including amount borrowed, interest rate, repayment schedule, etc.

  - specifies principal loan amount, which is initial amount borrowed; typically purchase price of home minus down payment.

  - specifies interest rate at which loan will accrue interest; can be fixed rate, adjustable rate, or another agreed-upon rate

  - outlines repayment terms, including number of monthly payments, due date of each payment, and total repayment period

  - may include provisions for late payment fees and penalties if borrower fails to make timely payments

  - defines what constitutes default on loan and outlines lender's rights and remedies in event of default, including foreclosure

  - often stipulates that loan is secured by property itself; if borrower defaults on loan, lender has right to foreclose on property to recover outstanding debt

- **mortgage**: security instrument and legal contract that **pledges the property as collateral** for repayment of loan; key characteristics include:

  - establishes lien on the property, providing lender with security interest in the property and giving lender right to foreclose and sell property if borrower defaults on loan

- primary parties involved in mortgage document are borrower (**mortgagor**) and lender (**mortgagee**); document outlines roles and responsibilities of each

- includes a detailed description of property being pledged as collateral; typically includes property's legal description, address, and other identifying information

- specifies loan terms and conditions, including loan amount, interest rate, repayment schedule, and any provisions related to late payments or default

- outlines rights and remedies of lender in case of borrower default, including right to foreclose on property and sell it to recover outstanding debt

- recorded in public records of county where property is located; recording serves as public notice of lender's lien on property

- certain provisions include:

  - acceleration clause (aka due-on-sale clause): allows lender to demand immediate repayment of entire loan balance if certain conditions are not met
  - alienation clause: prohibits borrower from transferring mortgaged property title without lender's consent
  - defeasance clause: allows borrower to "defease" or eliminate mortgage lien by meeting specific conditions, usually repaying loan in full

- **deed of trust** (aka trust deed): legal document **used in some U.S. states as mortgage alternative in real estate transactions**; key characteristics include:

  - serves as security instrument that pledges the property as collateral for loan. providing lender with legal interest in the property; gives lender right to foreclose and sell property if borrower defaults on loan
  - involves three primary parties: borrower, lender, and trustee, neutral third party, often title company or attorney, who holds legal title to property on behalf of lender until loan is repaid
  - borrower retains equitable ownership and right to possess and use property, while trustee holds legal title for security purposes
  - often include "power of sale" provision, which allows trustee to initiate non-judicial foreclosure sale in event of borrower default
  - recorded in public records of county where property is located; recording provides public notice of lender's interest in property
  - deed of reconveyance issued when loan is fully paid, which releases lien on property and transfers legal title back to borrower

> **Funding synopsis**

- financial transactions that take place at closing

- buyer and seller complete property sale, and all necessary payments and financial adjustments are made

- funds used for necessary payments typically made through wire transfers or certified funds

- **closing agent** / settlement agent oversees funding and disbursal of funds at closing, ensuring all payments are made correctly and the transaction is completed according to contract terms

- **closing costs**: fees and expenses associated with purchase or sale of property; typically divided between buyer and seller, although specific arrangements can vary depending on local customs and negotiations; include:
    - loan-related fees such as origination fees, appraisal fees, and credit report fees
    - title-related fees such as title insurance, title search, and recording fees
    - escrow or attorney fees for handling the closing process
    - taxes such as property taxes and transfer taxes
    - prepaid expenses including homeowners insurance and property taxes
    - miscellaneous fees such as courier fees, document preparation fees, and inspection fees

- **buyer's down payment**: portion of purchase price buyer pays upfront

- **earnest money**: money buyer provides as sign of good faith when making offer on the property; typically held in escrow and applied toward buyer's closing costs or down payment

- **mortgage loan**: if buyer is financing purchase with a mortgage loan, lender disburses loan funds at closing to cover remaining purchase price after down payment and earnest money are considered

- **prorations and adjustments**: made to ensure that buyer and seller are responsible for their respective portions of certain costs based on the closing date

- **closing statement**: provides itemized breakdown of all funds involved in closing; outlines buyer's costs, seller's proceeds, and any adjustments that need to be made

Financial Calculations Used in Mortgage Lending

➢ **Period interest**

- period interest, or periodic interest: interest that accumulates over a specific time period, often on a regular basis, such as monthly or annually

- this interest represents cost of borrowing; calculated based on outstanding loan balance, applicable interest rate, and terms of loan for given period

- lenders generally quote interest rates using annual percentage rate (APR); but interest on most mortgages compounds on monthly basis, i.e., 12 times per year

- **formula:**

Monthly Interest Payment = (Annual Interest Rate in Decimal Form ÷ Number of Compounding Periods) x Principal Balance

example: Data: outstanding loan balance $100,000; 4% annual interest rate; 12 compounding periods (monthly)

Monthly Interest Amount = (0.04 ÷ 12) x 100,000 = 0.00333 x 100,000 = 333.33

Monthly Interest = $333.33

➢ **Per diem interest**

- per diem interest: interest that accumulates every day instead of monthly or another period; aka daily interest
    - o note: lenders may use 365 days or 360 days for calculation

- **formula**

Daily Interest = (Monthly Interest Rate in Decimal Form ÷ 365) x Principal Balance

example: outstanding loan balance $250,000; 6% annual interest rate

Daily Interest = (0.06 ÷ 365) x 250,000 = 0.0001644 x 250,000 = $41.10

➢ **Prepaid interest**

- mortgage interest is paid in arrears; each monthly payment includes interest from the prior month
- first monthly mortgage payment generally due first day of second month after closing
- interest will typically accrue starting day after closing to end of that same month, so borrower will pay for that interest at closing; term: prepaid interest or interest on closing

- **formula:**

Prepaid Interest Owed at Closing = (Interest Rate in Decimal Form ÷ 365) x Principal x Number of Days

scenario example: The closing date for Caroline's home purchase is scheduled for March 15. So, her first regular mortgage payment will be due May 1, and it will contain the interest owed for April (interest is paid in arrears). Her mortgage loan has an annual interest rate of 5%, and the loan amount is $375,000. Using the 365-day year, the MLO calculates the interest that accrues from March 15 to March 31 to determine the amount of prepaid interest Caroline will owe at closing.

Prepaid Interest Owed at Closing = (0.05 ÷ 365) x 375,000 x 16 = 0.0001369 x 375,000 x 16 days = $821.92

➢ **PITI payments; escrow payments & limits**

- PITI: four components of a typical monthly mortgage payment, i.e., principal, interest, taxes, insurance

Total Monthly Mortgage Payment = Monthly Principal + Monthly Interest + Monthly Taxes + Monthly Insurance

- escrow: collected by lenders to ensure certain expenses related to homeownership, e.g., property taxes and homeowners insurance, are paid on time and in full
  - escrow cushion: per RESPA, lenders permitted to hold no more than one-sixth (1/6) of estimated total annual disbursements from escrow account
  - property taxes: levied by local governments on the value of real property to fund public services and infrastructure
  - homeowners insurance: insurance policy that provides financial protection to homeowners and lenders if property is damaged

Monthly Property Tax Escrow Payment = Annual Property Tax Bill ÷ 12

Monthly Homeowners Insurance Escrow Payment = Annual Insurance Premium ÷ 12

scenario example: Jon's annual property tax bill is $15,000, paid in two installments in June and September each year. His closing is in January, so his first mortgage payment is due March 1. To prepare for closing, the MLO needs to determine how many payments Jon will pay into escrow before each installment is due. The MLO also needs to figure any shortage and also add in the permissible cushion to find the amount Jon will have to pay at closing.

1. Six months of taxes are due June 1. By then, Jon will have paid monthly taxes into the escrow account for March, April, and May.

2. Six months of taxes are also due September 1. By then, Jon will have paid monthly taxes into the escrow account for June, July, and August.

3. Jon's mortgage payments (which include escrow amounts for taxes) will cover six months of tax payments. That leaves six months unaccounted for, as well as the permissible two months of cushion, for a total of eight months to be paid at closing.

4. Jon's monthly property tax bill: $15,000 ÷ 12 = $1,250

5. At closing, Jon will pay eight months of monthly tax payments into the escrow account: $1,250 x 8 = $10,000

➢ **Mortgage insurance**
- monthly payment may also include applicable mortgage insurance (PMI or MIP), which offer several payment options
  - PMI generally required for conventional loan when down payment is less than 20% of property's purchase price
  - MIP required for borrower taking out FHA loans

- PMI premium amounts are calculated by multiplying the loan principal by a given factor

  - factor is expressed as an annual premium rate
  - annual premium rates typically range from around 0.22% to 2.25%, depending on details such as:
    - borrower's credit score

85

- loan amount
- LTV ratio
- mortgage term
  - often rolled into monthly payment

example: $350,000 principal loan amount; 0.75% annual premium rate; paid monthly

1. Convert all percentages to decimals to calculate.

Principal Loan Amount x Annual Premium Rate Percentage = Annual PMI

$350,000 x 0.0075 = $2,625 annual PMI

2. Calculate monthly PMI.

Annual PMI ÷ 12 = Monthly PMI

$2,625 ÷ 12 = $218.75

- MIP: borrower pays upfront MIP at closing, as well as annual payment
  - upfront MIP (UFMIP): 1.75% of the loan amount; may be paid in cash at closing or rolled into loan
  - annual MIP: between 0.15% and 0.75% of loan amount; rate depends on:
    - base loan amount
    - LTV ratio
    - mortgage term

examples: $250,000 FHA loan; 1.75% UFMIP; 0.75% annual MIP rate

1. To calculate UFMIP.

Principal Loan Amount x 1.75% = UFMIP
$250,000 x 0.0175 = $4,375

2. To calculate monthly MIP. First, find the annual MIP, divide by 12, round to 2 decimal places.

Principal Loan Amount x 0.75% = Annual MIP
$250,000 x 0.0075 = $1,875

Annual MIP ÷ 12 = Monthly MIP
$1,875 ÷ 12 = $156.25

➢ **Down payment**

- down payment: initial lump sum borrower pays upfront when purchasing a property, typically percentage of total purchase price

- earnest money accompanying offer will be credited toward purchase price at closing, reducing amount of cash required from borrower at closing

- formula to calculate down payment percentage:

$$Down\ Payment \div Purchase\ Price = Down\ Payment\ Percentage$$

example: $360,000 purchase price; $36,000 down payment; calculate down payment percentage

$$\$36,000 \div \$360,000 = 0.1 \text{ (convert to percentage: 10\%)}$$

- formula to calculate loan amount when loan-to-value ratio is known:

$$Purchase\ Price\ x\ LTV = Loan\ Amount$$

example: $590,000 purchase price; 73% LTV

$$\$590,000\ x\ 0.73 = \$430,700$$

- formula to calculate down payment amount

$$Purchase\ Price - Loan\ Amount = Down\ Payment\ Amount$$

example: Use scenario above to continue.

$$\$590,000 - \$430,700 = \$159,300$$

example: In same scenario, borrower's earnest money was $20,000, which will be applied to down payment amount at closing, reducing borrower's required down payment amount.

$$\$159,300 - \$20,000 = \$139,000 \text{ required down payment at closing}$$

➢ **Loan-to-Value ratio**

- loan-to-value ratio (LTV): ratio between amount of mortgage loan and appraised value or purchase price of property being financed
  - o critical factor in determining risk level with mortgage
  - o calculated by dividing principal loan amount by either purchase price <u>or</u> appraised value, whichever is lower

$$Principal\ Loan\ Amount \div Purchase\ Price\ OR\ Appraised\ Value = LTV$$

example: $500,000 purchase price; $490,000 appraised value; $400,000 loan amount

$$\$400,000 \div \$490,000 = 81.6\%\ LTV$$

example: $500,000 purchase price; $505,000 appraised value; $375,000 loan amount

$$\$375,000 \div \$500,000 = 75\%\ LTV$$

- combined loan-to-value ratio: considers total amount of all outstanding loans secured by property, including primary mortgage and any secondary loans or liens, in relation to property's appraised value or purchase price

o calculated by dividing total outstanding balance of mortgage loans secured by property by either purchase price or appraised value, whichever is lower

Total of All Mortgage Balances ÷ Appraised Value OR Purchase Price = CLTV

example: $300,000 purchase price; $250,000 loan amount; $40,000 piggyback loan; $50,000 down payment; $295,000 appraised value

($250,000 + $40,000) ÷ $295,000 = 98.3%

- home equity combined loan-to-value ratio (HCLTV): evaluates risk of borrower taking out multiple loans secured by property, resulting in total loan amount that is significantly higher than property's appraised value or purchase price

  o calculated by dividing total outstanding balances of all loans secured by property <u>plus</u> any available credit on a HELOC by either purchase price or appraised value, whichever is lower

(Total of All Mortgage Balances + HELOC Available Credit) ÷ Appraised Value OR Purchase Price = HCLTV

example: $700,000 appraised value; $500,000 first mortgage amount; $100,000 available HELOC

($500,000 + $100,000) ÷ $700,000 = 85.7%

➤ **Debt-to-Income ratios**

- debt-to-income (DTI) ratio: compares borrower's gross monthly income (earnings before any payroll deductions or taxes) with debt load; two ratio types:

  o housing (front-end) ratio: calculated by adding all proposed housing expenses and dividing by gross income; expenses include:

    - principal
    - interest
    - property tax
    - hazard insurance
    - flood insurance
    - homeowner association dues

Housing DTI = All Proposed Housing Expenses ÷ Gross Income

  o total (back-end ratio): calculated by adding all of borrower's debt and dividing by gross income; debts include:

    - proposed PITI (principal, interest, property tax, insurance)
    - consumer debt payments, e.g., car loans, credit cards, bank loans
    - negative rental income
    - alimony, child support

Total DTI = All Borrower Debt ÷ Gross Income

- for housing ratio, standard acceptable maximum typically ranges from 33% to 36% of borrower's income
- for total ratio, standard acceptable maximum typically ranges from 36% to 43% of borrower's income
- automated underwriting systems will often allow conforming conventional debt ratios to exceed standard guidelines by balancing high debt ratios with strong assets and good credit; may allow a DTI of 50%
- manually underwritten loans have Fannie Mae maximum DTI of 36% of borrower's monthly income; maximum rises to as much as 45% if borrower meets certain credit score and reserve requirements

housing DTI example: (all figures are monthly) $1,800 principal and interest payment; $130 real estate taxes; $25 hazard insurance; $36 HOA; $6,840 gross income

1. Add up all proposed housing expenses.
$$\$1,800 + \$130 + \$25 + \$36 = \$1,991$$

2. Divide housing expenses total by gross income.
$$\$1,991 \div \$6,840 = 0.29108 = 29\%$$

total DTI example: (all figures are monthly) $1,991 total proposed housing expenses; $290 total credit card payments; $560 car payment; $75 car insurance

1. Add up all monthly expenses:

$$\$1,991 + \$290 + \$560 + \$75 = \$2,916$$

2. Divide total expenses by gross income:

$$\$2,916 \div \$6,840 = 0.4263 = 43\%$$

- Fannie Mae/Freddie Mac allow exclusion of <u>installment</u> loans' monthly payments when 10 or fewer payments remain

➤ **Buydowns**

- allows borrower to pay lower interest rate and mortgage payments by paying discount points up front
    - discount point: fee equal to 1% of total loan amount
- temporary buydown: when loan's interest rate is reduced for a specific time period, generally 3 years or fewer
    - 3-2-1 buydown: temporarily lowers interest rate by 3 percentage points in first year, 2 percentage points in second year, and 1 percentage point in third year; reverts to original rate after that
- permanent buydown, aka fixed-rate buydown: when borrower obtains lower interest rate over life of loan

➤ **Closing costs; prepaid items; prorated items**

- **prepaid items**: costs borrowers pay upfront at closing to ensure in advance that certain bills are covered; typically related to property and mortgage, including:

  - property tax portion
  - homeowners insurance premium portion
  - mortgage interest from day of closing until end of month
  - PMI premium portion
  - escrow account funding to cover future property tax and insurance payments

- **prorated items**: costs of certain ongoing expenses divided proportionately between buyer and seller based on the time each party owns property during billing period, including:

  - property taxes
  - HOA dues
  - rent (if property is a rental)
  - utilities

  proration scenario: On January 1, seller Damon pays his annual property taxes ($16,500) in advance. That summer, Damon lists property, and buyer Lucy contracts to buy the property. Closing is scheduled for August 1. Because Damon already paid that year's property taxes, Lucy owes him for the taxes from August 2 through December 31, when Lucy will own the property. At closing, Damon will be credited $6,871.92 from Lucy.

  $16,500 annual tax ÷ 365 = $45.21 daily tax
  $45.21 daily tax x 152 days = $6,871.92 Lucy owes Damon

➤ **Calculating ARM fully-indexed rate**

- ARM mortgages adjust interest rates at certain times over life of loan, generally after a set fixed-rate period; tied to particular index; e.g. Constant Maturity Treasury (CMT)

- **index rate**: benchmark interest rate that mirrors general market conditions; changes based on market fluctuations

- **teaser rate**: initial discount lender provides to borrower; last for a specific duration, after which rate adjusts

- **adjustment date**: when a new rate goes into effect

- **margin**: number of percentage points added to index by lender to set interest rate on ARM after initial rate period ends; set in your loan agreement and will not change after closing

- **fully indexed rate**: variable interest rate calculated by adding a margin to specified index interest rate; may not exceed periodic cap or lifetime cap

- to calculate interest that will go into effect on adjustment date, three values are needed:

  - index rate at date of adjustment
  - margin that will be added to interest rate
  - periodic cap, aka adjustment cap

- formula to calculate fully indexed rate

Fully Indexed Rate = Margin + Index Rate

example: Flynn is going with a 3/1 ARM. At closing, the index rate is 3%, and the margin is 2%. Added together, that results is a 5% fully indexed rate, but the lender is offering a 4% teaser rate for the first three years of the loan. When the first adjustment date arrives three years later, the index rate is 4%. So, the fully indexed rate is now 6%, which is the rate that now goes into effect until the next adjustment date.

Section III Quiz: Mortgage Loan Origination Activities

3.1 At which point(s) does a borrower complete a Uniform Residential Loan Application?

    a. On initial application only
    b. At closing
    c. On initial application and at closing
    d. On conditional loan approval

3.2 For a lender to accept a loan application, it must include specific minimum details, such as

    a. declarations.
    b. borrower's desired loan amount.
    c. military service details.
    d. demographic data.

3.3 MLOs are responsible for ensuring loan applications are completed accurately and thoroughly, which includes

    a. analyzing information for inconsistencies.
    b. determining demographic data.
    c. researching the property's chain of title.
    d. Verifying accuracy of appraisal.

3.4 A borrower using financial gifts to cover mortgage costs is subject to permissions and restrictions. Which of the following is true regarding these permissions and restrictions?

    a. For any loan product, any borrower with excellent credit may use a financial gift to cover 80% of mortgage costs, regardless of down payment amount.
    b. For government loans, a borrower with a credit score of 700 or greater may use a gift to cover all costs no matter how much the borrower puts down.
    c. A VA loan borrower may use a financial gift to cover all costs.
    d. A borrower putting 20% down on a conventional loan may use financial gifts to cover all costs.

3.5 What is the purpose of the VOE form?

    a. Verifies the availability and source of funds borrower intends to use for down payment, closing costs, or reserves
    b. Confirms a borrower's current and past employment history, income, and job stability
    c. Validates a borrower's eligibility for certain loan programs including financial assistance for down payments or mortgage costs and fees
    d. Endorses loan product suitability for borrower in terms of goals and eligibility

3.6 Which of the following is one action an MLO can take to understand how to match the applicant with a suitable loan product?

    a. Inquiring about the loan's purpose
    b. Confirming the availability and source of down payment funds
    c. Determining the applicant's legal history
    d. Electing whether to retain or sell the proposed loan

3.7 What is another name for Form 1003?

    a. Uniform Residential Appraisal Report
    b. Verification of Employment Form
    c. Unmarried Addendum
    d. Uniform Residential Loan Application

3.8   Lenders typically verify _____ year(s) of a borrower's income for qualification purposes.

      a. one
      b. two
      c. four
      d. five

3.9   Regarding TRID's tolerance thresholds, which of the following tolerances applies to fees that must remain the same between the initial Loan Estimate to the final Closing Disclosure?

      a. 10% comprehensive tolerance
      b. Unrestricted tolerance
      c. Zero tolerance
      d. Cumulative tolerance

3.10   MLO Sarah's financial institution makes mortgage loans and then sells them. Which disclosure that explains this policy is she required to provide to loan applicants?

      a. Mortgage Loan Servicing Disclosure
      b. Affiliated Business Arrangement Disclosure
      c. Homeownership Counseling Disclosure
      d. Revised Loan Estimate

3.11   Regarding the "3-7-3" rule, what does the 7 indicate?

      a. Lenders are generally required to provide borrowers with initial disclosures within 7 business days of receiving mortgage loan application.
      b. Borrowers must receive redisclosures with updated terms when certain significant changes are made to loan terms seven days after initial disclosures have been provided.
      c. The earliest a lender can close a mortgage loan is on the seventh business day after providing initial disclosures to the borrower.
      d. All disclosures must be provided within 7 days of loan application.

3.12   Which of the following best describes the mailbox rule for disclosures?

      a. Loan applicants may only receive required disclosures via U.S. Mail.
      b. Disclosures are deemed to be received on the third business day after they're placed in the mail.
      c. No matter the choice of delivery method, lenders must send required disclosures 3 business days after loan application.
      d. For electronic delivery of disclosures, applicants must send a return receipt to the lender within 3 business days of receipt.

3.13   The _____ provides a detailed breakdown of final loan terms and closing costs.

      a. revised LE
      b. CFPB Home Loan Toolkit
      c. Adjustable-Rate Mortgage Disclosure
      d. Closing Disclosure

3.14   Which of the following disclosures must be provided within three business days of loan application for all ARM applications?

      a. Revised Loan Estimate
      b. AfBA disclosure
      c. Closing Disclosure
      d. Adjustable-Rate Mortgage Disclosure

3.15 Regarding an MLO's considerations for an applicant's assets, which of the following is a true statement?

 a. Lenders consider only liquid assets; fixed assets do not play a role in the borrower analysis process.
 b. Lenders often consider the seasoning of funds, meaning how long the funds have been in the borrower's account.
 c. Business accounts are not part of the asset analysis.
 d. Liquid assets and real property are considered assets in an MLO's analysis, but stocks and bonds are not.

3.16 Regarding income verification, income with an expiration date, such as alimony, must be likely to continue for _____ after closing.

 a. six months
 b. 2 years
 c. 3 years
 d. 5 years

3.17 A borrower's income is usually required to be verifiable

 a. over the past 2 years.
 b. when considering bonus and commission income.
 c. when the borrower is an hourly employee.
 d. for employment income only, no other type of income.

3.18 Which of the following is true regarding unemployment compensation when used for income purposes on a loan application?

 a. It is acceptable as long as three years of tax returns are included as documentation.
 b. It is only acceptable if it is part of a regular annual work cycle.
 c. It can be used as qualifying income when it is due to layoffs.
 d. It is treated as non-taxable income.

3.19 What type of qualifying income can be subject to "grossing up"?

 a. Non-taxable income
 b. Capital gains income
 c. Bonuses and commissions
 d. Non-employment income

3.20 TRID's 10% cumulative tolerance applies to:

 a. fees for services the borrower shops for and chooses one that is not on the lender's list
 b. fees paid to the lender or loan originator
 c. fees paid to third-party service providers not affiliated with the lender
 d. fees for services provided by the lender's / MLO's affiliates

3.21 Which of the following factors in determining a person's credit score is correct?

 a. A mix of credit types is considered to be disadvantageous.
 b. Newer credit accounts are considered more reliable information sources.
 c. The number of credit report inquiries is not a consideration.
 d. Paying bills on time accounts for 35% of a credit score.

3.22 For which loan application would the CFPB Home Loan Toolkit be a required disclosure?

  a. Single-family home purchase application
  b. Home refinance application
  c. HELOC application
  d. Reverse mortgage application

3.23 Which of the following is one purpose of the initial Loan Estimate (LE)?

  a. Explains whether the lender intends to service the loan or transfer it to another entity
  b. Outlines estimated closing costs, so borrowers can compare offers from different lenders
  c. Provides a written list of prospective settlement service providers typically involved in the closing process
  d. Presents borrowers with information about their rights and responsibilities, as well as the various stages of obtaining a mortgage

3.24 Select the correct formula for calculating the housing ratio.

  a. All Recurring Monthly Debt ÷ Gross Monthly Income
  b. Loan Amount ÷ Property Value
  c. PITI on Primary Residence ÷ Gross Monthly Income
  d. Purchase Price x LTV

3.25 What is total DTI?

  a. Ratio between gross income and all monthly debt obligations
  b. Percentage of all monthly expenses in relation to net income
  c. Relationship between the mortgage loan amount and the property's appraised value
  d. Assessment of a borrower's ability to repay the mortgage loan

3.26 Which statement about LTV is true?

  a. LTV ratios measure the relationship between the mortgage loan amount and the borrower's gross income.
  b. LTV ratios exceeding 80% generally mean conventional loan borrowers must purchase PMI.
  c. All mortgage loan programs have the same LTV ratio requirements.
  d. A lower LTV suggests smaller down payment and potentially higher risk.

3.27 _____ are prohibited under the CFPB's ability to repay rules.

  a. Jumbo loans
  b. Temporary financing
  c. Amortization
  d. Balloon payments

3.28 Which of these is the best definition of "tangible net benefit"?

  a. Net difference between financial advantages and disadvantages in a rent vs. purchase comparison
  b. Long-term interest savings and reduced monthly mortgage payments when an interest rate is reduced
  c. Financial advantages or benefits that a borrower is expected to gain from refinancing an existing mortgage loan
  d. Refinancing loans in order to generate fees and charges for a lender

3.29   In which appraisal approach does the appraiser identify recently sold properties similar to subject property in terms of location, size, condition, and features?

   a. Sales comparison
   b. Cost
   c. Income
   d. Sales contrast

3.30   Functional obsolescence, one type of depreciation, involves _____ that reduce(s) the property's value.

   a. factors off property, like changes in the neighborhood,
   b. damage or wear to property itself
   c. adding land value separately
   d. issues related to property's layout or design

3.31   Which of the following statements accurately describes the independent appraisal requirement?

   a. It encourages lenders to rely solely on the borrower's self-assessment of the property's value.
   b. It mandates that appraisers must always be selected and paid by the borrower.
   c. It ensures that appraisals are conducted by unbiased and qualified professionals.
   d. It allows lenders to use in-house appraisers without any external oversight.

3.32   In a typical real estate transaction, which party is the appraiser's client?

   a. Borrower
   b. Lender
   c. Seller
   d. Listing agent

3.33   Appraiser Lynn is using the cost approach to estimate the value of a subject property. To do so, she'll

   a. identify comparable properties, make adjustments to them based on differences from the subject property, and use comps' adjusted sales prices to estimate the subject's fair market value.
   b. calculate the cost to rebuild or replace the subject property, account for depreciation, and add in the value of the land.
   c. estimate the property's potential income, subtract its operating expenses, and then divide that by the cap rate.
   d. identify comparable properties, subtract any operating expenses, account for depreciation, and then average the values.

3.34   Appraisers generally use the cost approach for

   a. income-producing properties, such as hotels, apartments, or complex commercial buildings.
   b. residential properties and vacant land.
   c. properties that are not frequently bought or sold, such as unique or specialized properties.
   d. hospitality, tourism, or entertainment properties.

3.35   Which of the following is included in the debt-to-income ratio?

   a. Medical insurance premiums
   b. Revolving credit accounts
   c. Childcare expenses
   d. Educational expenses

3.36 When using the income approach, how does an appraiser determine the property's net operating income (NOI)?

    a. Estimating the potential income and subtracting the operating expenses
    b. Estimating the potential income and adding the operating expenses
    c. Adding the potential income and operating expenses, and then dividing by the cap rate
    d. Dividing the potential income by the cap rate

3.37 The capitalization rate for an income-producing property is

    a. an estimation of an income producing property's fair market value.
    b. a factor an appraiser uses to account for depreciation.
    c. the depreciated cost of a structure expressed as a percentage.
    d. the expected rate of return an investor would require to invest in the property.

3.38 In a real estate transaction, what is the primary focus of a title report?

    a. Estimating property taxes
    b. Identifying any existing liens, encumbrances, or defects related to ownership rights
    c. Assessing the property's physical condition
    d. Determining the property's potential rental income

3.39 In which report would one find any potential complications for transferring property, such as liens, easements, or restrictions?

    a. Title report
    b. Appraisal report
    c. Inspection report
    d. Credit report

3.40 Regarding title insurance, who is the insured when the buyer finances the home purchase?

    a. Buyer
    b. Lender
    c. Seller
    d. All interested parties

3.41 Which type of insurance is typically a component of homeowners insurance?

    a. Flood insurance
    b. Hazard insurance
    c. Title insurance
    d. Mortgage insurance

3.42 Which of the following is true about flood insurance?

    a. The National Flood Insurance Program is a type of private flood insurance.
    b. Lenders typically require flood insurance for properties in any FEMA-designated flood zones.
    c. Flooding is generally covered by standard homeowners insurance policies.
    d. If the actual structure is not located in SFHA, no flood insurance is required.

3.43 Which party is responsible for coordinating and conducting closing process, ensuring all necessary documents are prepared, reviewed, and signed by relevant parties?

a. Lender
b. MLO
c. Settlement agent
d. Listing agent

3.44 What is one purpose of loan origination fees?

a. Cover the cost of evaluating a borrower's creditworthiness
b. Allow a borrower to "buy down" the interest rate
c. Cover charges associated with finalizing a mortgage loan
d. Protects the lender from lost interest income in case a borrower pays off the loan before a specified period of time

3.45 A(n) _____ is an optional fee that is paid upfront to lower the interest rate on a mortgage.

a. origination fee
b. discount point
c. recording fee
d. prepayment fee

3.46 Which of the following is considered a closing cost?

a. Origination fee
b. Prepayment penalty
c. Title insurance
d. Discount point

3.47 A _____ is a legally binding contract between a borrower and lender outlining the borrower's promise to repay the loan amount under specific terms and conditions.

a. Mortgage
b. Security instrument
c. Trust deed
d. Promissory note

3.48 Which document establishes a lien on the borrower's property?

a. Closing disclosure
b. Mortgage
c. Promissory note
d. Acceleration clause

3.49 Which security instrument involves three parties?

a. Mortgage
b. Promissory note
c. Deed of trust
d. Certificate of title

3.50 When a mortgage is used as a security instrument, which party is the mortgagor, and which party is the mortgagee?

a. The borrower is the mortgagor, and the lender is the mortgagee.
b. The MLO is the mortgagor, and the borrower is the mortgagee.
c. The lender is the mortgagor, and the borrower is the mortgagee.
d. The borrower is the mortgagor, and the MLO is the mortgagee.

3.51 Which document often includes a "power of sale" provision?

    a. Deed of trust
    b. Mortgage
    c. Promissory note
    d. Security instrument

3.52 What is the purpose of a defeasance clause in a mortgage?

    a. Prohibits the borrower from transferring a mortgaged property's title without the lender's consent
    b. Permits the lender to demand immediate repayment of the entire loan balance if certain conditions are not met
    c. Allows the borrower to eliminate the mortgage lien by meeting specific conditions
    d. Releases the lien on a property and transfers legal title back to the borrower

3.53 MLO Shauna is going over some calculations with borrower Tomas to see what his monthly payments would be at different interest rates for a 30-year loan. For one calculation, she uses his loan amount of $200,000 and an annual interest rate of 6%. What would his monthly interest payment be? (note: interest, not PITI!)

    a. $360
    b. $1,000
    c. $72
    d. $33.33

3.54 Using 365 days, calculate the per diem interest for an outstanding loan balance of $150,000 and a 5% annual interest rate.

    a. $20.55
    b. $18.25
    c. $1.22
    d. $1.37

3.55 The closing date for a home purchase is scheduled for May 20. The first regular mortgage payment will be due July 1, and it will include the interest owed for June. The mortgage loan has an annual interest rate of 6%, and the loan amount is $475,000. Using the 365-day year, calculate the interest that accrues for the remainder of May to determine the amount of prepaid interest the borrower will owe at closing.

    a. $936.99
    b. $2,375
    c. $858.90
    d. $2,590.91

3.56 Lenders most often collect escrow to pay which two expenses?

    a. Property taxes and homeowners insurance
    b. Property taxes and HOA dues
    c. Homeowners insurance and mortgage insurance
    d. Mortgage insurance and upcoming special assessments

3.57 Per RESPA, lenders are permitted to hold no more than _____ of estimated total annual disbursements from an escrow account as a cushion.

    a. 1/2
    b. 1/4
    c. 1/6
    d. 1/10

3.58 Calculate monthly PMI for a principal loan amount of $350,000 for 20 year-loan and a 0.55% annual premium rate.

a. $1,925
b. $160.42
c. $96.25
d. $8.02

3.59 What is the UFMIP for a borrower with a $325,000 FHA loan and a 0.65% annual MIP?

a. $5,687.50
b. $2,112.50
c. $176.04
d. $473.96

3.60 What is the monthly MIP for a borrower with a $450,000 FHA loan and a 0.65% annual MIP rate?

a. $2,925
b. $243.75
c. $656.25
d. $54.69

3.61 What is the down payment percentage when a borrower puts $125,000 down on a property with a purchase price of $559,000?

a. 4.5%
b. 44%
c. 22.4%
d. 25%

3.62 Erik and Tanya made an offer of $499,000 on a home and paid $15,000 in earnest money. To avoid PMI, they're putting down 20% on the loan. At closing, what will their required down payment be net of the earnest money put down?

a. $99,800
b. $96,800
c. $77,400
d. $84,800

3.63 Calculate the LTV on a property with a $525,000 purchase price, a $530,000 appraised value, and a $415,000 loan amount.

a. 79%
b. 1.26%
c. 78%
d. 1.28%

3.64 Using the appropriate information given, calculate the HCLTV: $700,000 appraised value, $690,000 purchase price, $475,000 principal loan balance, $85,000 available HELOC.

a. 80%
b. 81.2%
c. 56.5%
d. 55.7%

3.65 What is the main purpose of the two DTI ratios?

   a. Compare a mortgage loan amount to the appraised value or purchase price of the property
   b. Compare the total amount of all outstanding loans secured by the property to its appraised value or purchase price
   c. Compare borrowers' gross monthly income to their debt load
   d. Compare the difference between a property's purchase price and appraised value to the principal loan amount

3.66 Calculate the front-end ratio using data from the following information (all figures are monthly): $2,900 principal and interest payment; $250 real estate taxes; $20 hazard insurance; $25 HOA; $200 total credit card payments; $430 car payment; $12,840 gross income

   a. 22.6%
   b. 29.8%
   c. 24.9%
   d. 27.5%

3.67 What is a buydown?

   a. A type of mortgage that allows for an extended repayment period
   b. A financial incentive offered by sellers to buyers in a competitive housing market
   c. A reduction in the interest rate and monthly payments on a mortgage loan
   d. The process of acquiring a property below its market value through negotiation

3.68 How do borrowers obtain a buydown?

   a. Paying upfront discount points
   b. Making a larger down payment
   c. Reducing their DTI
   d. Increasing their earnest money amount

3.69 Clive is buying Sandra's property, and closing is set for September 20. Sandra paid the $5,500 annual property taxes in advance on January 1. How much will Clive owe Sandra at closing for his portion of the property taxes that she has already paid? Use 365 in your calculations and round to the nearest tenth.

   a. $1,558.56
   b. $1,374.99
   c. $1,552.21
   d. $1,537.14

3.70 Adele has chosen a 3/1 ARM. The lender offered a(n) _____ as a discount for the first three years of her loan.

   a. initial rate
   b. teaser rate
   c. intro rate
   d. inducement rate

3.71 Amelia is working with MLO Sam on her 3/1 ARM to determine what her fully indexed rate will be on the first adjustment date for her loan. At closing three years ago, the index rate was 3%, and the margin was 2%. Now, the index rate is 5%. What is the fully indexed rate?

   a. 7%
   b. 5%
   c. 2%
   d. 3%

Section IV: Ethics

➢ **Ethical Issues Related to Federal Laws**

- **Violations of federal law**
- **Prohibited acts (RESPA)**
- **Fairness in lending**
- **Fraud detection**
- **Mortgage fraud categories; red flags**
- **Advertising**
- **Predatory lending and steering**

➢ **Ethical Behavior and Loan Origination Activities**

- **Financial responsibility**
- **Proper handling of consumer complaints**
- **Company compliance**
- **Fiduciary relationships with customers**
- **Truth in marketing and advertising**
- **General business ethics**

Ethical Issues Related to Federal Laws

➢ **Violations of federal law**

- **Unfair, Deceptive, or Abusive Acts or Practices** (UDAAP)

  - originated as result of the Dodd-Frank Act; refined and enforced by Consumer Financial Protection Bureau (CFPB)
  - designed to protect consumers and ensure they are treated fairly and honestly
  - regulators **use UDAAP standards to evaluate all mortgage-related entities** for practices such as:

    - using misleading advertising
    - impeding consumer's understanding of transaction
    - obscuring information that causes consumer to take out an unaffordable loan.

- **TILA definitions relating to UDAAP**

  - **unfair**: an act or practice that:

    - causes substantial injury to consumer, and
    - cannot be reasonably avoided by consumer, and
    - is not outweighed by offsetting benefits

  - **deceptive**: an act or practice that misleads consumer

- o **abusive**: an act or practice that:
    - ▪ hinders consumer's ability to comprehend a transaction and exploits the consumer's lack of comprehension

➤ **Prohibited acts**

- • Per RESPA, lenders and MLOs prohibited from:

    - o **compromising client interests**: compromising borrower or investor interests in order to benefit a referral source

    - o **kickbacks**: giving or receiving any **thing of value** in exchange for referral fees or kickbacks from settlement services

        - ▪ thing of value: any item, service, benefit, or consideration that has worth or can be beneficial to an individual or entity, e.g., cash, gifts, perks, special benefits or advantages, unearned fees, exclusive discounts, etc.

        - ▪ example: A title insurance company offers gifts like vacations, expensive dinners, or cash bonuses, to MLOs in exchange for referring clients to them for title insurance services.

    - o **must use a certain provider**: requiring consumers to use particular settlement service provider a lender or MLO suggests

    - o **steering consumers** to specific settlement service providers

        - ▪ **example**: An MLO strongly recommends that a borrower use a specific escrow agent for their settlement services, claiming that this agent offers the best rates and service. In reality, the MLO has a financial interest for referring borrowers to this particular escrow agent.

- • **Gramm-Leach-Bliley Act**: includes provisions for consumer privacy and data protection related to their personal financial information; prohibits lenders and MLOs from *pretexting*:

    - o **pretexting**: using false pretenses to obtain customer information from financial institutions

        - ▪ example: To save time, an MLO impersonates a client in order to gain access to the client's financial accounts

➤ **Fairness in lending**

- • **No credit discrimination: Equal Credit Opportunity Act** (ECOA): prohibits lenders and MLOs from discriminating against borrowers based on factors such as race, color, religion, national origin, sex, marital status, age, or receipt of public assistance

    - o all consumers applying for credit or seeking information to be treated equally

    - o equal access to credit does not equate to identical loan terms; individual circumstances apply

    - o applicants in similar financial situations should receive similar loan terms regardless of protected class status

- **example**: An MLO routinely processes loan applications from various clients seeking mortgage financing. However, the MLO holds biased beliefs against certain protected classes under ECOA. The MLO systematically denies or offers less favorable terms to applicants belonging to these protected classes, despite their creditworthiness and ability to repay the loan. The MLO justifies these actions by citing vague reasons or subjective factors that are not relevant to the borrower's financial qualifications.

- **No housing discrimination**: Fair Housing Act (FHA): prohibits discrimination in housing-related transactions, including mortgage lending, based on similar protected classes as ECOA; prohibitions include:

  - **redlining**: refusing loans based on neighborhood characteristics

    - **example**: A mortgage lender systematically refuses to provide mortgage loans or offers less favorable terms to applicants residing in certain neighborhoods where the majority of residents belong to minority racial / ethnic groups. On review of lending patterns and loan application data, it is evident that these "redlined" neighborhoods consistently receive disproportionately fewer mortgage loan approvals or are subject to higher interest rates and fees compared to similarly situated neighborhoods. Further investigation reveals that the lender's discriminatory practices are not based on the individual creditworthiness or financial qualifications of the applicants residing in these neighborhoods. Instead, the decisions to deny or limit mortgage lending are motivated by stereotypes, biases, or prejudices against residents living there.

  - **steering**: guiding borrowers to certain loan products based on protected characteristics

    - **example**: An MLO is working with a single parent whose spouse recently died. The borrower plans to own the home for just a few years and then move to another state where other family members live. The MLO strongly believes an ARM loan is the best choice for the borrower, but the borrower prefers a fixed-rate loan. The MLO decides to show the borrower fixed-rate loans for which the borrower will have trouble qualifying, and then compare them to favorable ARMs. The borrower ultimately chooses an ARM yet continues to feel uncomfortable, despite the MLO's assurances.

- **Americans with Disabilities Act** (ADA): requires reasonable accommodations be made to serve borrowers living with a disability

  - discrimination in form of denial of credit, unfavorable terms, or unequal treatment based on disability prohibited under ADA

- **disparate impact**: neutral policy that disproportionately affects particular group can still be considered discriminatory

  - **example**: A mortgage lender implements a minimum credit score requirement of 700 for all applicants seeking conventional mortgage loans. This policy appears neutral and applies equally to all applicants regardless of their demographic characteristics. However, upon analysis of the lender's loan data, it becomes evident that this requirement disproportionately impacts minority applicants, specifically Black and Hispanic borrowers.

Further investigation reveals that the credit score requirement is not directly related to assessing a borrower's creditworthiness or ability to repay the loan. Instead, it serves as a barrier that disproportionately excludes minority applicants from accessing mortgage financing, continuing systemic inequalities in homeownership opportunities.

- **role disclosure**: ensures borrowers understand who represents their interests, potential implications of these relationships, and potential conflicts of interest

➢ **Fraud detection**

- **fraud**: deceiving others for personal gain or to cause harm
- **mortgage fraud**: any intentional, deceptive, or fraudulent act designed to misrepresent information in a mortgage application, loan approval, or real estate transaction
  - can include false statements about income, employment, assets, property value, or borrower's financial situation; altered documentation; failure to disclose debts, etc.
  - can occur at different stages of lending process, from application to closing
  - defrauding parties include
    - **borrower**: may inflate income or assets to look better for loan qualification
    - **real estate professional**: may facilitate undisclosed second mortgage from the seller (aka silent second)
    - **lender**: may provide borrower with loan documents containing different terms than those agreed upon
    - **MLO**: may steal identities to create fraudulent loan applications
    - **appraiser**: may falsify appraisal report so borrower obtains a larger loan approval
- **intentional misrepresentation**: one party intentionally provides false information or conceals material facts to deceive another party involved in transaction, e.g., omitting important fact(s) that would impact lender's credit decision
  - involves intent to deceive: party making false statement or concealing information must do so knowingly and with intent to induce other party to rely on false information, e.g., providing inaccurate financial information
  - serious legal offense; can lead to civil liability, financial penalties, and criminal charges
- **negligence: <u>unintentional</u> misrepresentation**
  - breaches in duty of care, e.g., errors, omissions, failures to fulfill responsibilities
  - can result in legal actions, including civil lawsuits seeking damages or compensation for harm suffered by aggrieved party
- **fraud for property**: intentional fraud where individual(s) or entity engages in deceptive practices in order to obtain ownership, possession, or control of property

- **straw buyer**: someone who serves as a front for buyer / borrower but has no association with the property, i.e., will not actually own, possess, or control the property

- straw buyers often have better credit and stronger financial qualifications than actual buyer
  - if intentional fraud, straw buyer may agree to scheme for compensation
  - if unknowing, straw buyer may co-sign not knowing another person is using confidential financial details,

- **fraud for profit**: type of intentional misrepresentation activity in which individuals scheme to gain money for themselves via transaction process

  - industry professionals are typical culprits, often work together
  - creditor suffers significant financial loss
  - **air loan**: individuals or groups fabricate loan applications for nonexistent properties or for properties they do not own

    - falsified documentation, including appraisals and financial records, create appearance of legitimate transaction
    - once lender approves and funds loan, fraudsters take funds and lender discovers collateral is fake or non-existent

- ➢ **Mortgage fraud categories and red flags**

  - **asset and liability fraud**: manipulating financial information related to assets and liabilities to deceive lenders into approving loans under false pretenses

    - **asset fraud**: individuals misrepresent their assets to inflate financial standing and improve chances of qualifying for mortgage

      - **example**: overstating value of real estate holdings, bank accounts, or investment portfolios

    - **liability fraud**: concealing or understating existing debts or financial obligations to appear stronger financially

      - **example**: not disclosing outstanding loans, credit card debt, or other liabilities during mortgage application process

    - **potential red flags**: shortage of information from borrower; information provided is sketchy. Examples:

      - discrepancies between loan application information and supporting documentation
      - significant fluctuations in asset balances or debt levels with no reasonable explanation
      - failure to adequately verify authenticity of assets or liabilities claimed by borrower
      - history of frequent loan applications or multiple credit inquiries within short period
      - failure to disclose all assets, liabilities, or financial obligations during application process
      - large deposits or transfers of funds from undisclosed sources, particularly if labeled as gifts or loans

- - **prevention methods** for MLO include:
    - scrutinize documents for irregularities or inconsistencies that may indicate falsified information
    - verify authenticity of assets and liabilities directly with financial institutions, creditors, and other relevant sources
    - paying close attention to unusual or suspicious financial transactions

- **income and employment fraud**: misrepresenting income or employment history to boost creditworthiness
  - examples include borrowers who:
    - inflate reported income to meet lender requirements for loan approval
    - provide false or misleading information regarding employment history and status
    - fabricate employment positions and income sources
    - conceal unverifiable or under-the-table income streams to avoid scrutiny or taxation
  - potential red flags include:
    - suspicious gaps or inconsistencies in borrower's employment history, such as extended periods of unemployment or frequent job changes
    - borrower's unwillingness or inability to provide supporting documentation for stated income sources
    - discrepancies between borrower's reported income and employment history, industry norms, or standard wage levels for occupation
    - borrower claiming rapid or unrealistic income growth over short period without corresponding evidence
    - incomplete or inconsistent employment verification documentation
    - borrower providing vague or unverifiable details about employers
    - borrower reluctance to disclose employer information
  - prevention methods for MLO include:
    - asking detailed questions and following up on discrepancies or missing information
    - conducting thorough verification of income and employment documentation with third parties, e.g., financial institutions, employers

- **occupancy fraud**: providing false or misleading information regarding intended occupancy status of property in mortgage loan application; often intended to help borrower qualify for favorable loan terms reserved for owner-occupied properties or to help borrowers lacking sufficient income to qualify for desired loan amount
  - examples include:
    - claiming property will be a primary residence when it is actually intended to be second home or investment property
    - misrepresenting property as primary residence when it is actually vacant or intended for speculative purposes

- misrepresenting intent to occupy a property as primary residence may pose a higher risk of default, as borrower may have less commitment to maintaining property and fulfilling mortgage obligations compared to owner-occupants

- potential red flags include:
  - property intended as investment but borrower does not own a primary residence (example of *reverse occupancy fraud* in which borrower uses potential rental income to help qualify for loan)

  - borrower moving from single-family home to multi-unit in same area

  - borrower purchasing property in area with high concentration of vacation homes or investment properties, but claiming it as primary residence

  - borrower moving from larger home to smaller one but keeping larger one as investment property

- prevention methods for MLO include:
  - **requiring borrowers to certify intended occupancy status** in loan application

  - **conducting post-closing occupancy verification** to ensure compliance, e.g., physical inspection, utility bill review, HOA confirmation of occupancy

- **suspicious activity reports (SARs)**: document filed by financial institutions, including banks and mortgage lenders, to report potentially suspicious or unusual activities that may indicate money laundering, fraud, or other illicit financial transactions

  - lenders and MLOs have legal obligation to identify and report any unusual or suspicious financial activities that may indicate potential fraud in mortgage lending process

  - all suspicious activity should be reported to appropriate Bank Secrecy Act compliance workers per company's anti-money laundering policies
    - **Bank Secrecy Act** (aka Anti-Money Laundering [AML] law): combats money laundering and other financial crimes by imposing recordkeeping and reporting requirements on financial institutions

    - compliance requirements designed to help detect and prevent money laundering activities, terrorist financing, illicit financial transactions

  - MLOs protected from legal liability for filing SARs in good faith, even if reported activity does not result in criminal charges or prosecution

➢ **Advertising**

- **Truth in Lending Act** (TILA) imposes rules and requirements for lender advertising to ensure transparency and accuracy, such as:

- including **clear and conspicuous disclosures of important terms and conditions**, such as:
  - mortgage type
  - interest rate details
  - annual percentage rate (APR) expressed in same font and type size as interest rate
  - repayment terms
  - applicable fees

- **prohibiting false, misleading, or deceptive statements in advertising**, either express or implied; falls under Unfair, Deceptive or Abusive Acts or Practices (UDAAP)

- **disclosing additional facts for "trigger terms,"** such as:
  - amount or percentage of down payment
  - number of payments
  - repayment period
  - finance charge
  - APR

- **prohibiting bait-and-switch tactics**, e.g., advertising attractive loan terms but offering less favorable terms in reality

- **maintaining records of mortgage advertisements**, including copies of advertisements and documentation of compliance with TILA's advertising rules
  - retained for specified period
  - made available to regulatory authorities upon request

- **due diligence**
  - advertisements to be reviewed for compliance before publication
  - must be truthful
  - must state that certain terms and conditions are subject to change

- **Fair Housing Act's advertising** provisions
  - should be fair and inclusive
  - should not focus on people based on protected class status

> **Predatory lending and steering**

- **predatory lending**: unethical or abusive lending practices that exploit vulnerable borrowers, often resulting in financial harm or disadvantage

  - targets individuals who may have limited financial knowledge, poor credit history, or low income
  - uses deceptive tactics to entice borrowers into loans with unfavorable terms and conditions
  - uses deceptive advertising, false promises, and bait-and-switch tactics to lure borrowers into loans they cannot afford or understand
  - misrepresents loan terms or conceal fees to exploit borrower's lack of financial knowledge

- o **often results in borrowers not being able to repay loans**

- predatory lending examples include:

  - o **loan flipping**: encouraging borrowers to refinance or "flip" their loans repeatedly, charging exorbitant fees each time and extending repayment period, ultimately increasing cost of loan

  - o **asset-based lending**: offering loans based on equity in borrower's home or other assets, rather than ability to repay the debt, putting borrower's property at foreclosure risk

  - o **excessive fees and charges**: imposing excessive fees, penalties, and charges on borrowers, often without their knowledge or understanding, increasing overall cost of loan

  - o **high prepayment penalty loans**: imposing excessive or unfair prepayment penalties to trap borrowers in unfavorable loans, inhibit ability to refinance, and hinder ability to pay off debts

- **steering**: directing or encouraging borrower toward certain loan products or lenders based on factors other than borrower's best interests

  - o reasons include:

    - ▪ financial incentives or commissions for promoting certain loan products or lenders over others
    - ▪ higher-cost loans or subprime mortgages that result in greater profits for lender or MLO
    - ▪ focus on loans more lucrative for MLO or lender, limiting borrower's ability to shop around for best terms

  - o **prohibited under** various laws and regulations, including Real Estate Settlement Procedures Act **(RESPA)** and Truth in Lending Act **(TILA)**

  - o example: An MLO receives a bonus for originating certain types of mortgage loans that carry higher interest rates, fees, or prepayment penalties. The MLO consistently steers borrowers towards these high-cost loan products, even though the borrowers may qualify for more affordable or suitable alternatives, such as fixed-rate mortgages or government-insured loans.

Ethical Behavior and Loan Origination Activities

- ➢ **Financial responsibility**

  - per federal SAFE Act, **MLOs expected to maintain a level of personal financial integrity and responsibility**

    - o **examples**: clean financial record, no recent bankruptcies due to financial mismanagement, no patterns of poor money handling

110

- o essentially, for MLOs to advise others and manage those funds, they must demonstrate they successfully manage their own
- loan applicants also expected to have achieved acceptable level of financial responsibility to be approved for loan
  - o involves lender review of applicant's credit history, income, debt-to-income ratio, savings
  - o MLOs / underwriters determine if applicants:
    - are capable of handling financial obligations of mortgage loan along with other financial responsibilities
    - can make payments on time
    - solidly qualify for desired loan amount

➢ **Handling consumer complaints**

- MLOs must always act professionally even if consumer complaint seems unjustified or unfair
  - o acknowledge consumer's feelings whether fair or otherwise
  - o communicate steps that will be taken to address issue
  - o follow company's policies and procedures for managing complaints
- federal law: **all received complaints must be recorded in complaint log**
  - o details to record include complaint facts, date received, and final disposition
  - o log to be made available to state or CFPB examiner on request
- CFPB requires responses be made to formal complaints within 15 days
  - o when more time needed, alert consumer within 15-day period
  - o final response should be delivered within 60 days
- fair lending standards apply to complaint management; process should be uniform for all consumers

➢ **Company compliance, self-reporting**

- **mortgage lending entities required to comply with federal and state mortgage laws**
- expected to monitor compliance management system continuously
- companies expected to report all detected compliance violations to applicable regulatory entities, in other words, lenders are responsible for *self-reporting*. Must report
  - o what violation occurred
  - o what steps were taken to correct the violation
  - o what procedures were enacted to prevent recurrence
- self-reporting lessens penalties for violations; concealing violations results in harsh penalties once uncovered

➢ **MLOs relationships with consumers, company, and investors**

- fiduciary relationship: MLOs considered to have fiduciary relationship with clients, i.e., those who have decided to move forward with mortgage application process

- o paramount obligation to act in interests of clients
- o MLOs must maintain commitment to transparency, integrity, and unwavering loyalty to client's welfare throughout mortgage transaction process
- o must follow all client's lawful instructions
- o must keep client's private information confidential
- o may not benefit personally from client's private information

- responsibility to protect company and / or investor

  - o adhere to employer's / investor's established policies, procedures, and regulatory guidelines
  - o disclose client-provided information that is material to the transaction, e.g., the applicant is demoted during underwriting process
  - o follow all legal and regulatory guidelines and mandates
  - o complete tasks in timely manner to protect rate lock expiration dates and closing dates

- **Cybersecurity issues**: significant risks to mortgage industry; compromise consumers' sensitive information, financial transactions, and integrity of lending process

  - o specific threats include:

    - **wire fraud**: cybercriminals intercepting or diverting funds during closing process

    - **ransomware**: malicious software that encrypts files or systems, effectively locking users out until ransom is paid

    - **phishing**: deceptive emails, messages, or websites designed to trick recipients into divulging sensitive information or clicking on malicious links

  - o **Gramm-Leach-Bliley Act Safeguards Rule**
    - **requires financial institutions to develop written cybersecurity program** outlining how they will protect the security, confidentiality, and integrity of consumer information; should include steps to:

      - identify and assess potential risks to security of consumer information in their possession, such as unauthorized access, data breaches, or cyberattacks

      - implement safeguards to address identified risks; may include access controls, encryption, firewalls, etc.

      - regularly monitor, evaluate, test and update information security program to adapt to changing threats and ensure its effectiveness in safeguarding consumer information

      - train all employees on the program details

- o **proper precautions to protect sensitive information** include:
  - adhere to company's cybersecurity program

  - utilize antivirus software and spam filters

  - implement multi-factor authentication for accessing sensitive systems and accounts

  - use encryption technologies for email communications, file storage, and data transmission to ensure confidentiality

  - connect to secure, password-protected Wi-Fi networks

➤ **Truth in marketing and advertising**

- **CFPB's Reg N** purpose: prevent deceptive advertising practices in mortgage lending

- **Reg N** implements Mortgage Acts and Practices – Advertising rule, aka MAP Rule

- **MAP Rule** intent: ensure accuracy and transparency regarding rates, fees, and terms; foster integrity and fairness in mortgage advertising

- MAP Rule expressly **prohibits** mortgage advertising from:
  - o disseminating false statements or misrepresentations
  - o using the word "fixed" to describe rate or payment unless it genuinely remains fixed for entirety of loan term
  - o stating or implying any affiliation with any government program, benefit, or entity
  - o using ambiguous presentation of credit terms

- lenders essentially required to provide advertising that is accurate, comprehensible, and comprehensive regarding mortgage products and terms, including:
  - o disclosing rates, fees, terms, and other pertinent details
  - o using easily understandable and accessible language
  - o presenting credit terms and other critical facts clearly and conspicuously for potential borrowers

- focal point: consumers gain a sense of risks and rewards related to advertised product; can assess if product aligns with consumer's risk tolerances

➤ **Consumer education**

- consider legal obligations as a minimum to professional, successful loan origination practice
- ethical standards also crucial, particularly regarding consumer education
- **example**: providing a Loan Estimate within 3 days of loan application (legal obligation) vs. taking time to thoroughly explain — in plain language — the LE's contents to borrower (ethical consideration)

  - o explanation ensures borrower:

113

- understands rights, obligations, and loan terms' implications for borrower
- empowers borrower to make informed decision about loan

- ethical consumer education considerations often take form of personalized, professional service in helping borrowers understand their financial situation and options for mortgage financing

> **General business ethics**

- description: **moral principles and standards that guide conduct and decision-making of individuals and organizations in the business world**

- **purpose for mortgage industry**: upholding highest standards of integrity and service benefits MLOs / associated professionals, clients and consumers, and entire mortgage industry

- values: **honesty, integrity, fairness, respect, and responsibility** in all aspects of business operations, including:

    o interactions with customers, employees, suppliers, competitors, and community
    o decisions that balance business finances / stakeholders with ethical considerations

- companies' codes of ethics serve as formal set of guidelines and principles outlining expected standards of behavior and conduct for everyone in the organization; specifics include:

    o sets **clear standards and expectations** regarding ethical behavior for employees
    o serves as a **reference point for employees** when faced with ethical challenges
    o **promotes accountability** by holding individuals responsible for their actions and behaviors
    o **helps mitigate legal, financial, and reputational risks** associated with unethical behavior

- corporate code of ethics should be reviewed and updated periodically

    o ensure code stays in line with latest legal requirements
    o incorporate new standards and benchmarks to at forefront of ethical conduct
    o identify and address new ethical challenges as they emerge
    o confirm code aligns with company values, culture, strategic objectives, etc.
    o reduce risk of legal battles and reputational harm
    o foster culture of accountability in upholding ethical standards

- **National Association of Mortgage Brokers** (NAMB) established comprehensive Code of Ethics that sets forth ethical standards and expectations for members

    o expectations include:

        - acting with honesty, integrity, and fairness in all professional dealings

- maintaining high level of professionalism in business practices

- providing clear and accurate information to clients regarding mortgage products, terms, and costs

- complying with all applicable laws, regulations, and licensing requirements

- providing guidance and assistance to help clients make informed decisions about mortgage financing options

- disclosing any potential conflicts of interest that may arise in business relationships

- acting in best interests of clients at all times

Section IV Quiz: Ethics

4.1 Which of the following actions could potentially violate UDAAP dictates (Unfair, Deceptive or Abusive Acts & Practices)?

   a. Providing misleading information about loan terms
   b. Failing to disclose a property's lien status to the borrower
   c. Offering a discount on closing costs for borrowers who submit their application in a timely manner
   d. Recommending a mortgage product based on the borrower's financial situation

4.2 What is considered an example of an unfair practice under UDAAP?

   a. Charging excessive origination fees
   b. Offering incentives to borrowers who refer friends and family to the lending institution
   c. Providing accurate and transparent information about loan options
   d. Misrepresenting the interest rate of a loan to a borrower

4.3 A loan applicant deliberately understates her existing debts on the loan application. What is this an example of?

   a. Asset fraud
   b. Fraud for profit
   c. Loan flipping
   d. Liability fraud

4.4 An example of occupancy fraud is

   a. concealing unverifiable income streams to avoid scrutiny or taxation.
   b. misrepresenting a property as primary residence when it is actually vacant.
   c. not disclosing outstanding loans, credit card debt, or other liabilities during mortgage application process.
   d. using a straw buyer to qualify for a loan and purchase the property.

4.5 _____ is when a financial entity refuses to fund a loan based on neighborhood characteristics.

   a. Disparate impact
   b. Pretexting
   c. Redlining
   d. Steering

4.6 Which of the following best describes pretexting in the context of consumer protection laws and privacy regulations?

   a. Providing false information to obtain someone's personal or confidential information from financial institutions
   b. Using encryption methods to secure sensitive data from unauthorized access
   c. Conducting thorough background checks on potential clients to verify their identity
   d. Implementing strict password policies to prevent unauthorized access to sensitive systems

4.7 Which of the following would be a potential red flag for income fraud?

   a. Borrower's unwillingness or inability to provide supporting documentation for stated income
   b. Suspicious gaps or inconsistencies in borrower's employment history
   c. Significant fluctuations in asset balances or debt levels with no reasonable explanation
   d. History of frequent loan applications or multiple credit inquiries within short period

4.8   Which of the following laws includes provisions for consumer privacy and data protection relating to personal financial information?

   a. Gramm-Leach-Billey Act
   b. Equal Credit Opportunity Act
   c. Unfair, Deceptive or Abusive Acts or Practices
   d. Truth in Lending Act

4.9   A mortgage lender offers to provide a 50% discount on closing costs for clients referred by a specific real estate agent. This arrangement could be construed as an illegal kickback under:

   a. TILA
   b. GLBA
   c. RESPA
   d. ECOA

4.10   _____ is primarily concerned with fairness in lending practices.

   a. ECOA
   b. TILA
   c. RESPA
   d. UDAAP

4.11   In the context of a mortgage loan, a straw buyer is someone who

   a. applies for the loan on someone else's behalf, concealing the true buyer's identity.
   b. gets a loan to buy a property with the intention of flipping it for a higher price.
   c. uses funds obtained from an illegal source for the down payment.
   d. obtains a property without getting the necessary financing or mortgage approval.

4.12   Which of these is a description of reverse occupancy fraud?

   a. Rachel purchases a property in an area with a high number of vacation homes or investment properties, but claims it will be her primary residence.
   b. Suzanne and her mother co-apply for a loan on a property in which her mother will live full-time but she will only live there in the winter and autumn seasons.
   c. Karl uses potential rental income to help qualify for a loan to buy a property but plans to use it as his primary residence.
   d. After his divorce, Gabriel is moving to a smaller home but keeping the larger home as a rental property.

4.13   Which of the following scenarios could be considered to have a disparate impact on borrowers?

   a. A credit union offers a special mortgage program exclusively for first-time homebuyers, which includes down payment assistance and lower interest rates.
   b. A mortgage banker requires all applicants to provide a minimum down payment of 20% to qualify for a mortgage loan.
   c. A mortgage company offers adjustable-rate mortgages (ARMs) as a financing option for home purchases.
   d. A lender's investors allow for a 650 credit score for loan qualification, but the lender requires a minimum credit score of 750.

4.14   Financial institutions file a _____ to report potentially suspect or unusual activities that may indicate money laundering, fraud, or other illicit financial transactions.

   a. Financial Investigation Alert (FIA)
   b. Suspicious Activity Report (SAR)
   c. Transaction Red Flag (TRF)
   d. Bank Secrecy Act Report (BSAR)

4.15 Deceiving others for personal gain or to cause harm is known as

a. negligence.
b. fraud.
c. unintentional misrepresentation.
d. intentional mistake.

4.16 MLO Eric relied on incomplete information provided by the borrower without verifying its accuracy. This is an example of

a. negligence.
b. fraud.
c. intentional misrepresentation.
d. intentional mistake.

4.17 In a fraud for property scheme, who is most typically the culprit?

a. MLO
b. Lender
c. Real estate agent
d. Borrower

4.18 The _____ imposes rules and requirements for lender advertising to ensure transparency and accuracy.

a. RESPA
b. TILA
c. ECOA
d. GLBA

4.19 Which of the following would be considered a trigger term in a lender's advertisement, requiring further disclosure?

a. Get a quote now.
b. Fixed-rate mortgage
c. Rates subject to change
d. $10,000 down

4.20 _____ is a type of intentional misrepresentation in which an individual or individuals engage in deceptive practices in order to obtain ownership, possession, or control of real property.

a. Fraud for profit
b. Loan flipping
c. Fraud for property
d. Occupancy fraud

4.21 Which of the following is the BEST definition of predatory lending?

a. Predatory lending occurs when lenders offer loans with high interest rates to borrowers with poor credit history.
b. Predatory lending consists of unethical or abusive lending practices that exploit vulnerable borrowers, often resulting in financial harm or disadvantage.
c. Predatory lending involves providing financial assistance to borrowers who may not fully understand the terms of the loan agreement.
d. Predatory lending is characterized by lenders offering adjustable-rate mortgages (ARMs) to borrowers who may not be able to afford potential increases in monthly payments.

4.22 _____ is / are an example of predatory lending.

   a. Asset-based lending
   b. Subprime mortgages
   c. Debt consolidation lending
   d. Payday loans

4.23 Per the federal SAFE Act, MLOs are expected to

   a. regularly attend industry conferences and seminars.
   b. demonstrate proficiency in using mortgage software applications.
   c. maintain a level of financial integrity and responsibility.
   d. provide detailed financial reports to clients upon request.

4.24 In the mortgage industry, to what does *self-reporting* refer?

   a. MLOs reporting their personal financial information to clients
   b. Mortgage companies reporting their quarterly earnings to shareholders
   c. Borrowers reporting their income and assets on mortgage applications
   d. Mortgage companies reporting detected compliance violations to the applicable regulatory entity

4.25 MLOs are generally considered to have a fiduciary relationship with their clients. Which of the following is one responsibility an MLO has in this fiduciary relationship?

   a. Keep the client's private information confidential.
   b. Keep all transactional facts confidential.
   c. Act in the highest interest of the client over all others.
   d. Follow all the client's instructions.

4.26 What does the Gramm-Leach-Bliley Act Safeguards Rule require of financial institutions, including mortgage companies?

   a. Annual audits of their financial statements
   b. Free credit monitoring services to all consumers
   c. A written cybersecurity program to protect consumer information
   d. A minimum level of capital reserves to protect against financial losses

4.27 What is the main purpose of the CFPB's Reg N?

   a. Streamline the mortgage application process for borrowers
   b. Establish guidelines for mortgage loan officer compensation
   c. Standardize the types of properties eligible for mortgage financing
   d. Prevent deceptive advertising practices in mortgage lending

4.28 The MAP Rule expressly prohibits mortgage advertising from

   a. stating or implying any affiliation with any government entity.
   b. including testimonials or endorsements from satisfied customers.
   c. making claims about potential risks to borrowers.
   d. mentioning any facts about the particular loan products.

4.29 Which of the following statements is true regarding MLOs and consumer education?

    a. Educating consumers about the mortgage loan process is not an ethical consideration.
    b. Ethical consumer education considerations often take the form of personalized, professional service.
    c. Consumer education is solely the responsibility of government agencies, and MLOs have no obligation to provide such guidance.
    d. An MLO's legal requirements are sufficient to serve as consumer education about the mortgage loan process.

4.30 _____ focus(es) on moral principles and standards that guide the conduct and decision-making of individuals and organizations in the business world.

    a. Regulatory standards
    b. General business ethics
    c. Corporate social responsibility
    d. Business etiquette

4.31 What purpose do companies' codes of ethics serve within organizations?

    a. Companies' codes of ethics serve as formal guidelines and principles outlining expected standards of behavior and conduct for everyone in the organization.
    b. Codes of ethics are primarily designed to restrict employee behavior and limit individual autonomy within the organization.
    c. The main function of codes of ethics is to increase profitability and shareholder value.
    d. Codes of ethics are only relevant for senior management and do not apply to lower-level employees within the organization.

4.32 Which of the following statements is true regarding regular review and updating of a company's codes of ethics?

    a. A static code of ethics promotes stability and consistency within the organization, leading to better employee morale.
    b. Frequent updates to the code of ethics can be time-consuming and distract from core business activities.
    c. Regular review and updates ensure that the code remains at the forefront of ethical conduct and aligned with the latest legal requirements.
    d. Ethical considerations are subjective and can vary widely among individuals, making regular updates unnecessary.

4.33 How does the Bank Secrecy Act impact financial institutions' activities?

    a. Requires recordkeeping and reporting to help detect and prevent money laundering activities
    b. Mandates a written anti-identity theft policy to protect consumers' personal data
    c. Manages fair lending undercover testers to expose discriminatory practices
    d. Expects financial institutions to provide free credit monitoring services to consumers

4.34 Which of the following statements is true about an MLO's legal obligations and ethical conduct?

    a. MLOs primarily focus on meeting minimum regulatory standards, which also meets ethical conduct considerations.
    b. Ethical conduct for MLOs involves prioritizing their own financial interests over those of the consumer.
    c. MLOs' legal obligations are far more crucial than ethical matters related to consumers.
    d. Both legal obligations and ethical standards are crucial to a professional, successful loan origination practice.

4.35 TILA's rules and requirements for lender advertising to ensure transparency and accuracy, such as:

    a. permitting bait-and-switch tactics along as the ad discloses that loan specifics may change.
    b. stipulating that copies of mortgage advertisements be submitted to TILA for review.
    c. requiring clear and conspicuous disclosures of important terms and conditions.
    d. prohibiting "trigger terms."

Section V: Uniform State Content

➢ **SAFE ACT and CSBS /AARMR Model State Law**

- **State mortgage regulatory agencies**
- **Regulatory authority**
- **Responsibilities and limitations**

➢ **State Law and Regulation Definitions**

- **Definitions**

➢ **License Law and Regulation**

- **Persons required to be licensed**
- **License qualifications and application process**
- **Grounds for denying license**
- **License maintenance**
- **NMLS requirements**
- **Temporary authority to operate**

➢ **Compliance**

- **Prohibited conduct**
- **Required conduct**
- **Advertising**

SAFE Act and CSBS / AARMR Model State Law

➢ State mortgage regulatory agencies

- **Secure and Fair Enforcement for Mortgage Licensing Act of 2008** (SAFE Act)
  - established minimum national standards for licensing and registering MLOs
  - launched consumer protection benefits such as:
    - improved consumer protection standards
    - required background checks and training
    - greater transparency via MLO public registry
  - SAFE ACT regulatory administrators are not responsible for licensing MLOs directly; each state executes own licensing system per SAFE Act standards
  - effected formation of **Nationwide Multistate Licensing System** (NMLS) and **Nationwide Mortgage Licensing System and Registry** (NMLS-R)

- State Regulatory Registry, LLC (SRR) oversees both NMLS and NMLS-R operations; formed by CSBS

- NMLS regulatory context

    - Conference of State Bank Supervisors (CSBS) and American Association of Residential Mortgage Regulators (AARMR) formed NMLS in 2006 in support of state regulators in participating states

    - these regulatory entities centralized the licensing system for individuals and companies so that they could obtain, maintain, and renew licenses

    - covers non-depository financial services industries, e.g., money services businesses, mortgage lenders, securities firms, etc.

- NMLS-R overview

    - created within broader NMLS system specifically for MLOs

    - serves as registry for all state-licensed MLOs

    - consumers can research MLOs, check their licensing status, review any disciplinary history

- NMLS-R essential characteristics

    - purposes:

        - standardize application forms and requirements for state-licensed loan originators across the board

        - maintain central database with comprehensive licensing and supervision information

        - consolidate and optimize flow of data between regulatory bodies

        - strengthen accountability and tracking mechanisms for loan originators

        - make licensing process smoother and less burdensome for regulators

        - reinforce consumer protections and anti-fraud efforts

        - grant consumers free access to information about loan originators

        - create system that mandates loan originators to prioritize consumer best interests

        - encourage responsible practices in subprime mortgage market

        - expedite, facilitate handling consumer complaints

    - licensees / registrants may be charged fees to maintain NMLS-R; consumers access system information free or charge

- o **Consumer Financial Protection Bureau (CFPB)** will establish and maintain similar systems for states choosing not to participate in NMLS-R

- o CFPB also empowered to:
  - replace NMLS-R with similar system if NMLS-R is found to be unsatisfactory

  - oversee a state's licensing system if found to be deficient per SAFE Act standards

- **Regulatory environment**
  - o names of specific state agencies / entities overseeing state licensing vary

  - o **such entities required to meet certain standards to avoid CFPB intervention**, such as:
    - enforcing state licensing laws for loan originators

    - mandating registration with NMLS-R for all state-licensed loan originators

    - regularly reporting enforcement actions and licensing violations to NMLS-R

    - offering process for loan originators to contest information reported to NMLS-R

    - levying civil penalties against unlicensed loan originators

    - requiring loan originators to demonstrate financial stability through minimum net worth, surety bond, or contribution to recovery fund; company bonding is common

  - o **Regulation H** created by CFPB after SAFE Act; sets forth details on **required standards for state licensing authorities**, such as:
    - minimum requirements for state-chartered licensing programs for MLOs

    - criteria for licensing eligibility, education, training, continuing education, and testing

    - permission for CFPB to review and approve state licensing programs for Regulation H compliance

    - process for investigation MLO / state officials' violations and imposing penalties

  - o CSBS and AARMR jointly developed model state law including recommended wording
    - states with regulations aligning with or surpassing model law stringency generally deemed compliant with SAFE Act standards

- ➢ **Regulatory authority**
  - **SAFE Act confers important regulatory powers to state licensing agencies**, such as:
    - developing and implementing licensing systems that meet minimum standards established by law
    - investigation and examination powers based on violations / complaints; includes:
      - gathering information and evidence
      - reviewing documents and records
      - conducting interviews
      - issuing subpoenas (depending on state-specific laws)
      - taking disciplinary action, e.g., fines, reprimands, license suspension or revocation (depending on state laws)
  - **states required to report to CFPB on licensing activities** and ensure compliance with SAFE Act's mandates
  - CFPB has authority to establish and maintain state's licensing system when CFPB determines existing licensing system fails to meet SAFE Act's minimum requirements
    - CFPB then creates and oversees federal licensing system for that state
    - CFPB's licensing system does not entirely replace state's regulatory authority; state can still enact stricter licensing requirements within jurisdiction; must still meet minimum federal standards
  - CFPB has authority to establish and maintain its own national licensing system if NMLS-R fails to meet minimum regulatory requirements
  - per SAFE Act, definition of *state* includes:
    - the 50 U.S. states
    - Washington, D.C.
    - U.S. territories, including: Puerto Rico, Guam, Virgin Islands, American Samoa, Northern Mariana Islands

- ➢ **Responsibilities and limitations**
  - **state agency responsibilities**:
    - enforce state licensing laws
    - report licensing violations to NMLS-R
    - penalize unlicensed MLOs
  - regulators may take possession of MLO's documents when MLO is under formal investigation

- MLO retains right to access documents to conduct normal business operations <u>unless</u> a risk of document breach, exposure, disclosure, etc., exists

State Law and Regulation Definitions

➢ **Definitions**

- **administrative and clerical tasks**: tasks for which no license is required, e.g., receiving, collecting, and distributing information that is common to mortgage loan process; communication to and from consumers meant to obtain common information

- **American Association of Residential Mortgage Regulators** (AARMR): national organization representing state residential mortgage regulators responsible for directing and controlling mortgage lending, brokering, or servicing activities

- **application**: official document consumers submit to lender expressing their interest in obtaining mortgage loan
  - lenders use application information to consider consumer's request
  - those who take or receive consumer applications considered to be loan originators

- **Conference of State Bank Supervisors** (CSBS): nationwide organization representing state regulators overseeing all types of banks, including those involved in mortgage lending
  - plays central role in creation and ongoing oversight of NMLS-R and model licensing law

- **immediate family member**: spouse, child, sibling, parent, grandparent, grandchild; originating loan(s) with or on behalf of immediate family member requires <u>no</u> MLO license

- **independent contractor**: self-employed, finds clients, sets fees, manages taxes; may specialize in certain loan products or specific borrower characteristics; responsible for obtaining and maintaining individual MLO licenses in states where they operate

- **loan originator**:
  - individual or entity that initiates process of securing loan for borrower in exchange for some sort of compensation; in general, can encompass wide range of loan types, including mortgages, personal loans, car loans, business loans, etc.

  - mortgage loan originator: more specific term within mortgage industry, referring to individual licensed to originate mortgage loans

- **loan processor / underwriter**: individual who performs support and clerical tasks under loan originator supervision;
  - o **need to be licensed only under certain circumstances**
  - o unlicensed loan processors / underwriters required to be supervised by licensed MLO
  - o SAFE Act requires *actual nexus* between unlicensed processor / underwriter and licensed MLO acting as supervisor
    - ▪ **actual nexus**: connection in which supervisor provides training, guidance, and compliance review for processor / underwriter; supervisor actively assigns, authorizes, and monitors processor / underwriter's work

- **non-traditional mortgage product**: mortgage product that is not 30-year, fixed-rate loan, e.g., ARM, balloon, interest-only, non-QM

- **registered loan originator**: loan originator who is registered with NMLS-R; employed by depository institution, subsidiary of depository institution, or institution regulated by Farm Credit Administration; **generally do not need licensure**

- **residential mortgage loan**: specific type of loan used to finance purchase or refinance of property intended for use as residence; used for primary, secondary, or investment property purposes

- **state-licensed loan originator**: individual who has obtained specific license from state(s) where they operate to originate residential mortgage loans; also registered with NMLS-R, typically work for mortgage companies, mortgage brokers, mortgage lenders

- **State Regulatory Registry**: wholly-owned subsidiary of CSBS; operates NMLS-R

- **unique identifier**: primary and essential identifier assigned by NMLS-R to every entity and individual MLO that maintains an account on the platform
  - o allows regulators, industry, and consumers to easily track activity and history of MLOs regardless of location
  - o must appear on advertisements and other documents

License Law and Regulation

➢ **Persons required to be licensed**

- **loan originator**: person who:
  - o takes residential mortgage loan applications and either offers or negotiates terms of residential mortgage loan in order to earn compensation or another type of gain
  - o presents themselves to public as a person who can or will do above activities

- **taking an application occurs when**:
  - o receiving borrower's application directly from borrower <u>or</u> from third party

127

- entering application information into automated system, whether receiver has authority to approve application or not

- **taking an application is NOT**:

    - accepting an application package and routing it to the appropriate department or individual for processing without reviewing its contents or making any preliminary decisions

    - answering general questions about application process, fees, or deadlines without engaging in fact-finding or eligibility assessments

    - describing loan products or services offered by a company without discussing specific terms or rates that would apply to a particular individual

    - gathering general borrower information, e.g., name, contact information, etc., to forward to licensed MLO or set up appointment with same

- **offering or negotiating loan** terms includes activities such as:

    - presenting specific interest rates, loan amounts, or repayment terms to potential borrower
    - discussing terms and conditions of specific loan product with borrower
    - attempting to reach mutual understanding with borrower regarding loan terms
    - recommending lender or specific loan terms to borrower per an agreement with someone other than borrower
    - providing revised loan offer on pending application in response to borrower request for different rate or different fees

- offering or negotiating loan terms does NOT include activities such as:

    - **providing general information** about different loan types, interest rates, and repayment options without recommending specific products or lenders
    - **sharing educational resources** about mortgage process, loan qualifications, and financial literacy or eligibility requirements without analyzing individual financial information
    - making an underwriting decision regarding borrower qualifications for loan
    - communicating with borrower that loan offer has been sent
    - offering / negotiating loan offer via third-party loan originator without communicating directly with borrower or presenting oneself to public as loan originator, e.g., seller offering financing to buyer via loan originator

- **all requirements apply to residential mortgage loans only**; SAFE Act does not cover commercial loans

- **loan originators must be licensed and registered with NMLS-R, or just registered with NMLS-R**; requirements depend on lending entity:

    - **loan originators who work for non-depository entities with state-regulated licenses must be licensed** (e.g., mortgage bank or mortgage broker)

- **loan originators who work for depository institutions**, subsidiaries of depository institution, or Farm Credit Administration-regulated institution generally **do <u>not</u> need licensure** but do need to be registered

- companies engaged in loan origination activities generally required to be licensed

- sole proprietor companies engaged in loan origination required to hold two licenses: one for business owner as an individual and one for business itself

- **other exemptions** to loan originator license requirement include:

    - **clerical workers performing strictly administrative tasks** for loan originators

        - <u>off-limits activities</u> include: offering/negotiating rates, terms; counseling consumers about loan rates, terms; taking loan applications

    - licensed real estate professionals not being compensated by lender

    - **loan processors / underwriters performing duties under a licensed individual's / registered company's supervision**

        - note: underwriting / loan processing managers almost always licensed due to supervisory role; but no NMLS-R registration typically required

    - individuals performing loan originating activities when:

        - loan secured by lender's own residence
        - originating business loans; state licensure may be required, but no federal requirements
        - offering or negotiating loan terms / arranging credit for immediate family member
        - arranging timeshare credit
        - performing official activities as government or non-profit employee
        - originating loans as an attorney as part of an attorney-client relationship
        - working as a registered loan originator

> **Licensee qualifications and application process**

- **education and exam requirements**

    - successful completion of 20-hour pre-license course that includes:

        - 3 hours on federal laws and regulations
        - 3 hours of ethics (various topics)
        - 2 hours on nontraditional mortgage products

    - National SAFE Exam with Uniform State Content

        - 120 questions; 115 are scored and 5 or not
        - 75% or better required to pass
        - 30-day waiting period between tests when applicant fails and wants to retest
        - 3 consecutive failures: 6-month waiting period before retest; failure at this point resets wait period cycle (3 monthly waiting periods followed by 6-month waiting period)

- application requirements
  - submit proof of identity and fingerprints to NMLS-R
  - agree to criminal background check and credit check:
    - purpose: verify financial responsibility, character, general suitability to serve consumers
  - borderline applicants may be required by state to:
    - maintain net worth based on dollar amount of loans originated
    - maintain surety bond based on dollar amount of originated loans; generally fulfilled at company level; most common approach
    - pay into state-maintained recovery fund used to pay claims from borrowers harmed by MLO improper actions
  - unique identifier
    - NMLS-R assigns number or other identifier to each loan originator
    - used to distinguish individual and track conduct
    - must be included on all applications, business cards, advertisements, etc.
    - often used in place of Social Security number regarding SAFE Act and its rules

➢ **Grounds for denying license**
- **financial reasons**
  - outstanding judgments, other than medical expense-related
  - tax or other government liens
  - foreclosure(s) within past 3 years
  - pattern of delinquent account(s) during past 3 years

- **legal issues**
  - convicted of or pleaded guilty to felony in past 7 years, unless pardoned
  - convicted of or pleaded guilty to felony for any of following (unless pardoned):
    - fraud
    - dishonest
    - breach of trust
    - money laundering

- **license revoked in another state**

➢ **License maintenance**
- **licenses renewed annually**

- licensees required to continue to meet license qualifications, e.g., financial accountability, criminal stipulations

- **minimum required continuing education (CE)**: 8 hours annually of NMLS-approved CE courses

    o specific requirements may vary by state; courses typically include:

      ▪ 3 hours federal law and regulations
      ▪ 2 hours ethics (must include fraud, consumer protection, and fair lending issues)
      ▪ 2 hours of non-traditional mortgage lending
      ▪ 1 hour elective education

    o CE credits apply to same year in which course is completed

    o may not take same course 2 years in a row

- **renewal period**: November 1 through midnight December 31

    o failure to renew by deadline causes license to expire

      ▪ license reactivation: required to complete CE courses from last year of licensure via Late CE courses

    o some states recognize late renewal period: January 1 through February 28; failure to renew during this period <u>terminates</u> license

- MLO's state laws may mandate additional courses or requirements for renewal; <u>check state particulars</u> to be sure

- **extended absence renewals**

    o for MLOs who leave industry and want to return

    o **if license expired for fewer than 3 years:**

      ▪ take Late CE course; will serve as last year of licensure's CE requirement

      ▪ apply for new license

    o **license expired for 3 to 5 years:**

      ▪ retake pre-license education (which is valid for only 3 years)

      ▪ submit new license application

    o no valid MLO license or federal registration **for more than 5 years**:

      ▪ retake pre-license education

      ▪ retake and pass NMLS SAFE exam (score valid for only 5 years)

➢ **NMLS requirements**

- licensees must register with NMLS-R

- states required to report MLOs' license violations and enforcement actions taken to NMLS-R

- NMLS-R unique identifier must appear on all MLO's advertisements, transaction documents, solicitation materials (emails, social media posts, etc.), websites / online profiles, business cards / stationery

- courses and education providers must be NMLS-R-approved

- state-licensed companies and companies employing state-licensed MLOs required to submit quarterly *Mortgage Call Reports* to NMLS-R
    o detailed reports of state-licensed mortgage companies' mortgage activity from previous quarter
    o includes data on loan application activity, origination, and servicing

- required NMLS-R updates:
    o employment change
    o address change
    o profile must be current in order to renew license

➢ **Temporary authority to operate (TA)**

- new provision that streamlines transition for:

    o **federally-registered MLOs seeking state licensure** to work in state-licensed mortgage company

    o **state-licensed MLOs seeking licensure in another state**

- **grants eligible MLOs authority to originate loans** before obtaining full state licensure

- conditions / limitation include:
    o must have submitted state's license application via NMLS-R
    o no disqualifying issues, such as denial of license in any state, revocation of MLO license, convictions of certain financial crimes, disciplinary actions
    o must have completed pre-licensure education requirements and passed MLO licensing exam

- if conditions are satisfied, TA is granted within 48 hours of applying for new state license

- approval period may extend to 9 days if more information is needed based on background check results

- duration: lasts 120 days after license application submitted; MLO can originate loans while license application processes

132

- TA ends when:
  - license application approved
  - MLO withdraws TA application
  - application denied
  - 120-day period expires and application incomplete in NMLS-R

Compliance

➤ **Prohibited conduct**

- making false, misleading, or deceptive statements / representations in connection with mortgage loan transaction

- misrepresenting or omitting relevant details about loan terms, conditions, fees, etc.

- attempting to influence appraiser's independent judgment of property's value

- engaging in fraud, theft, or any dishonest act in connection with mortgage loan transaction

- forging, altering, or fabricating documents related to mortgage loan transaction

- conducting MLO business without an active license

- failing to provide required disclosures to loan applicants or using disclosures to mislead applicants

- engaging in activity that represents conflict of interest in loan transaction

- mishandling, misappropriating, or failing to properly account for funds held in connection with mortgage loan transaction

- violating applicable state or federal laws related to settlement procedures

- originating loans without adhering to established underwriting guidelines

- failing to cooperate with regulatory authorities during investigations or audits

- penalties for violations: up to $25,000 per offense

➤ **Required conduct**

- demonstrate good character, financial responsibility, general suitability to serve consumers

- include unique identifier on applications, transaction documents, advertisements, solicitations

- employ proper record keeping practices, including security of paper / electronic document copies

➢ **Advertising**

- include unique identifier in ads

- avoid deception, intentional misrepresentation, bait and switch schemes, etc.

5.1   Which of the following activities requires an MLO license?

    a. answering general questions about the application process, fees, or deadlines
    b. presenting specific interest rates, loan amounts, or repayment terms to a potential borrower
    c. sharing educational resources about the mortgage process
    d. performing strictly administrative tasks

5.2   As part of her work for Midtown Mortgage, Shelly uses an automated underwriting service to determine borrowers' qualifications for a loan. Shelly is not licensed, so which of the following must be true?

    a. Shelly works under a licensed MLO's supervision.
    b. Midtown Mortgage is a non-depository entity with a state regulated license.
    c. Shelly only works on residential mortgage transactions.
    d. Shelly is a sole proprietor.

5.3   What did the CSBS and AARMR jointly develop?

    a. Nationwide Mortgage Licensing System and Registry
    b. A registry for all state-licensed MLOs
    c. Model state law
    d. SAFE Act

5.4   MLOs must complete a minimum of _____ hours of continuing education courses during each renewal period.

    a. 5
    b. 8
    c. 12
    d. 16

5.5   Which of the following is true about the Nationwide Multistate Licensing System (NMLS)?

    a. It covers non-depository financial services industries.
    b. It serves as registry for all state-licensed MLOs.
    c. It addresses depository institutions and their subsidiaries.
    d. It is a wholly-owned subsidiary of CSBS.

5.6   What is the minimum passing score for the NMLS SAFE licensing exam?

    a. 70%
    b. 75%
    c. 80%
    d. 85%

5.7   Nick is an unlicensed loan processor who works under MLO licensee Drake's supervision at Loan-Stars Lending & Co. When the state regulator investigates Loan-Stars for compliance, what type of relationship between Nick and Drake will the regulator look for?

    a. Professionally cordial interaction
    b. Direct report status
    c. Actual nexus
    d. Mutual professional affiliations

5.8   The _____ has authority to establish and maintain a state's licensing system when that state's existing licensing system fails to meet the SAFE Act's minimum requirements.

   a. NMLS
   b. CFPB
   c. NMLS-R
   d. AARMR

5.9   One purpose of the NMLS-R is to:

   a. maintain a central database with comprehensive licensing and supervision information.
   b. create a nationwide licensing system for all 50 states and U.S. territories.
   c. establish minimum national standards for licensing and registering MLOs.
   d. confer investigation and examination powers based on violations and/or complaints.

5.10   Which of the following is true about loan originators who work for depository institutions?

   a. They are required to be licensed and registered with the NMLS-R.
   b. They are only required to be licensed.
   c. They do not need to be licensed but do need to be registered.
   d. They do not need to be licensed or registered as long as proper supervision is given.

5.11   Davis is a sole proprietor with his own loan origination business. Which of the following is true regarding his licensing requirements?

   a. Two licenses are required: one for himself and one for the business.
   b. As a sole proprietorship, Davis's individual license is sufficient.
   c. Because Davis owns the company, the company's license covers the company and himself.
   d. Sole proprietors do not need to be licensed, but they do need to be registered with NMLS-R.

5.12   Cheryl failed the NMLS SAFE licensing exam on her first try and wants to take it again. What are the requirements?

   a. She has to take the pre-license education again and then retest.
   b. She has to wait 30 days before she can retake the test.
   c. She has to wait 6 months before she can retake the exam.
   d. She must pass the exam on the first try to work in loan origination.

5.13   Based on her MLO license application, Susan is considered a borderline applicant. Which of the following is a common approach for dealing with more marginal MLO applicants?

   a. Maintaining a net worth based on a dollar amount of loans originated
   b. Paying into state-maintained recovery fund used to pay claims from harmed borrowers
   c. Maintaining a surety bond based on a dollar amount of originated loans
   d. Registering a unique identifier so her actions may be tracked

5.14   _____ is grounds for denying an application for an MLO license.

   a. A tax lien
   b. An outstanding medical expense
   c. A foreclosure 5 years ago
   d. A misdemeanor conviction

5.15   Heath worked as an MLO for several years and then took on a new role in another area of banking 2 years ago. Now, he would like to return to his MLO work. To become re-licensed, he will have to:

   a. retake the pre-license education coursework and apply for a new license.
   b. take a Late CE course and apply for a new license.
   c. apply for a new license.
   d. take the CE courses for the current year and apply for a new license.

5.16   To avoid regulatory intervention, state agencies overseeing MLO licensure are required to meet certain standards, such as:

   a. replacing the NMLS-R with similar system if it is found to be unsatisfactory.
   b. granting consumers free access to information about loan originators.
   c. requiring commercial mortgage lenders to participate in the state's MLO licensing process.
   d. regularly reporting enforcement actions and licensing violations to NMLS-R.

5.17   An MLO's _____ must appear on their advertisements and all other consumer-facing materials.

   a. Social Security number
   b. unique identifier
   c. email address
   d. phone number

5.18   Who of the following would benefit from the new temporary authority (TA) provisions?

   a. A former MLO seeking to reestablish licensure
   b. An unlicensed underwriter who wants to work as an underwriting supervisor
   c. A state-licensed MLO who wants to be licensed in another state as well
   d. A license applicant who is appealing an application denial

5.19   Lamar's MLO license was revoked in the state where he lived 3 years ago. He moved to another state and wants to work in as an MLO in the mortgage industry again. Which of the following is true?

   a. Lamar will need to take both pre-license education and an additional ethics course before he can apply for a license in his current state.
   b. Lamar's previous license revocation is grounds for his license application to be denied in his current state.
   c. Because his license was revoked 3 years ago, the statute of limitations has expired.
   d. A license revocation bars an individual from working in the mortgage industry in any capacity.

5.20   A(n) _____ initiates the process of securing any loan for a borrower in exchange for some form of compensation.

   a. mortgage loan originator
   b. underwriter
   c. loan originator
   d. loan processor

5.21   What power does the SAFE Act confer to state agencies related to complaint and violation investigations?

   a. Taking disciplinary action when a violation occurred
   b. Suing the perpetrator in civil court
   c. Bringing criminal action against the violator
   d. Suspending the licensee and licensed company until the investigation is complete

5.22 _____ is a connection in which a supervisor provides training, guidance, compliance review, and work assignment for a processor / underwriter.

a. Overt administration
b. Actual nexus
c. Arm's length
d. Direct oversight

5.23 The MLO pre-license course consists of _____ hours of coursework.

a. 10
b. 15
c. 20
d. 30

5.24 What is the main purpose of an MLO's unique identifier?

a. To verify an MLO's current employment status with a specific company
b. To allow MLOs to access exclusive discounts from NMLS partner companies
c. To generate revenue for the NMLS Consumer Access website
d. To distinguish the MLO and track his or her conduct

5.25 Which entity is a nationwide organization representing state regulators overseeing all types of banks, including those involved in mortgage lending?

a. CSBS
b. AARMR
c. CFPB
d. NMLS

5.26 An MLO has not had a license for six years. What must this party do to become re-licensed?

a. Retake pre-license education coursework
b. Retake and pass the NMLS SAFE exam
c. Take a Late CE course and then retake and pass the NMLS SAFE exam
d. Retake pre-license education coursework and then retake and pass the NMLS SAFE exam

5.27 Under which of these circumstances would an individual be exempt from MLO licensing requirements?

a. Counseling consumers about loan rates
b. Supervising loan processors and underwriters
c. Negotiating loan terms for an immediate family member
d. Originating loans as a sole proprietor

5.28 Which of the following is true regarding business loan origination?

a. Both state and federal licensure is required.
b. No universal federal requirements apply.
c. The SAFE Act affects business loan origination activities.
d. Licensure is mandated at the federal level but not the state level.

5.29 Which of the following actions is prohibited for MLOs?

a. Adhering to an appraiser's independent judgment of a property's value
b. Conducting MLO business with an active license
c. Engaging in an activity that represents a conflict of interest in a loan transaction
d. Making statements in connection with a mortgage loan transaction

5.30   What's the main purpose of the TA provision?

a. Grants eligible MLOs authority to originate loans before obtaining full state licensure
b. Streamlines the MLO license renewal process
c. Makes the MLO registration process the NMLS-R easier for licensees
d. Enables unlicensed mortgage professionals to "test out" of the pre-license coursework requirement for MLO licensure

5.31   What is one task that would be considered administrative / clerical and would not require a license to perform?

a. Negotiating specific repayment terms to a potential borrower
b. Soliciting a borrower's application directly from the borrower
c. Originating a residential loan
d. Gathering general borrower information to set up an appointment with an MLO

5.32   Which activity would fall under the "offering or negotiating terms of a residential mortgage loan" category of duties requiring an MLO license?

a. Sharing educational resources about the mortgage process, loan qualifications, and financial literacy
b. Providing a revised loan offer on a pending application in response to the borrower's request for a different rate
c. Making an underwriting decision regarding a borrower's qualifications for a loan
d. Providing general information about different loan types without recommending a specific product

5.33   Which of the following is true about underwriting / loan processing managers?

a. They are almost always licensed due to their supervisory role.
b. They are permitted to oversee the work of underwriters and loan processors, but cannot engage in those activities themselves.
c. They are required to register with the NMLS-R.
d. They are generally not licensed because they do not perform loan origination activities.

5.34   What information are states required to report to the NMLS-R?

a. MLO employment changes
b. MLO license violations
c. Number of MLOs in the state
d. State MLOs' unique identifiers

5.35   What is the purpose of the *Mortgage Call Report*?

a. Alert NMLS-R of MLOs in violation of SAFE Act requirements
b. Flag MLO advertisements that do not display a unique identifier
c. Detail a company's mortgage activity from the previous quarter
d. Update an MLO's profile in the NMLS-R

Comprehensive Practice Exams I and II

Practice Exam I

1. Hometown Mortgage Loans and Superior Loans have a business arrangement in which Hometown originates home loans and Superior services those loans. Per RESPA, how is Hometown required to disclose this business arrangement with Superior to borrowers?

    a. Hometown notes the arrangement on the loan closing documents at settlement.
    b. Hometown issues a Servicing Transfer Statement within 10 business days of loan application.
    c. Hometown provides the Affiliated Business Arrangement Disclosure within three business days of the loan application.
    d. Hometown's Loan Estimate clearly delineates the relationship.

2. Brian works for a mortgage lending institution that is a subsidiary of a large regional bank. For which of these tasks would he need an MLO license?

    a. He answers an email from a potential borrower about the application process.
    b. He calls a borrower to talk through a Loan Estimate that he emailed the day before.
    c. He responds to an online chat question and sends links to mortgage education websites.
    d. He manages the company's mailing list and distributes the quarterly newsletter.

3. At closing, which party or parties sign the mortgage note and deed of trust / mortgage?

    a. Borrower
    b. Borrower and lender
    c. Lender
    d. Borrower, lender, and seller

4. Which if the following is true about ECOA?

    a. ECOA prohibits lenders from considering an applicant's credit history.
    b. Per ECOA, equal access to credit does not equate to identical loan terms.
    c. Per ECOA, lenders must offer the lowest current interest rate to all applicants.
    d. ECOA prohibits lenders from verifying income information from loan applicants.

5. Which of the following is the best definition of *unique identifier*?

    a. A tag that MLOs use to identify their advertisements for compliance purposes
    b. A numerical / character series that NMLS-R assigns to each entity and individual who has an account on the NMLS-R platform
    c. A numerical label that lenders designate for each loan applicant so they can more efficiently complete their SARs
    d. A publicly accessible code that reveals the personal details and transaction history of an entity or individual on the NMLS-R platform

6. Which of the following is a potential penalty for an MLO who exhibits prohibited conduct?

    a. Probation for one year
    b. Fine of much as $25,000 per offense
    c. Mandatory completion of community service hours
    d. Reduction in commission rates for one year

7. _____ occurs when a borrower's monthly payments are not large enough to cover interest due on a loan. The unpaid interest is added to the principal balance, so the total amount of debt increases over time.

    a. Loan subordination
    b. Negative amortization
    c. A 2-1 buydown
    d. A yield spread premium

8. Which of the following is one purpose of the initial escrow statement?

    a. Reviews the past year's escrow account activity and projects the coming year's expenses
    b. Details estimated interest rates, monthly payments, and total closing costs due at settlement
    c. Provides an itemized accounting of all escrow items to be paid from the account in the first year
    d. Notes escrow shortages or surplus, and how either will be managed

9. Which of the following is true about RESPA's stipulations on escrow accounts?

    a. Lenders may only require an escrow account per government loan program requirements for a given loan.
    b. RESPA does not address any limitations for borrowers' escrow accounts.
    c. Lenders must require borrowers to deposit an amount equal to three months' worth of the annual estimated payment to serve as a cushion in their escrow accounts.
    d. RESPA sets borrower monthly escrow deposits at 1/12 of the annual estimated payment for taxes, insurance, and other impounds.

10. A borrower's estimated annual escrow amount for taxes and insurance is $4,800. Calculate the maximum permissible cushion for the escrow account.

    a. $400
    b. $480
    c. $800
    d. $1,200

11. A loan application submits a borrower's _____ to a lender so that the lender can make an informed credit decision involving a federally related mortgage loan.

    a. credit report
    b. property details
    c. financial information
    d. official proof of identification and fingerprints

12. _____ is one aspect of non-qualified mortgages.

    a. A DTI below 43%
    b. Conventional documentation for income
    c. Stringent regulatory protection for borrowers
    d. A more lenient application process

13. Which of the following is true regarding an escrow surplus?

    a. Any surplus amount is credited to the next year's escrow amount.
    b. An escrow surplus can be added to the account's cushion.
    c. When the surplus is $50 or more, the surplus must be returned to the borrower within 30 days after it is discovered.
    d. The lender can apply the surplus directly to the loan's principal balance without consulting the borrower.

14.   _____ are exempt from qualified mortgages requirements.

    a. FHA loans
    b. Fixed-rate loans
    c. Thirty-year ARMs
    d. Reverse mortgages

15.   Evelyn is using an FHA loan to buy a:

    a. duplex, and she will live in one unit.
    b. large Victorian home divided into six apartments, and she will live in one.
    c. winter home in Arizona.
    d. bed and breakfast inn with five guest suites and several common areas.

16.   Federally related mortgage loans are

    a. non-conforming.
    b. insured or guaranteed by the federal government.
    c. are not sold on the secondary market.
    d. made by lenders that fund more than $5,000,000 each year.

17.   Which of the following is true about HELOCs?

    a. The home's equity decreases over the life of the loan.
    b. Lenders generally utilize alternative documentation for income qualification.
    c. They typically involve two phases: a draw period and a repayment period.
    d. They are a strategy often used by borrowers who anticipate moving during the loan term.

18.   Lenders must notify borrowers of the intent to transfer loan servicing rights to another entity within _____.

    a. 10 or fewer days before transfer occurs
    b. 15 or fewer days before transfer occurs
    c. 5 days before transfer occurs
    d. 20 or fewer days before transfer occurs

19.   Which of these is considered a conforming loan?

    a. Subprime loan
    b. FHA loan
    c. Conventional fixed-rate loan
    d. Alt-A loans

20.   A loan application is required to include certain information. Which of the following is one piece of required information?

    a. Desired loan amount
    b. A detailed list of the borrower's debts and assets
    c. A photo of the property
    d. The seller's name and contact information

21.   Which of the following describes non-conforming loans?

    a. Loans that involve negative amortization
    b. Government loans that are not guaranteed
    c. Conventional loans that do not adhere to Fannie Mae or Freddie Mac rules
    d. Unconventional loans that can be sold in the secondary market

22. A(n) _____ is useful for high-value properties, especially in markets where housing prices exceed national average. Strict qualifications apply, such as excellent credit, downpayment of 20% or more, and rigorous documentation and income verification processes.

   a. jumbo loan
   b. Alt-A loan
   c. USDA loan
   d. subprime loan

23. Julia takes out a(n) _____ at the same time as her primary mortgage to help finance her purchase.

   a. jumbo loan
   b. reverse mortgage
   c. purchase money second mortgage
   d. balloon mortgage

24. What type of mortgage insurance continues over the life of the loan?

   a. PMI
   b. UFMIP
   c. VA funding fee
   d. MIP

25. What is one purpose of the CFPB Home Loan Toolkit?

   a. Informs borrowers about options for essential services related to mortgage transaction
   b. Assists borrowers in understanding mortgage loan process
   c. Discloses any financial or ownership interests that settlement service providers may have in affiliated businesses
   d. Informs borrowers about adjustable-rate mortgages and helps them make informed decisions

26. Which of the following is as aspect of the primary mortgage market?

   a. Existing mortgages are bought and sold via mortgage-backed securities.
   b. Borrowers and lenders work directly together to create new mortgages.
   c. Liquidity is provided to lenders to fund more mortgage loans.
   d. Entities do not interact directly with borrowers.

27. The _____ addresses consumer privacy and data protection regarding their personal financial information.

   a. Gramm-Leach-Billey Act
   b. Equal Credit Opportunity Act
   c. Unfair, Deceptive or Abusive Acts or Practices
   d. Truth in Lending Act

28. When a borrower uses unemployment compensation for income purposes on a loan application,

   a. it is averaged with employment income on 2 required years of tax returns.
   b. it renders the applicant a bad risk for the lender.
   c. it can be due to layoffs or terminations.
   d. it is treated as non-taxable income.

29. For which of the following reasons might license applicants have their application denied?

   a. A foreclosure in the past 5 years
   b. A license revoked in another state
   c. An HOA lien on their primary residence
   d. An outstanding judgment for an unpaid medical bill

30. _____ help Fannie Mae and Freddie Mac manage the risks of buying and guaranteeing mortgages by aiming to offset potential losses from defaults.

   a. Adjustable-rate mortgages (ARMs)
   b. Government-sponsored enterprises (GSEs)
   c. Qualified mortgages (QMs)
   d. Loan-Level Price Adjustments (LLPAs)

31. Which of the following is the formal title of the industry standard loan application?

   a. Uniform Residential Loan Application
   b. Freddie Mac Form 65
   c. Mortgage Loan Servicing Application
   d. Standardized Property Loan Application

32. What do financial institutions do when they discover potentially suspect or unusual activities that may indicate money laundering, fraud, or other illicit financial transactions?

   a. Report the activity to the local law enforcement authorities before conducting an internal review
   b. File a Suspicious Activity Report (SAR) with the appropriate compliance workers
   c. Directly confront the individuals or entities involved to gather more information before taking any further action
   d. Immediately freeze all accounts associated with the suspicious activity without any investigation

33. A _____ is an initial discount a lender provides to ARM borrowers that is lower than fully indexed rates and lasts for a specific duration.

   a. primary rate
   b. teaser rate
   c. flux rate
   d. benchmark rate

34. The closing date for Matt's home purchase is scheduled for April 15. So, his first regular mortgage payment will be due June 1, and it will contain the interest owed for May (interest is paid in arrears). His mortgage loan has an annual interest rate of 5%, and the loan amount is $475,000. Using the 365-day year, calculate the interest that accrues from April 15 to April 30 to determine the amount of prepaid interest Matt will owe at closing.

   a. $1,041.10
   b. $976.03
   c. $273.75
   d. $11.25

35. For MLOs working as sole proprietors,

   a. the company's license covers the MLO and the business.
   b. the MLO must be licensed and so must the business.
   c. only the MLO needs to be licensed.
   d. registration, not licensure, is required.

36. Per TILA definitions relating to UDAAP, an unfair act or practice is one that

   a. conceals material property defects.
   b. hinders a consumer's ability to comprehend a transaction, product or service.
   c. causes substantial injury to a consumer.
   d. exploits a consumer's lack of comprehension.

37. _____ are designed for borrowers with poor credit scores or other financial challenges making them a higher risk for lenders.

   a. Subprime loans
   b. Non-qualified mortgages
   c. Jumbo loans
   d. Adjustable rate loans

38. To which one of these loan types does RESPA apply?

   a. A mortgage that is assumable without the lender's approval
   b. A commercial refinance
   c. A home equity line of credit
   d. A construction loan

39. An example of predatory lending is

   a. income verification lending.
   b. asset-based lending.
   c. graduated payment mortgages.
   d. government-insured lending.

40. What is one approach an MLO can take to help match borrowers with suitable loan products for their particular situations and goals?

   a. Determining which type of tolerance threshold applies
   b. Verifying the borrower's employment history
   c. Deciding whether to hold or sell the mortgage in question
   d. Inquiring about the applicant's purchase timing

41. LTV ratios exceeding _____ generally mean a borrower must purchase PMI.

   a. 70%
   b. 75%
   c. 80%
   d. 85%

42. Which of the following is one aspect of ECOA?

   a. Using false pretenses to obtain customer information from financial institutions
   b. Refusing loans based on neighborhood characteristics
   c. Offering similar loan terms to applicants in similar financial situations
   d. Guiding borrowers to certain loan products based on protected characteristics

43. What is the formula for DTI?

   a. PITI on Primary Residence ÷ Gross Monthly Income
   b. Loan Amount ÷ Property Value
   c. Gross Monthly Income ÷ All Recurring Monthly Debt
   d. All Recurring Monthly Debt ÷ Gross Monthly Income

44. Darren is applying for an FHA loan, and his aunt Helen is helping him with a financial gift. Darien's credit score is 680. Which of the following statements is true?

   a. Darren is responsible for 3.5% of the down payment.
   b. Helen's gift may cover all costs regardless of Darren's down payment amount.
   c. Darren may not accept a financial gift from his aunt, per FHA.
   d. Darren must use 5% of his own funds for a down payment on the purchase.

45. The _____ requires that reasonable accommodations be made to serve borrowers living with a disability.

   a. ADA
   b. FHA
   c. ECOA
   d. UDAAP

46. MLO Jean noticed certain transactional activities that raised a red flag. She filed an SAR, but the investigation resulted in no finding of actual illegal activity. What happens to Jean now, per the Bank Secrecy Act?

   a. She is protected from any legal liability.
   b. She is required to take advanced training in recognizing potential red flags for fraud.
   c. She loses her job based on this error.
   d. She faces legal action against her for defamation and breach of privacy.

47. The declarations section of Form 1003 includes details about

   a. the loan's purpose.
   b. the borrower's assets and liabilities.
   c. any outstanding judgments against the borrower.
   d. the borrower's military service status.

48. TILA requires that lenders disclose additional facts for "trigger terms" used in advertisements, such as

   a. the minimum credit score required to qualify.
   b. annual operating costs of the property being financed.
   c. the number of payments.
   d. availability of loan modification options.

49. Which of these actions is a RESPA violation?

   a. Using false pretenses to obtain customer information from financial institutions
   b. Impeding consumer's understanding of transaction
   c. Giving or receiving something of value in exchange for referrals of settlement service business
   d. Discriminating against borrowers based on factors such as race, color, religion, national origin, sex, marital status, age, or receipt of public assistance

50. Which of the following fees relates to the 10% cumulative tolerance threshold?

   a. Fees paid to the lender or loan originator
   b. Transfer taxes
   c. Fees paid to third-party service providers not affiliated with the lender
   d. Fees for optional services

51. Which mortgage product is generally best suited for borrowers who plan to stay in their homes for a long time?

   a. Adjustable-rate
   b. Interest-only
   c. Fixed-rate
   d. Balloon

52. Which disclosure provides a detailed breakdown of final loan terms and closing costs?

    a. Loan Estimate
    b. CFPB Home Loan Toolkit
    c. Adjustable-Rate Mortgage Disclosure
    d. Closing Disclosure

53. What is one preventive measure MLOs can take against fraud?

    a. Requiring borrowers to certify the property's intended occupancy status in the loan application
    b. Conducting thorough verification of income and employment documentation with third parties, such as financial institutions and employers
    c. Verifying authenticity of assets and liabilities directly with financial institutions, creditors, and other relevant sources
    d. Performing post-closing occupancy verifications to ensure the borrower is in compliance

54. Which is a true statement about LTVs?

    a. The LTV ratio helps ensure borrower's debt responsibilities are less than net income.
    b. All conforming mortgage loan programs have the same LTV ratio requirements.
    c. Government-backed loans may allow for higher LTV ratios compared to conventional loans.
    d. LTV ratios exceeding 80% generally mean FHA loan borrowers must purchase MIP.

55. Which of the following defines fraud? Choose the best option.

    a. Breaching duty of care, e.g., errors, omissions, failures to fulfill responsibilities
    b. Deceiving others for personal gain or to cause harm
    c. Unintentionally concealing material facts that may deceive another party involved in a transaction
    d. Making a mistake on a mortgage loan application

56. Which of the following loan products require that the property meet minimum property requirements (MPR)?

    a. ARM loans
    b. VA loans
    c. Conventional loans
    d. Qualified loans

57. What is one requirement of the Bank Secrecy Act (aka Anti-Money Laundering law)?

    a. Verifying the identity of individuals who want to open an account
    b. Reporting SAR findings to the public
    c. Sharing customer information with other financial institutions
    d. Terminating employees who fail to recognize instances of fraud

58. What is a GSE?

    a. A financial service corporation that Congress created to enhance credit flow, particularly in the housing sector
    b. A system that provides stable, low-cost funding to financial institutions for home mortgage and economic development loans
    c. A tool that protects consumers from predatory lending practices and from obtaining loans they cannot afford
    d. A risk-based fee that primary mortgage market lenders assess on borrowers based on certain perceived risk factors, such as low credit scores

59. Which of the following disclosures may be necessary if the loan amount or interest rate changes?

    a. Revised Loan Estimate
    b. AfBA disclosure
    c. Closing Disclosure
    d. Mortgage Loan Servicing Disclosure

60. The NMLS-R serves several purposes, one of which is

    a. enforcing state licensing laws for loan originators.
    b. maintaining a nationwide licensing system for all 50 states and U.S. territories.
    c. creating a system that mandates loan originators to prioritize consumers' best interests.
    d. operating a "whistle blower" network for consumer complaints and investigations.

61. Limiting points and fees charged to borrowers to help prevent excessive costs is a key feature of

    a. USDA loans.
    b. qualified mortgages.
    c. FHA loans.
    d. subprime mortgages.

62. For what purpose would a borrower submit a loss mitigation application to the lender?

    a. To request more time before the lender starts the foreclosure process
    b. To kickstart the short sale negotiations between the borrower and lender
    c. To give the lender information that may determine if the borrower qualifies for a foreclosure alternative
    d. To render an accounting of fees and costs the lender will cover for the borrower

63. Certain borrower-supplied information must be verified by third parties listed on application. For example, to confirm the availability and source of funds the borrower intends to use for the down payment and closing costs, the financial institution would use the _____ authorization form.

    a. VOE
    b. CD
    c. VOD
    d. AfBA

64. Smooth Talk Mortgage's policies forbid making loans in certain parts of town where average income levels are less than $80,000. Which statement about this policy is true?

    a. It is a conservative policy based on financial data.
    b. It is a discriminatory practice that is prohibited by the FHA.
    c. It is a violation of UDAAP.
    d. It is legal but questionable ethically.

65. How many hours of CE do MLOs need to complete during each renewal period?

    a. 8
    b. 12
    c. 16
    d. 20

66. The loan to value ratio (LTV):

    a. measures the relationship between the mortgage loan amount and the property's appraised value or purchase price.
    b. of less than 80% generally means conventional loan borrowers must purchase PMI.
    c. has the same requirements no matter the mortgage loan program.
    d. suggests a smaller down payment and potentially higher risk when it is low.

67. When may a lender legally send a first notice of default to a borrower?

    a. Borrower fails to make two payments.
    b. Borrower violates a due-on-sale clause.
    c. Lender and borrower initiate short sale discussions.
    d. Borrower moves out of the property.

68. _____ is part of the loan origination pre-qualification phase.

    a. Asking for details regarding borrowers' employment, income, assets, and liabilities
    b. Assessing borrowers' information to estimate their potential qualifying mortgage amount
    c. Evaluating an application to determine the risk involved in lending to a borrower
    d. Approving, suspending, or denying an application

69. A neutral policy that disproportionately affects a particular group can still be considered discriminatory. What is this type of discrimination called?

    a. Disparate impact
    b. Steering
    c. Direct impact
    d. Pretexting

70. Loan applicant Sabrina is writing a letter of explanation for her employment gap earlier in the year. After eight years with the same company, she was laid off, and it took her three months to find a new job. In general, what might this gap mean for her loan application?

    a. Sabrina will be required to make a larger down payment to lower her LTV due to the employment gap.
    b. Because the gap is fewer than 6 months, Sabrina can qualify with her current job verification, as long as she meets other criteria.
    c. Sabrina will need a co-signer for her mortgage loan because of her employment gap.
    d. Sabrina will need to be with her new full-time job for at least 6 months before qualifying for a loan.

71. When might the CFPB deem it necessary to establish and maintain a state's MLO licensing system?

    a. It finds that the state's exam pass rate is far below the national average.
    b. It believes the state's existing licensing system fails to meet the SAFE Act's minimum requirements.
    c. There is a significant increase in consumer complaints regarding mortgage loan transactions within the state.
    d. The state exceeds the national average in MLO licensing approvals.

72. The _____ is responsible for ensuring loan applications are complete, accurate and thorough.

    a. underwriter
    b. MLO
    c. underwriting manager
    d. borrower

73. What is the 90-day rule that pertains to FHA mortgages?

   a. An FHA loan is not assumable if the original borrower has owned the home for 90 days or more.
   b. FHA will not insure a mortgage when a potential buyer contracts to buy a home within 90 days of the previous sale.
   c. Borrowers must have been employed for more than 90 days to be eligible for an FHA loan.
   d. FHA borrowers must occupy the property within 90 days after closing.

74. Jeff and Lucy applied for a mortgage loan for a primary residence. They actually plan to rent the house as an investment property. This is an example of

   a. asset fraud.
   b. fraud for profit.
   c. occupancy fraud.
   d. redlining.

75. Conforming loans set seller concession limits based on down payment percentages for primary or secondary homes. For example, when borrowers put less than 10% down, concessions are capped at _____ of the home's purchase price.

   a. 2%
   b. 3%
   c. 6%
   d. 9%

76. For which property would an appraiser typically choose the cost approach?

   a. A single-family home built in 1995
   b. A large hotel
   c. A museum
   d. A two-acre unimproved lot

77. A breach in one's duty of care, such as errors, omissions, and failures to fulfill responsibilities, is a form of

   a. intentional misrepresentation.
   b. fraud.
   c. mistake.
   d. negligence.

78. What is the maximum LTV on an FHA loan used for a home purchase?

   a. 93.5%
   b. 97.75%
   c. 80%
   d. 96.5%

79. What type of relationship are MLOs considered to have with their clients?

   a. Advisory
   b. Fiduciary
   c. Consultative
   d. Transactional

80. A mortgage loan originator

    a. initiates the process of securing a mortgage loan for a borrower in exchange for some form of compensation.
    b. gathers all the necessary paperwork from borrowers and ensures that everything is in order for the underwriting process.
    c. reviews all the documentation provided, assesses the risk of lending to a borrower, and decides whether the loan should be approved.
    d. acts as a neutral third party to handle the exchange of documents and money between buyers, sellers, and lenders.

81. An underwriter's credit decision is based on

    a. an evaluation of the borrower's creditworthiness and where the property is located.
    b. verification of the borrower's provided information and the inspector's judgment of the property's condition.
    c. the borrower's completion of a formal application and credit report data.
    d. an assessment of the borrower's likelihood of repaying the loan and the property's value as collateral.

82. Molly worked as an MLO for a few years and then went back to school to train for a new career. Fifteen years later, she decides she would like to work in the mortgage industry again. What does she need to do to regain her license?

    a. Take a Late CE course and submit a renewal application
    b. Retake the pre-license education and submit a new license application
    c. Retake both the pre-license education and the NMLS SAFE exam, and then submit a new license application
    d. Take a Late CE course and submit a new license application

83. Ted is 100 days delinquent on his mortgage payment. He received a notice of default from his lender. Why might the lender have sent this notice of default?

    a. RESPA allows the lender to send a first notice of default when a borrower is three months delinquent on payments.
    b. Lenders may send such notices once a borrower misses a payment.
    c. The lender is responding to Ted's loss mitigation application.
    d. Another lienholder has already begun foreclosure action against Ted, and the lender is joining that action.

84. When a consumer files a complaint and an investigation begins, the SAFE Act permits state agencies to

    a. revoke the license of the MLO under investigation.
    b. gather information and evidence as part of the investigation.
    c. seek legal reparations from the MLO on behalf of the complainant.
    d. have the MLO under investigation arrested.

85. Regarding TRID's tolerance thresholds, which one applies to fees that can change from Loan Estimate to final Closing Disclosure without restrictions?

    a. No tolerance
    b. Unrestricted tolerance
    c. Zero tolerance
    d. Cumulative tolerance

86. One condition an MLO must satisfy before taking advantage of the Temporary Authority (TA) provision is that the MLO must

   a. have submitted the license application to the state agency.
   b. already be federally registered.
   c. have no disqualifying issues.
   d. have a licensed company's sponsorship.

87. Jake applies for a mortgage loan to buy an investment property, but he plans to reside in the home. He uses the potential rental income to help him qualify for the loan. This is an example of

   a. occupancy fraud.
   b. reverse occupancy fraud.
   c. creative financing.
   d. second-home financing.

88. Which of the following scenarios describes a short sale? Assume each borrower has received a first notice of default from the lender.

   a. Lance's lender has agreed that the property may be sold for less than Lance's principal loan balance.
   b. Claire's lender has accepted and is reviewing her loss mitigation application.
   c. Devin's lender has seized the house and will sell it as an REO.
   d. Selena's lender is selling the home at a public auction.

89. All MLOs are prohibited from

   a. omitting relevant details about loan terms.
   b. requiring an appraisal to fund a loan.
   c. conducting clerical MLO-related activities as a registered but not licensed MLO.
   d. counseling consumers about loan rates and terms.

90. A borrower's loan has as interest-only period of five years. After that, the borrower will typically

   a. convert the loan to a standard amortizing fixed-rate or adjustable-rate loan.
   b. make one balloon payment to pay off the loan.
   c. take out a second mortgage to cover principal payments not paid during the interest-only period.
   d. convert the loan to a reverse mortgage.

91. Which action relates to a straw buyer scheme?

   a. Applying for a loan on someone else's behalf to conceal the true buyer's identity
   b. Obtaining a loan to buy a property and then flipping it for a higher price
   c. Using ill-gotten funds for a down payment
   d. Buying a property without financing measures

92. The _____ informs borrower of lender's intent to service the loan or transfer it to another lender.

   a. Closing Disclosure
   b. Loan Estimate
   c. Mortgage Servicing Disclosure Statement
   d. Affiliated Business Arrangement Disclosure

93. An FHA loan assumption in which a new borrower takes over the original borrower's payments, but the original borrower remains liable if new borrower defaults is called a(n) _____.

a. assignment
b. basic assumption
c. simple assumption
d. novation

94. Which of the following changes would require an MNLS-R profile update?

a. Job title
b. CE coursework taken
c. Salary raise
d. Address change

95. The pre-qualification phase of the loan origination process serves as a preliminary assessment of a borrower's financial capability, therefore, it is _____.

a. exceptionally thorough
b. often unnecessary
c. generally non-binding
d. typically formal

96. Which of the following is one purpose of the Loan Estimate?

a. Finalize the loan terms and other non-closing cost fees
b. Details projected interest rates, monthly payments, and total closing costs
c. Inform borrower of lender's intent to service the loan or transfer it to another lender
d. Notify borrower when the lender has a business arrangement with another service provider involved in the transaction

97. Regarding the relationship between a supervising MLO and an unlicensed processor / underwriter, what does *actual nexus* mean?

a. A formal partnership where the processor/underwriter shares financial liabilities and profits with the supervising MLO
b. A peer-to-peer collaboration where the supervising MLO and processor/underwriter work as equals, without a defined hierarchy or oversight
c. An independent contractor scenario where the processor/underwriter operates separately from the MLO, only consulting for specific issues without direct oversight
d. A supervisory connection where the MLO provides training, guidance, and work oversight to the processor/underwriter by the MLO

98. Which of the following would be a prepaid item a borrower pays upfront at closing?

a. Mortgage interest from the day of closing until the end of the month
b. HOA monthly dues for the initial month of occupancy
c. MLO compensation
d. Title insurance

99. Fannie Mae/Freddie Mac allow the exclusion of _____ in DTI calculations when 10 or fewer payments remain.

a. auto insurance payments
b. alimony
c. an installment loan's monthly payments
d. HOA annual dues

100.   MLO Carlo is calculating a borrower's LTV to determine the risk level for his mortgage company. The property was appraised at $625,000, and the contracted sales price is $631,000. The proposed loan amount is $450,000, and the proposed down payment is $181,000. What's the LTV, rounded to the nearest whole number?

    a. 72%
    b. 71%
    c. 40%
    d. 99%

Practice Exam II

1. What does the acronym UDAAP stand for?

    a. Underwriting Disclosure and Asset Protection Protocol
    b. Unfair, Deceptive or Abusive Acts or Practices
    c. Universal Disclosure and Affordability Act Provisions
    d. Unrestricted Debt Assessment and Approval Program

2. What type of loans protect lenders against borrower lawsuits, serving particularly as a "safe harbor" in proving lender compliance with ability-to-repay rules?

    a. Negative amortization loans
    b. Interest-only loans
    c. ARMs
    d. QMs

3. Per federal regulations, individuals who perform loan origination activities are required to be licensed when

    a. originating loans as part of volunteer work for a community bank's outreach program.
    b. engaging in loan process activities solely to provide market analysis data for real estate professionals, without negotiations on loan terms.
    c. originating loans as employees of non-depository institutions.
    d. originating loans as an attorney as part of an attorney-client relationship.

4. In the primary mortgage market

    a. interest earned on loans helps lenders fund more mortgage loans.
    b. borrowers and lenders work directly together to create new mortgages.
    c. GSEs enhance credit flow, particularly in housing sector.
    d. existing mortgages are bought and pooled into mortgage-backed securities.

5. What is meant by *tangible net benefit*?

    a. The decrease in interest rates in the general market at the time a borrower refinances a mortgage, giving the borrower more monthly savings
    b. The reduction in the number of payments left on a mortgage after extending the loan term through refinancing
    c. The increase in property value a borrower can expect in a given market over the first five years after purchasing a home
    d. The financial advantages or benefits that a borrower is expected to gain from refinancing an existing mortgage loan into a new one

6. Which of these loans is exempt from RESPA requirements?

    a. Loan intended to be sold to a GSE
    b. Vacant lot purchase loan
    c. Conventional home loan
    d. Reverse mortgage

7. Claire and Cameron are buying a home for $625,000, and their LTV is 75%. They paid $20,000 in earnest money with their offer. How much will they need to bring to closing?

    a. $162,250
    b. $171,250
    c. $136,250
    d. $156,250

155

8. The Gramm-Leach-Bliley Act Safeguards Rule requires financial institutions to develop

   a. consumer complaint management policies that reflects federal requirements and professional conduct.
   b. consumer education programs that help borrowers understand their financial situation and options for mortgage financing.
   c. codes of ethics to serve as a formal set of guidelines and principles outlining expected standards of behavior and conduct for everyone in the organization.
   d. written cybersecurity programs outlining how they will protect the security, confidentiality, and integrity of consumer information.

9. MLO Margaret's supervisory activities over her team of unlicensed loan originators, processors, and underwriters include training, guidance, compliance review, and work assignments. The term for this working relationship is called

   a. professionally cordial interaction.
   b. direct report status.
   c. actual nexus.
   d. mutual professional affiliations.

10. The _____ is designed to bolster lending in local communities by providing stable, low-cost funding to financial institutions for home mortgage and economic development loans.

    a. Government National Mortgage Association (Ginnie Mae)
    b. *HomeReady* Program
    c. Federal Housing Administration (FHA)
    d. Federal Home Loan Bank System (FHLB)

11. Which of the following is true about title reports?

    a. After the title search, the title report notes any outstanding liens, mortgages, or encumbrances on the property.
    b. Issues noted in the report have no impact on the loan's approval or terms.
    c. RESPA requires professional title companies to conduct title searches and provide comprehensive reports.
    d. The survey, not the title report, provides a legal description of the property, including the precise property location and boundary identification.

12. Regulators use UDAAP standards to evaluate all mortgage-related entities for practices such as

    a. obscuring information so a consumer takes out an unaffordable loan.
    b. giving or receiving anything of value in exchange for referrals of settlement service business.
    c. using false pretenses to obtain customer information from financial institutions.
    d. discriminating against borrowers based on protected class factors.

13. An MI factor

    a. relates to an appraiser's utilization of a cap rate to determine a property's NOI.
    b. is a numerical value or percentage of the loan amount that is used to calculate the annual PMI premium.
    c. goes into the calculation for both the upfront and annual premiums for an FHA loan's mandatory MIP.
    d. works alongside Form 1003 in automated underwriting systems applications.

14. Optional fees paid upfront to lower interest rates on mortgages are referred to as

    a. discount points.
    b. origination fees.
    c. closing costs.
    d. funding fees.

15. Which of the following is part of ECOA's rules for independent appraisals?

    a. Lenders may hire appraisers to work directly for them as employees.
    b. Lenders are permitted to directly compensate appraisers based on an appraisal's outcome.
    c. Lenders may suggest a range of values for appraisers to use as a guide, but the appraiser males the final determination.
    d. Lenders must select independent appraisers with the necessary qualifications and experience to perform reliable appraisals.

16. A _____ is a legally binding contract between a borrower and a lender outlining the borrower's promise to repay the loan amount to the lender under specific terms and conditions.

    a. mortgage
    b. deed of trust
    c. promissory note
    d. security instrument

17. In this type of fraudulent activity, individuals often work together to gain money for themselves via the transaction process.

    a. Fraud for property
    b. Asset fraud
    c. Fraud for profit
    d. Liability fraud

18. Fannie Mae/Freddie Mac key conforming loan standards include

    a. a general credit score requirement of at least 580.
    b. a typical down payment minimum of 10%.
    c. current (2023) baseline loan limit for single-unit properties of $726,200 in most areas.
    d. a typical borrower DTI of 40% or less.

19. Calculate the period interest amount for an outstanding loan balance of $250,000 with a 7% annual interest rate and 12 compounding periods.

    a. $336
    b. $1,458.33
    c. $1,614.58
    d. $1,215.28

20. The ECOA prohibits lenders and MLOs from discriminating against borrowers based on factors such as

    a. receipt of public assistance.
    b. employment status.
    c. geographic location.
    d. primary language.

21. Which of the following would be considered a mortgage brokerage service as it relates to settlement services?

   a. Forecasting interest rates
   b. Loan counseling
   c. Title search
   d. Appraisal

22. When an MLO considers a borrower's DTI, which of these monthly expenses would be included in the income calculations?

   a. Alimony
   b. Daycare expenses
   c. Medical insurance
   d. Groceries / food

23. Lenders prefer that financial assets in accounts are seasoned. What does this mean?

   a. The assets were moved from a retirement account to a checking or savings account.
   b. The assets are fixed and can be easily converted to cash or cash equivalents.
   c. The assets are liquid and have been held in the account for 60 days or more.
   d. The assets are earnings from the borrower's current employer.

24. An example of asset fraud is when a mortgage loan applicant

   a. provides false or misleading information regarding the intended occupancy status of the property.
   b. misrepresents income earned or employment history to boost their creditworthiness.
   c. misrepresents their holdings to inflate their finances to improve their chances of qualifying.
   d. conceals or understates existing debts or financial obligations to appear stronger financially.

25. Providing the CFPB's Home Loan Toolkit booklet to borrowers is required for

   a. all federally regulated mortgage loans.
   b. borrowers who assume a loan.
   c. borrowers entering the pre-foreclosure phase.
   d. home purchase loans only.

26. Elizabeth and Joe are buying a home for $560,000. They would like a first mortgage that is 80% or the purchase price and also a purchase money second mortgage for the maximum allowable amount. Their chosen loan has a maximum combined LTV (CLTV) of 95%. What is the amount of their second mortgage?

   a. $28,000
   b. $65,000
   c. $84,000
   d. $112,000

27. Fannie Mae:

   a. creates mortgages on the primary market and sells them to commercial banks.
   b. buys loans to provide local banks with federal money to finance home mortgages.
   c. issues government guarantees on bond pools of government-backed loans.
   d. guarantees investors will receive timely principal and interest payments of MBS, unless the original borrower defaults.

28. RESPA disclosure requirements impact several services and their fees related to transactions and settlement. Which of the following transaction-related fees or costs are typically exempt?

    a. Fees for property inspections
    b. Fees for over-standard LTVs
    c. Fees for loan origination
    d. Fees for mortgage broker services

29. Borrower Gene has a 30-year mortgage on his home. Five years into the loan, he loses his job and fails to make payments for four months. He receives a notice of default from his lender. Gene's mortgage incudes a power of sale clause, so the lender proceeds with the foreclosure process. The lender sends Gene notice of sale, publishes the notice in local newspapers, and waits a specified period to give Gene a chance to get caught up. What type of foreclosure does this scenario describe?

    a. Non-judicial foreclosure with no recording / publication requirement
    b. Judicial foreclosure
    c. Non-judicial foreclosure with recording / publication requirement
    d. Judicial foreclosure with grace period

30. States are required to report _____ to NMLS-R.

    a. MLO employment changes
    b. MLO license violations
    c. number of MLOs in supervisory roles
    d. MLOs who leave the profession

31. Which of the following is a prorated expense that the buyer and seller would divide between them at closing?

    a. Property taxes
    b. Mortgage interest from day of closing until end of month
    c. PMI
    d. Escrow account funding

32. Non-conforming loans

    a. follow Fannie Mae/Freddie Mac guidelines.
    b. are not conventional loans.
    c. typically have less stringent requirements.
    d. exceed FHFA loan limits.

33. Gloria's annual gross income is $85,000, and her monthly debts are a $300 car loan, $150 in student loans, and $200 in credit card bills. She has her eye on a $325,000 townhouse, and she has saved 20% for a down payment. The loan she has applied for has an estimated monthly payment of $1,500, and with taxes, interest, and insurance, it will be $1,800. What is Gloria's DTI with this loan?

    a. 25%
    b. 35%
    c. 30%
    d. 80%

34. An SAR report must be filed _____ after initial detection of suspicious activity or thresholds that may require an investigation.

    a. exactly 7 days
    b. at least 15 days
    c. no more than 30 days
    d. up to 60 days

35. What is the purpose of the Homeowners Protection Act?

    a. Restrict mortgage lenders from risky speculative investments
    b. Set ability-to-repay requirements
    c. Protect homebuyers from excessive PMI charges
    d. Limit pre-payment penalties

36. To which of the following does RESPA apply?

    a. Renovation contractor
    b. Seller-financed purchase
    c. ARM mortgage converting to fixed rate
    d. Home inspectors

37. The Nationwide Multistate Licensing System (NMLS)

    a. serves as registry for all state-licensed MLOs.
    b. grants consumers free access to information about loan originators.
    c. is a centralized licensing system for individuals and companies in the non-depository financial services sector.
    d. oversees a state's licensing system if it is found to be deficient per SAFE Act standards.

38. The lender's promise to hold a certain interest rate and specific number of points for a borrower for a specified period is called a _____ agreement.

    a. tolerance
    b. rate lock
    c. yield spread premium
    d. lender credit

39. _____ is defined as the point at which a borrower becomes contractually obligated to the lender on a loan.

    a. Loan assignment
    b. Application delivery
    c. Agreement
    d. Loan consummation

40. The minimum age for a reverse mortgage borrower is

    a. 55
    b. 60
    c. 62
    d. 65

41. Hometown Mortgage Loans is affiliated with Superior Loans, a company that services mortgage loans. Per their arrangement, Hometown originates home loans, and Superior services them. Hometown Mortgage is required to notify borrowers of this business affiliation _____.

    a. within three business days of loan application
    b. at least 15 days before settlement
    c. within three calendar days of loan application
    d. whenever it wants to. No specific timeframe applies.

42. What is a thrift?

a. A company or individual that provides discounted services to lenders or borrowers in the course of originating, processing, or closing a mortgage loan
b. A type of financial institution that is prohibited from offering mortgage loans
c. A financial institution that primarily accepts savings deposits and makes mortgage and other loans
d. A market where loans that originated in the primary market are sold to investors

43. Which government loan program offers both guaranteed loans and direct loans?

a. FHA
b. USDA
c. ADA
d. Fannie Mae

44. What is one action the Mortgage Acts and Practices (MAP Rule, or Reg N) expressly prohibits?

a. Disclosing client-provided information that is material to the transaction and / or other parties involved
b. Failing to implement safeguards to address identified cybersecurity risks
c. Directing a borrower toward certain loan products or lenders based on factors other than the borrower's best interests
d. Using the word "fixed" in advertising to describe a rate or payment unless it genuinely remains fixed for the entire loan term

45. Per TRID, situations in which a lender can issue a revised Loan Estimate, include

a. extraordinary events beyond anyone involved in the transaction's control.
b. borrower consultations with a financial advisor.
c. minor typographical errors in the borrower's name or address on the initial Loan Estimate.
d. the borrower's decision to use a different real estate agent.

46. A _____ meets certain CFPB standards, ensuring that lenders make loans that borrowers have ability to repay.

a. qualified mortgage
b. conforming mortgage
c. conventional mortgage
d. non-conforming mortgage

47. The Gramm-Leach-Billey Act prohibits lenders and MLOs from pretexting, which is

a. providing false information to obtain someone's personal or confidential information from financial institutions.
b. using encryption methods to secure sensitive data from unauthorized access.
c. conducting thorough background checks on potential clients to verify their identity.
d. implementing strict password policies to prevent unauthorized access to sensitive systems.

48. Which loan type typically disburses funds in stages known as "draws"?

a. HELOC
b. Reverse mortgage
c. Balloon mortgage
d. Construction loan

49. Dodd-Frank gives borrowers the private right of action. What does this mean?

   a. Borrowers can negotiate loan terms directly with lenders without involving an intermediary.
   b. Borrowers who feel they have faced discrimination can submit complaints to regulatory agencies about unfair lending practices.
   c. Borrowers who cannot afford their loan can sue creditors they feel did not properly determine their ability to repay.
   d. Borrowers whose application was denied can request a federal review of loan decisions they believe the creditor made in error.

50. _____ is one example of a high-cost mortgage under HOEPA.

   a. A mortgage with total closing costs, points, and fees that exceed 5% of the total loan amount threshold
   b. A first mortgage in which the APR exceeds APOR by at least 1.5 percentage points
   c. A reverse mortgage with an APR that exceeds APOR by 3.5 percentage points
   d. A first mortgage combined with a second purchase-money mortgage

51. A(n) _____ is an investment type that is issued by government-sponsored enterprises and typically consists of conforming loans.

   a. non-agency mortgage-backed securities (MBS) package
   b. agency MBS package
   c. CMO
   d. REMIC

52. Tracy's mortgage loan is through her branch of a large national bank. After five years, the bank recently alerted her that it was going to be no longer involved in the day-to-day management of her loan. Per RESPA, how must the bank notify Tracy of this decision?

   a. Servicing Transfer Statement
   b. Closing Disclosure
   c. Affiliated Business Arrangement Disclosure
   d. Mortgage Servicing Disclosure Statement

53. Which types of loan are exempt from RESPA's requirements for closing costs and fees disclosure?

   a. Loans secured by a lien
   b. Home equity loans, home equity lines of credit, and reverse mortgages
   c. Business, commercial, and agricultural loans
   d. Lender-approved loan assumptions

54. Valerie works for a mortgage lending company as an unlicensed employee. Which of these tasks could Valerie perform because it is exempt from MLO licensing requirements?

   a. Counseling consumers about the most advantageous loan products
   b. Supervising loan processors and underwriters in their work activities
   c. Negotiating loan terms for a friend who is buying their first home
   d. Collecting required documents from borrowers and passing them along to an MLO

55. When would a loan subordination be necessary?

   a. When a prepayment penalty applies to the mortgage
   b. When refinancing a first mortgage and a second mortgage exists
   c. When a loan that originated on the primary market is sold on the secondary market
   d. When a lender agrees to an assumption

56. Which of the following is true of Qualified Mortgages (QMs)?

    a. Balloon payments at the end of the loan term are not permitted under QM standards.
    b. Temporary QMs were created to provide a transition period when QM rules were established under Dodd-Frank.
    c. Per Dodd-Frank, small lenders have less flexibility when determining a borrower's DTI ratio than larger lenders do.
    d. To meet CFPB standards, all QMs have the same key features and requirements.

57. Lauren is a registered loan originator, but she's not licensed. Which of the following must be true?

    a. She works at a depository institution and is registered with the NMLS-R.
    b. She works for a non-depository entity that has a state-regulated license.
    c. She supervises other loan originators and underwriters at her place of business.
    d. She works at a mortgage company and is registered with the AARMR.

58. Which of these is considered an acceptable practice under RESPA?

    a. A settlement service provider requiring the buyer to use a specific title insurance company as a condition of the sale
    b. An MLO charging a fee to a real estate agent for including the agent on a list of recommended service providers
    c. A mortgage broker accepting payment for referring a buyer to a specific home inspector
    d. An MLO providing a Loan Estimate (LE) of settlement costs to borrowers no more than 3 days after receiving a loan application

59. Which type of illegal discrimination occurs when a financial entity refuses to fund a loan based on neighborhood characteristics?

    a. Disparate impact
    b. Pretexting
    c. Redlining
    d. Steering

60. _____ is a financing technique that reduces the mortgage interest rate in a stepped fashion during the loan's initial years.

    a. A discount point
    b. Negative amortization
    c. A 2-1 buydown
    d. A lender credit

61. With an adjustable-rate mortgage, what is the margin?

    a. The number of percentage points the lender adds to the index to determine the ARM interest rate after the initial rate period ends
    b. The benchmark interest rate that mirrors general market conditions, e.g. Constant Maturity Treasury (CMT)
    c. The interest rate on an ARM loan at closing that is tied to a particular index
    d. An initial discount the lender provides to the borrower, which lasts for a specific duration

62. Which regulation is primarily concerned with fairness in lending practices?

    a. ECOA
    b. TILA
    c. RESPA
    d. UDAAP

63. One expectation of the National Association of Mortgage Brokers (NAMB) comprehensive Code of Ethics is

a. meeting minimum regulatory standards, which also meets ethical conduct considerations.
b. prioritizing their own financial interests over those of the consumer.
c. acting with honesty, integrity, and fairness in all professional dealings.
d. developing a written cybersecurity program outlining steps to protect consumer information.

64. What is the point of prorations and adjustments included in the financial transactions that take place at closing?

a. To ensure that the buyer and seller are responsible for their respective portions of certain costs based on the closing date
b. To provide itemized breakdowns outlining the buyer's costs and the seller's proceeds at closing
c. To compare the ratio between the amount of the mortgage loan and the appraised value or purchase price of the property being financed
d. To direct legal document preparation to finalize the mortgage agreement

65. The CFPB's Reg N aims to

a. streamline the mortgage underwriting process.
b. establish guidelines for disclosure timelines.
c. standardize loan application administration.
d. prevent deceptive advertising practices in mortgage lending.

66. Which of the following is one type of fraud for profit?

a. Straw buyer
b. Air loan
c. Reverse occupancy fraud
d. Income fraud

67. To participate in *HomeReady* and *HomePossible* low down payment programs, a borrower's income must be

a. less than or equal to $50,000.
b. below the national poverty line.
c. no more than 80% of American median income.
d. equal to or less than American median income.

68. Someone who fails the NMLS SAFE exam on their first attempt and wants to retake it

a. may not do so.
b. has to retake the pre-license education and then retest.
c. must wait 30 days to retake the exam.
d. must wait 60 days to retake the exam.

69. Which of the following is true regarding qualifying ratios?

a. The DTI ratio carries more weight than the housing ratio.
b. Borrowers must qualify on both the housing ratio and the DTI ratio to be approved for a loan.
c. The housing ratio helps ensure the property's value supports the requested loan amount.
d. A lower LTV ratio suggests a smaller down payment and a potentially higher risk for the lender.

70. For consumers to receive and e-sign electronic loan disclosures and documents, what must first occur?

    a. Consumers must give their explicit consent to use electronic records and signatures.
    b. Lenders must send hard copies of all documents before consumers e-sign.
    c. Consumers must install lenders' proprietary firewall software on their devices.
    d. Consumers need to verify their identity using a government-issued ID in person at a bank or lender's office.

71. Professional appraiser Catherine is using the income approach to appraise an apartment building that is for sale. To calculate the building's NOI, what will she do?

    a. Estimate its potential income and subtract its operating expenses
    b. Estimate its potential income and add its operating expenses
    c. Add its potential income and operating expenses, and then divide by the cap rate
    d. Divide its potential income by the cap rate

72. Mortgage lending entities are expected to report_____, which is called *self-reporting*.

    a. their personal financial information to clients
    b. quarterly earnings to shareholders
    c. their income and assets on mortgage applications
    d. detected compliance violations to the applicable regulatory entity

73. The new Temporary Authority (TA) provision

    a. restructured the NMLS-R registration process for MLOs, creating a more straightforward platform.
    b. enables unlicensed mortgage professionals to "test out" of the pre-license coursework requirement for MLO licensure.
    c. streamlines the transition for federally-registered MLOs seeking state licensure to work at a state-licensed mortgage company.
    d. gives states a process by which to establish and maintain their own examination and licensing system.

74. Permitted MLO compensation includes

    a. consideration amounts based on the percentage of applications that close successfully.
    b. payments related to the total number of loans originated.
    c. compensation based on an interest rate.
    d. splitting fees with other loan originators and settlement service providers.

75. Trent's unique identifier

    a. verifies his past and current employment records.
    b. gives him exclusive discounts from NMLS partner companies.
    c. helps him measure his advertising success rates.
    d. distinguishes him from other MLOs and helps track his conduct.

76. Which of the following statements is true regarding Fannie Mae restrictions on financial gift donors?

    a. Donors must be related to the loan applicant by blood, marriage, adoption, or legal guardianship.
    b. The loan application must list a donor as a co-borrower.
    c. Donors are required to complete a VOD and VOE as part of the loan application.
    d. Loan applicants who use financial gifts for the purchase may only qualify for less attractive loan terms.

77. Under which circumstances may the CFPB exercise its authority to establish and maintain a state's licensing system?

    a. The state's exam pass rate is far below the national average.
    b. The CFPB believes the state's existing licensing system fails to meet the SAFE Act's minimum requirements.
    c. Consumer complaints regarding mortgage loan transactions within the state increase steadily over a three-year period.
    d. The state's number of MLO license violations considerably exceeds the national average.

78. The main purpose of the USA PATRIOT Act was that it

    a. introduced measures to enhance national security and prevent terrorist activities.
    b. enhanced the mortgage transaction process for first-time homebuyers.
    c. protected members of the armed services and veterans from unfair lending practices.
    d. established procedures to detect, report, and prevent money laundering and other financial crimes.

79. Which of the following is true regarding seller contributions per TILA?

    a. They may go toward closing costs, pre-paids, discount points, and down payment amounts.
    b. Maximum amounts are set across the board for all loan types.
    c. Conventional loans on primary residences with less than 10% down have a limit of 3%.
    d. For government insured /government guaranteed loans, the maximum amount is 4% of the purchase price.

80. Which federal legislation placed limitations on mortgage pre-payment penalties?

    a. Homeowners Protection Act
    b. Fair and Accurate Credit Transactions Act
    c. Dodd-Frank Act
    d. Equal Credit Opportunity Act

81. Per TILA's requirements for clear and conspicuous disclosures of terms in lender advertising, the APR must be

    a. expressed in the same font and type size as the interest rate.
    b. visible at the bottom of the advertisement in a footnote for clarity.
    c. conveyed as a range to account for potential rate changes over the life of the loan.
    d. highlighted in bold or italics to ensure it stands out more than the interest rate.

82. The Nationwide Multistate Licensing System (NMLS)

    a. covers non-depository financial service industries.
    b. serves as a registry for all state-licensed MLOs.
    c. serves all financial institutions and their activities.
    d. oversees the State Regulatory Registry.

83. Dodd-Frank introduced new mortgage lending standards and processes, including

    a. abolishing prepayment penalties on all mortgages.
    b. establishing ability-to-repay conditions such as minimum underwriting requirements for residential purchase mortgages.
    c. enforcing laws pertaining to discrimination in the mortgage lending industry.
    d. setting minimum borrower credit scores for the most common mortgage loan products.

84. When the CFPB uses its authority to establish and maintain a federal licensing system for a given state,

    a. the new system removes any regulatory authority the state previously had.
    b. the state has 2 years to revamp its licensing system or risk permanent CFPB authority.
    c. MLOs licensed in the state over the past 3 years must pass a federal exam to demonstrate a certain level of professional knowledge.
    d. the state can still enact stricter licensing requirements within its jurisdiction.

85. Which party initiates the process of securing a home loan for a borrower in exchange for compensation?

    a. Mortgage loan originator
    b. Underwriter
    c. Loan originator
    d. Loan processor

86. State agencies that oversee MLO licensing require loan originators to demonstrate financial stability. Which of these is the most common method for doing so?

    a. Individual minimum net worth
    b. Contribution to a recovery fund
    c. Individual surety bond
    d. Company surety bond

87. In an ARM, the periodic cap

    a. limits how much the rate can increase at the first adjustment after the fixed-rate period.
    b. sets the initial discount the lender provides to the borrower.
    c. sets the maximum increase for each adjustment period.
    d. limits the total rate increase over the life of the loan.

88. The *Mortgage Call Report*

    a. details a company's mortgage activity from the previous quarter.
    b. is used to update a mortgage company's profile in the NMLS-R.
    c. makes the licensing process smoother and less burdensome for state regulators.
    d. notes enforcement actions and licensing violations in each state.

89. Per the National Do-Not-Call Registry rules,

    a. consumers may file complaints against non-compliant businesses with the CFPB.
    b. potential penalties for telemarketers in violation can be as much as $25,000 per incident.
    c. telemarketers are required to check the list at least once every 31 days.
    d. surveys and political polls are required to abide by the list of Do-Not-Call participants.

90. A potential red flag for income and employment fraud is a

    a. discrepancy between a borrower's reported income and their employment history, industry norms, or standard wage levels for occupation.
    b. borrower purchasing property in an area with a high concentration of vacation homes or investment properties, but claiming it as a primary residence.
    c. seller listing a house for sale 30 days after buying it.
    d. failure to disclose all assets, liabilities, or financial obligations during the application process.

91.   _____ is included in the "offering or negotiating terms of a residential mortgage loan" category of duties that require an MLO license.

a. Providing educational resources to a consumer about the mortgage process
b. Attempting to reach a mutual understanding with a borrower regarding loan terms
c. Communicating with a borrower that a loan offer has been sent
d. Negotiating a loan offer via a third-party loan originator without communicating directly with the borrower

92.   Which of these is an example of a traditional mortgage product?

a. ARM
b. 30-year fixed rate loan
c. Balloon
d. Interest only loan

93.   An *adverse action* per the Fair Credit Reporting Act (FCRA) is

a. a negative action related to a credit application, such as an interest rate increase.
b. a consumer-requested credit freeze on their credit report.
c. an unfavorable decision against an applicant based in whole or part on credit information.
d. a red flag designed to combat identity theft in the lending industry.

94.   Created by the CFPB after the SAFE Act, Regulation H

a. standardized application forms and requirements for state-licensed loan originators across the board.
b. conferred important regulatory powers to state licensing agencies.
c. developed model state law including recommended wording.
d. set the criteria for licensing eligibility, education, training, continuing education, and testing.

95.   Which of the following is true regarding the license renewal requirements for MLOs?

a. Licenses must be renewed every two years.
b. Some states may require more than the federally-required hours of CE coursework.
c. Failure to renew by the deadline causes an MLO's license to terminate.
d. Extended absence renewals involve a Late CE course and new application for all formal MLOs.

96.   A minimum of _____ hours of continuing education courses is required during each MLO license renewal period.

a. 5
b. 8
c. 12
d. 16

97.   For which activity would a loan originator license requirement apply?

a. Counseling consumers about loan rates and terms
b. Performing official activities as a government employee
c. Originating a loan secured by the lender's own residence
d. Arranging credit for an immediate family member

98.   Loan originators who work for depository institutions

a. must be licensed and registered with the NMLS-R.
b. are only required to be licensed.
c. do not need to be licensed but do need to be registered.
d. do not need to be licensed or registered as long as proper supervision is given.

99. Which of the following is grounds for rejecting an application for an MLO license?

    a. A pattern of delinquent account(s) during past 2 years
    b. Pleading guilty to a felony for breach of trust
    c. Foreclosure in the past 5 years
    d. 3 or more traffic violations in 1 year

100. Karen's new mortgage loan is a 3/1 ARM. At closing, the index rate is 4%, and the margin is 2%, which results in a 6% fully indexed rate. Karen's lender offered a 3% teaser rate for the first three years of the loan. When the first adjustment date arrives three years later, what is the rate that goes into effect until the next adjustment date?

    a. 5%
    b. 6%
    c. 7%
    d. 9%

Quiz Answer Key

Section I Quiz: Federal Mortgage-Related Laws

1.1 (b) Consumer Financial Protection Bureau (CFPB)
The Consumer Financial Protection Bureau (CFPB) mission is to protect consumers from unfair, deceptive, or abusive practices in financial products and services like mortgages, credit cards, and student loans.

1.2 (c) Regulation X
Regulation X implements RESPA. Its primary focus is on mortgage settlement and servicing processes.

1.3 (a) Requires advance disclosure of financing costs to consumers
One of RESPA's primary aims is to help consumers by requiring certain disclosures about the nature and costs involved in the home buying process, particularly in the settlement phase.

1.4 (d) An individual other than a lender's employee who acts as a go-between for a borrower and a lender
RESPA defines "mortgage broker" as "a person (other than an employee of a lender) that renders origination services and serves as an intermediary between a borrower and a lender in a transaction..."

1.5 (b) Insured or guaranteed by the federal government
Per RESPA, a federally related mortgage loan is one secured by 1- to 4-unit residential property, including a loan insured or guaranteed by the federal government (FHA, VA, USDA), made by federally regulated lenders, (or whose deposits are federally insured, or who loan more than $1,000,000 per year), and intended to be sold to Fannie Mae or Freddie Mac.

1.6 (b) $203
Borrower Stan's estimated annual escrow amount for taxes and insurance is $2,436. RESPA mandates that monthly escrow payments cannot exceed 1/12 of the annual estimated payment. Thus, his monthly escrow payment, excluding the permitted cushion, would be $2,436 ÷ 12 = $203.

1.7 (d) A loan to purchase a residential duplex
RESPA applies to federally related mortgage loans that are secured by 1- to 4-unit residential property. Of these options, only the duplex meets the requirements.

1.8 (d) A lender pays its loan officer employees a bonus for closing a certain number of transactions per year.
RESPA prohibitions include receiving or giving any sort of compensation (e.g., kickback, fee split, unearned fee) for a referral in a mortgage transaction *without any actual service having been performed*. Lenders who pay employee bonuses based on performance are not in violation of RESPA provisions.

1.9 (b) A neighborhood developer requires all homebuyers to use her family's settlement company to close escrow.
RESPA prohibits sellers from requiring buyers to use a particular settlement company as a condition of sale.

1.10 (b) $1,007
RESPA permits escrow accounts to include a cushion of 1/6 (about two months) of the annual outlay for taxes, insurance, and other impounds. Maria's monthly outlay is $6,042 ÷ 12 = $503.50. So the permissible cushion is $503.50 x 2 = $1,007.

1.11 (c) High debt-to-income ratio
Lenders are permitted to deny a loan application when the applicant's debt-to-income ratio is too high.

1.12 (b) Prohibits creditors from discriminatory practices when granting credit
The main purpose of the Equal Credit Opportunity Act is to prohibit creditors from using discriminatory practices when granting or denying credit.

1.13 (c) His race
Although race, gender, and ethnicity questions appear on loan applications, applicants do not have to answer such questions.

1.14 (a) Information on Susan's right to receive a copy of the lender's appraisal
ECOA specifies that a notice of adverse action related to a loan application rejection must disclose the applicant's right to receive a copy of the lender's property appraisal when the property's unfavorable value is the basis for rejection.

1.15 (d) Creditors may consider applicants' immigration status, but only as it relates to the ability to repay the loan.
Considering immigration status strictly within the context of financial stability and loan repayment is permitted under ECOA because this context is not viewed as discriminatory.

1.16 (a) Overt discrimination
Overt discrimination is explicit or obvious, such as offering better loan terms to married couples than to single applicants.

1.17 (a) Requires disclosure of loans' terms and costs
One of TILA's primary purposes is to require lenders to disclose loans' terms and costs, such as interest rates, the amount financed, total payments, and payment schedule disclosures

1.18 (b) TILA applies to personal use loans with a minimum of four installment payments.
TILA applies to personal use loans with a minimum of four installment payments, such as residential mortgage loans, home equity loans, HELOCs, credit cards, personal loans, auto loans, etc. Business and commercial loans do not apply.

1.19 (d) the interest rate
The APR includes interest rates and any other costs such as points, broker fees, and closing costs. It does not include the appraisal, credit reporting, or inspection costs

1.20 (c) A fixed percentage of the loan amount
Permitted compensation types/terms for MLOs include: salary or set hourly wages, flat fee per transaction, bonuses and profit-sharing plans, retirement plans, amount based on percentage of applications that close successfully, and payment for tasks not specifically related to loan origination.

1.21 (d) Splitting fees with parties other than loan originators
Prohibited compensation types/terms include compensation based on interest rate or other loan terms, volume, loan or loan pool profitability, and splitting fees with parties other than loan originators.

1.22 (b) FHA, VA, and USDA loans.
TRID primarily focused on residential mortgage loans, such as fixed rate and adjustable rate mortgages, and FHA, VA, and USDA loans.

1.23 (c) Loan Estimate
The Loan Estimate was designed to help borrowers understand the key features, costs, and risks of a mortgage before they commit.

1.24 (a) the total interest that will be paid over the life of the loan
The Closing Disclosure breaks down final loan costs and terms, including the total interest that will be paid over the life of the loan.

1.25 (b) credit reports.
Lenders generally set fees for items like appraisals, credit reports, and flood determinations. Borrowers cannot shop for these services.

1.26 (d) No more than three days after lender receives borrower's loan application and no fewer than seven days prior to loan consummation
TRID requires that lender provide a Loan Estimate to borrowers no more than three days after a lender receives a borrower's loan application and no fewer than seven days prior to loan consummation.

1.27 (a) The borrower requests a larger loan amount.
Changes the borrower requests, such as a larger loan amount or a different loan product, constitute a "change of circumstances" per TRID, allowing the lender to issue a revised Loan Estimate within three business days after the lender learns of changed circumstances.

1.28 (d) Borrowers are permitted to cancel a home equity loan "no questions asked" within three days after closing.
Borrowers may cancel a refinance or home equity loan "no questions asked" within a period of three business days after closing. This right of rescission does not apply to home purchase loans.

1.29 (c) helps to ensure fair and equitable access to housing finance and to combat discriminatory lending practices
The primary purpose of the Home Mortgage Disclosure Act (MMDA) of 1975 is to help ensure fair and equitable access to housing finance and to combat discriminatory lending practices, such as redlining.

1.30 (b) An applicant's address history on the application shows frequent changes and is inconsistent with information on the credit report.
Application details that do not align with the credit report could indicate an attempt to obscure the borrower's true identity or financial situation.

1.31 (a) Consistent contributions to an investment portfolio
Financial institutions are required to file SARs with the Financial Crimes Enforcement Network when they detect certain types of suspicious activities. Regular contributions to savings accounts, retirement accounts, or investment portfolios that are in line with the customer's financial planning would generally be considered legal and typical activity.

1.32 (a) Gramm-Leach-Billey Act
The Gramm-Leach-Billey Act protects consumers' personal financial information; requires financial institutions to explain how they will share and protect such information; and requires financial institutions to provide customers with a written privacy notice when customer relationship is established and annually thereafter.

1.33 (c) actual repayments terms
A "triggering term" is specific language used in a mortgage loan advertisement that activates additional disclosure requirements. Using these terms necessitates including certain additional information in the advertisement to ensure that consumers are not misled.

1.34 (a) expanding the government's authority to collect bank and credit reporting records
One provision is that the act expands the government's authority to monitor phone and email communications, collect bank and credit reporting records, and track the activity of suspected terrorists through more lenient search warrant requirements.

1.35 (b) Electronic records must be accessible to all parties involved for the legally required retention period.
Electronic records must be properly stored and retrievable so they are readily accessible to all parties involved for the appropriate state's required retention period.

1.36 (a) To protect homebuyers from excessive private mortgage insurance (PMI) charges
The main purpose of the HPA is to protect homebuyers from excessive private mortgage insurance (PMI) charges, ensuring they do not pay PMI longer than necessary.

1.37 (d) Ability to repay requirements for borrowers
Dodd-Frank introduced new mortgage lending standards and processes to avoid risky lending practices that

contributed to the housing bubble and crash in 2008, such as ability-to-repay requirements, e.g., setting minimum underwriting requirements for residential mortgages.

1.38 (b) Consumer Financial Protection Bureau (CFPB)
The CFPB's overarching purpose is to protect consumers in the financial sector. For one, it regulates and supervises banks, credit unions, and other financial companies, including mortgage lenders, servicers, and brokers.

1.39 (c) Overseeing aspects of housing and mortgage lending, with a strong focus on fair practices and affordable housing
One of HUD's main purposes is overseeing aspects of housing and mortgage lending, with a strong focus on fair practices and affordable housing.

1.40 (d) Redlining
Redlining is arbitrarily denying mortgage loan applications in certain geographical areas without considering an applicant's qualifications.

1.41 (d) Redlining
The Home Mortgage Disclosure Act (HMDA) was enacted in part to combat discriminatory practices, such as redlining, the practice of arbitrarily denying mortgage loan applications in certain geographical areas without considering an applicant's qualifications.

1.42 (a) the private right of action
Dodd-Frank introduced new mortgage lending standards and processes to avoid risky lending practices that contributed to housing bubble and crash in 2008, such as giving borrowers private right of action, i.e., suing creditors when they realize they cannot afford their loan and they feel a creditor did not properly determine their ability to repay.

Section II Quiz: General Mortgage Knowledge

2.1 (b) borrowers and mortgage work directly together to create new mortgages
The primary mortgage market is where loans are originated. Borrowers and lenders work directly together to create new mortgages.

2.2 (c) Enables portfolio diversification; augments liquidity to primary market
The secondary mortgage market provides liquidity to primary market lenders so they can fund more mortgage loans, lessens interest-rate risk for lenders, enables portfolio diversification, and promotes industry standards for credit requirements, loan types, and loan documents.

2.3 (c) A government-sponsored enterprise (GSE)
A government-sponsored enterprise (GSE)is a financial service corporation created by Congress to enhance credit flow, particularly in the housing sector. Examples are Fannie Mae, Freddie Mac, and Ginnie Mae.

2.4 (d) It guarantees investors will receive timely principal and interest payments of MBS, even if original borrower defaults.
Among other functions and purposes, Fannie Mae guarantees investors will receive timely principal and interest payments of MBS, even if original borrower defaults.

2.5 (b) conforming loan
A conforming loan adheres to underwriting guidelines set by Fannie Mae and Freddie Mac.

2.6 (b) All conforming loans are conventional loans.
All conforming loans are conventional loans, but not all conventional loans conform to Fannie Mae and Freddie Mac guidelines.

2.7 (c) Jumbo loans
Non-conforming loans include jumbo loans, subprime mortgages, and Alt-A mortgages.

2.8 (a) qualified mortgage
Qualified mortgages meet certain CFPB standards, ensuring that lenders make loans that borrowers have ability to repay.

2.9 (d) limits on points and fees charged to borrowers
Qualified mortgage requirements include limits on points and fees charged to borrowers, which helps prevent excessive costs.

2.10 (c) conventional loan
A conventional loan is any loan the federal government does not insure or guarantee.

2.11 (d) ensure loans are stable and relatively low risk
Conforming loan standards ensure loans are stable and relatively low risk, making them more attractive for investors in secondary mortgage market.

2.12 (c) primary residences, second homes, and investment properties permitted
Key Fannie Mae/Freddie Mac key conforming loan standards permit property types such as primary residences, second homes, and investment properties. Different standards and requirements for each apply.

2.13 (c) VA loan
A VA loan can be a qualified mortgage if it meets the CFPB standards. The other loans listed here are exempt from qualified mortgage requirements.

2.14 (a) its purpose.
In mortgage lending, LLPAs vary based on several factors related to the borrower and the property, and the purpose of the loan is a significant component. Second homes, vacation homes, investment properties, and cash-out refinances are generally deemed higher risk, so they may trigger LLPAs.

2.15 (c) They offer low down payments.
FHA loans are designed to help lower-income and first-time homebuyers purchase homes. One feature is their low down payments, typically as low as 3.5% of purchase price

2.16 (a) A triplex, with one unit owner occupied
FHA loans can be used to purchase owner-occupied one- to four-unit residences, including single-family, multifamily, manufactured homes, etc.

2.17 (d) Novation
This arrangement is a novation.

2.18 (b) The FHA would not insure the mortgage, so Cliff cannot use an FHA loan to buy it.
FHA loans include anti-flipping provisions. For example, a property is ineligible for an FHA loan if the potential buyer contracts to buy the property within 90 days of the seller acquiring said property. So, if a potential buyer contracts to buy the home within 90 days of the previous sale, the FHA will not insure the mortgage.

2.19 (c) MIP
FHA loans require two types of mortgage insurance: upfront mortgage insurance premium (UFMIP) and annual mortgage insurance premium (MIP). MIP is an ongoing cost that is paid monthly. It is calculated by multiplying the base loan amount by a certain factor and then dividing by 12.

2.20 (d) It is often rolled into the loan amount.
The VA loan funding fee, which is typically 1.4% to 3.6% of the loan amount, is often rolled into loan amount instead of being paid up front.

2.21 (b) "The CRV is required to assess the home's value and ensure it meets VA-specified minimum property requirements for safety and condition."
The VA loan program requires a Certificate of Reasonable Value, which is based on an appraisal performed by a VA-approved appraiser to assess the home's value and ensure it meets VA-specific minimum property requirements (MPRs).

174

2.22 (b) offer assistance to borrowers to help avoid foreclosure
VA loans offer assistance to borrowers experiencing financial hardship to help avoid foreclosure.

2.23 (d) accessible to borrowers in certain eligible geographic areas
Both USDA guaranteed loans and USDA direct loans are only available in eligible areas, typically rural areas or towns of fewer than 35,000 people.

2.24 (a) conventional loans that do not adhere to Fannie Mae or Freddie Mac rules.
Non-conforming loans are conventional loans that do not adhere to Fannie Mae or Freddie Mac rules.

2.25 (b) a buyer looking for a loan that exceeds the FHFA's maximum limits.
Jumbo loans are useful for high-value properties, especially in markets where housing prices exceed national average. because loan limits exceed FHFA's maximum limits for conforming loans.

2.26 (a) negative amortization
The *Guidance on Non-Traditional Mortgage Product Risk* addresses risks associated with non-traditional mortgage products, including features like interest-only payments, negative amortization, balloon payment, and payment-option ARMs.

2.27 (b) alternative documentation for income
Non-QM loans may use forms of income verification other than traditional W-2 forms and tax returns, such as bank statements and asset depletion loans.

2.28 (c) Fixed-rate mortgage
Fixed-rate mortgages act as a form of insurance for borrowers against rising interest rates because the interest rate stays same over the life of the loan. Monthly principal and interest payments remain same from first payment to last, ensuring that housing costs remain unaffected by market changes.

2.29 (c) Purchase money second mortgage
A purchase money second mortgage is a secondary loan taken out at the same time as the primary mortgage to help finance a home purchase. It is often used to cover part of the purchase price that first mortgage does not cover.

2.30 (b) The loan typically converts to a standard amortizing loan.
With an interest-only loan, the loan typically converts to a standard amortizing loan once the interest only period ends.

2.31 (d) It is a short-term loan with a large final payment
Balloon mortgages are short-term loans, often 5 to 7 years, with large final payments.

2.32 (b) The home's equity decreases over the life of the mortgage.
Equity in the home decreases over the life of reverse mortgage, which can impact the amount heirs will inherit.

2.33 (c) Construction loan
Once a lender approves a construction loan, the lender then typically disburses funds to the builder in stages (aka "draws") as construction reaches specific milestones.

2.34 (b) 31%
For FHA loans, the percentage of a borrower's monthly gross income going toward housing costs (front-end ratio) cannot exceed 31%.

2.35 (b) $1,240
For FHA loans, the percentage of a borrower's monthly gross income going toward housing costs (front-end ratio) cannot exceed 31%. Calculate his maximum monthly mortgage payment by multiplying his gross monthly income by 31%: $4,000 x 0.31 = $1,240.

Section III Quiz: Mortgage Loan Origination Activities

3.1 (c) On initial application and at closing
The URLA is usually completed twice: on initial application and at closing.

3.2 (b) borrower's desired loan amount.
Minimum details required for a lender to receive a borrower's loan application includes the borrower's desired loan amount.

3.3 (a) analyzing information for inconsistencies.
MLOs' tasks in making sure that borrowers' applications are completed accurately and thoroughly include analyzing the provided information for inconsistencies.

3.4 (d) A borrower putting 20% down on a conventional loan may use financial gifts to cover all costs.
Borrowers putting 20% down on conventional loans are permitted to use financial gifts to cover all costs.

3.5 (b) confirms a borrower's current and past employment history, income, and job stability
The VOE form confirms a borrower's current and past employment history, income, and job stability.

3.6 (a) Inquiring about the loan's purpose
MLOs must understand a borrower's goals to match that borrower with a suitable loan product. MLOs are permitted to inquire about the proposed loan's purpose, e.g., buying a property, refinancing an existing mortgage, or tapping into a home's equity to meet other financial needs.

3.7 (d) Uniform Residential Loan Application
The Uniform Residential Loan Application (URLA) is also known as Form 1003, or the 1003, Fannie Mae's form number for the application.

3.8 (b) 2
Lenders typically verify 2 years of a borrower's income for qualification purposes.

3.9 (c) Zero tolerance
The term "zero tolerance" applies to fees that must remain the same from the initial Loan Estimate (LE) to the final Closing Disclosure (CD), including origination charges and transfer taxes.

3.10 (a) Mortgage Loan Servicing Disclosure
The Mortgage Loan Servicing Disclosure is a RESPA requirement that outlines whether the lender intends to service a loan or transfer it to another entity for servicing.

3.11 (c) The earliest a lender can close a mortgage loan is on the seventh business day after providing initial disclosures to the borrower.
The "7" in the "3-7-3 Rule" indicates the earliest a lender can close a mortgage loan is on the seventh business day after providing initial disclosures to the borrower.

3.12 (b) Disclosures are deemed to be received on the third business day after they're placed in the mail.
Per the mailbox rule, disclosures such as LE and CD are deemed to be received on the third business day after they're placed in the mail.

3.13 (d) Closing Disclosure
The Closing Disclosure provides a detailed breakdown of final loan terms and closing costs.

3.14 (d) Adjustable-Rate Mortgage Disclosure
The Adjustable-Rate Mortgage Disclosure must be provided within three business days of loan application for an ARM.

3.15 (b) Lenders often consider the seasoning of funds, meaning how long the funds have been in the borrower's account.
When considering a borrower's assets, lenders often consider seasoning of funds, meaning that funds have been in the borrower's account(s) for a certain time period.

3.16 (c) 3 years
For income verification purposes, income with an expiration date, such as alimony, must be likely to continue for 3 years after closing.

3.17 (a) over the past two years.
A borrower's income is usually required to be verifiable over the past 2 years.

3.18 (b) It is only acceptable if it is part of a regular annual work cycle.
Unemployment compensation is only acceptable as income on a loan application if it is part of a regular annual work cycle.

3.19 (a) Non-taxable income
Non-taxable income, such as permanent disability payments, Social Security benefits, and child support, can be subject to "grossing up," meaning the lender calculates what the tax would be and adds that amount to the gross amount received.

3.20 (c) fees paid to third-party service providers not affiliated with the lender
TRID's 10% cumulative tolerance applies to fees paid to third-party service providers not affiliated with the lender.

3.21 (d) Paying bills on time accounts for 35% of a credit score.
Paying bills on time accounts for 35% of a credit score, which means it carries the most weight of all the factors.

3.22 (a) Single-family home purchase application
The CFPB Home Loan Toolkit is a required disclosure for purchase transactions only.

3.23 (b) Outlines estimated closing costs, so borrowers can compare offers from different lenders
Outlining estimated closing costs so borrowers can compare offers from different lenders is one purpose of the initial Loan Estimate.

3.24 (c) PITI on Primary Residence ÷ Gross Monthly Income
Housing Ratio = PITI on Primary Residence ÷ Gross Monthly Income

3.25 (a) Ratio between gross income and all monthly debt obligations
Total DTI, aka back-end ratio, is the ratio between gross income and all monthly debt obligations.

3.26 (b) LTV ratios exceeding 80% generally mean conventional loan borrowers must purchase PMI
Conventional loan borrowers with LTV ratios exceeding 80% typically must purchase PMI.

3.27 (d) Balloon payments
Balloon payments are prohibited under the CFPB's ability to repay rules.

3.28 (c) Financial advantages or benefits that a borrower is expected to gain from refinancing an existing mortgage loan
"Tangible net benefit" means that a borrower is expected to gain financial advantages when refinancing an existing mortgage loan, such as reducing monthly mortgage payments, lowering the interest rate, or achieving other cost savings.

3.29 (a) Sales comparison
In the sales comparison appraisal approach, the appraiser compares the subject property to recently sold properties similar to subject property in terms of location, size, condition, and features.

3.30 (d) issues related to property's layout or design
Functional obsolescence involves issues related to the property's layout or design that reduce its value.

3.31 (c) It ensures that appraisals are conducted by unbiased and qualified professionals.
One benefit of the independent appraisal requirement is that it ensures that appraisals are conducted by unbiased and qualified professionals.

3.32 (b) Lender
The lender is the appraiser's client.

3.33 (b) calculate the cost to rebuild or replace the subject property, account for depreciation, and add in the value of the land.
With the cost approach, appraisers calculate the cost to rebuild or replace the subject property, account for depreciation, and add in the value of the land.

3.34 (c) properties that are not frequently bought or sold, such as unique or specialized properties.
Appraisers generally use the cost approach for appraising properties that are not frequently bought or sold, such as unique or specialized properties.

3.35 (b) Revolving credit accounts
The debt-to-income ratio is the percentage of all monthly debt obligations, including PITI, revolving debts, installment debts, alimony and / or child support, etc.

3.36 (a) Estimating the potential income and subtracting the operating expenses
An appraiser using the income approach determines the property's NOI by estimating the property's potential income and subtracting its operating expenses.

3.37 (d) the expected rate of return an investor would require to invest the in property.
The capitalization rate for an income-producing property is the expected rate of return an investor would require to invest in the property.

3.38 (b) Identifying any existing liens, encumbrances, or defects related to ownership rights
A title report is a detailed history of a property's ownership and any associated legal issues, such as outstanding liens, existing encumbrances or defects related to ownership rights.

3.39 (a) Title report
A title report is a detailed history of a property's ownership and any associated legal issues, such as outstanding liens, existing encumbrances or defects related to ownership rights.

3.40 (b) Lender
The lender is the insured party in the primary title insurance policy. Buyers may also purchase an owner's policy for themselves.

3.41 (b) Hazard insurance
Hazard insurance is typically a component of homeowners insurance.

3.42 (d) If the actual structure is not located in SFHA, no flood insurance is required.
FEMA flood zones range high-risk zones (SFHAs) to moderate-to-low-risk zones. When the actual structure is not located in an SFHA, no flood insurance is required.

3.43(c) Settlement agent
Settlement agents facilitate and oversee the final steps of the home buying or selling process, including document preparation, review, and signatures.

3.44 (a) Cover the cost of evaluating a borrower's creditworthiness
Among other purposes, loan origination fees cover the cost of evaluating a borrower's creditworthiness

3.45 (b) discount point
A discount point is an fee that is paid upfront to lower the interest rate on a mortgage.

3.46 (c) Title insurance
Title insurance is considered a closing cost.

3.47 (d) Promissory note
A promissory note is a legally binding contract between a borrower and lender outlining the borrower's promise to repay the loan amount under specific terms and conditions.

3.48 (b) Mortgage
A mortgage establishes a lien on the borrower's property.

3.49 (c) Deed of trust
A deed of trust involves three parties: borrower, lender, and trustee.

3.50 (a) The borrower is the mortgagor, and the lender is the mortgagee.
When a mortgage is used as a security instrument, the borrower is the mortgagor, and the lender is the mortgagee. Remember: **both lender and mortgagee have two 'E's**. If there are no E's then the party is the mortgagor, or buyer.

3.51 (a) Deed of trust
A deed of trust often includes a "power of sale" provision, meaning the trustee may initiate a non-judicial foreclosure sale if the borrower defaults.

3.52 (c) Allows the borrower to eliminate the mortgage lien by meeting specific conditions
A defeasance clause in a mortgage allows the borrower to eliminate the mortgage lien by meeting specific conditions, usually repaying the loan in full.

3.53 (b) $1,000
The formula for this calculation is: Monthly Interest Payment = (Annual Interest Rate in Decimal Form ÷ Number of Compounding Periods) x Principal Balance. So, (0.06 ÷ 12) x $200,000 = $1,000.

3.54 (a) $20.55
(0.05 ÷ 365) x 150,000 = $20.55

3.55 (c) $858.90
This is a prepaid interest calculation. The formula is: Prepaid Interest Owed at Closing = (Interest Rate in Decimal Form ÷ 365) x Principal x Number of Days. (0.06 ÷ 365) x 475,000 x 11 = $858.90.

3.56 (a) Property taxes and homeowners insurance
Lenders most often collect escrow to ensure that property taxes and homeowners insurance premiums are paid.

3.57 (c) 1/6
Per RESPA, lenders are permitted to hold no more than 1/6 of estimated total annual disbursements from an escrow account as a cushion.

3.58 (b) $160.42
First, find the annual PMI by multiplying the principal loan amount by the annual premium rate percentage (convert that to a decimal for calculations): $350,000 x 0.0055 = $1,925. Then divide the annual premium by 12 to get the monthly premium: $1,925 ÷ 12 = $160.42

3.59 (a) $5,687.50
The UFMIP for an FHA loan is currently 1.75% of the loan amount. So, $325,000 x 0.0175 = $5,687.50.

3.60 (b) $243.75
First find the annual MIP, then divide by 12. $450,000 x 0.0065 = $2,925 annual MIP. To find monthly MIP: $2,925 ÷ 12 = $243.75.

3.61 (c) 22.4%
The formula is: Down Payment ÷ Purchase Price = Down Payment Percentage. So, $125,000 ÷ $559,000 = 0.2236 = 22.4%.

3.62 (d) $84,800
First, calculate 20% of the purchase price: $499,000 x 0.20 = $99,800. Now, subtract the $15,000 they already paid as earnest money: $99,800 − $15,000 = $84,800. That is the balance on their down payment they'll owe at closing.

3.63 (a) 79%
The formula to calculate LTV is: Principal Loan Amount ÷ Purchase Price OR Appraised Value = LTV. Make sure to **use the lower of the purchase price or appraised value**. So, $415,000 ÷ $525,000 = 0.79 = 79%.

3.64 (b) 81.2%
The formula for HCLTV (home equity combined loan-to-value ratio) is: (Total of All Mortgage Balances + HELOC Available Credit) ÷ Appraised Value OR Purchase Price = HCLTV. So, ($475,000 + $85,000) ÷ $690,000 = 0.8115 = 81.2%. Remember to use the lower of the purchase price or appraised value.

3.65 (c) Compare borrowers' gross monthly income to their debt load
The main purpose of the two DTI ratios is to compare borrowers' gross monthly income to their debt load.

3.66 (c) 24.9%
The front-end ratio is also called the housing ratio. The formula is: Housing DTI = All Proposed Housing Expenses ÷ Gross Income. So, ($2,900 + $250 + $20 + $25) ÷ $12,840 = 0.2488 = 24.8%.

3.67 (c) A reduction in the interest rate and monthly payments on a mortgage loan
A buydown allows a borrower to pay a lower interest rate and mortgage payments by paying discount points up front.

3.68 (a) Paying upfront discount points
Borrowers obtain a buydown by paying upfront discount points.

3.69 (d) $1,537.14
First, calculate the daily tax amount: $5,500 ÷ 365 = $15.07. The count up how many days Clive will own the property: 10 days in September, 31 for October, 30 for November, and 31 for December. That is 102 days. $15.07 x 102 = $1,537.14.

3.70 (b) teaser rate
The lender offered Adele a teaser rate as a discount for the first three years of her loan.

3.71 (a) 7%
The formula for an ARM's fully indexed rate is: Fully Indexed Rate = Margin + Index Rate. The index rate is 5%, up 2 percentage points since closing occurred 3 years ago. The margin doesn't change, so it is still 2%. So, 2% + 5% = 7%.

Section IV Quiz: Ethics

4.1 (a) Providing misleading information about loan terms
Providing misleading information about loan terms violates UDAAP provisions.

4.2 (d) Misrepresenting the interest rate of a loan to a borrower
Misrepresenting the interest rate of a loan to a borrower is an unfair practice under UDAAP.

4.3 (d) Liability fraud
When loan applicants conceal or understate existing debts or financial obligations to appear stronger

financially, they are committing liability fraud.

4.4 (b) misrepresenting a property as primary residence when it is actually vacant.
An example of occupancy fraud is misrepresenting property as primary residence when it is actually vacant or intended for speculative purposes.

4.5 (c) Redlining
Redlining is when a financial entity refuses to fund a loan based on neighborhood characteristics.

4.6 (a) Providing false information to obtain someone's personal or confidential information from financial institutions
Pretexting can be defined as providing false information to obtain someone's personal or confidential information from financial institutions.

4.7 (a) Borrower's unwillingness or inability to provide supporting documentation for stated income
A borrower who is unwilling to or unable to provide supporting documentation for their stated income is a potential red flag for income fraud.

4.8 (a) Gramm-Leach-Billey Act
The Gramm-Leach-Billey Act includes provisions for consumer privacy and data protection related to their personal financial information.

4.9 (c) RESPA
RESPA prohibits lenders and borrowers for giving or receiving any thing of value in exchange for referrals of settlement service business, including exclusive discounts.

4.10 (a) ECOA
ECOA is primarily concerned with fairness in lending practices.

4.11 (a) applies for the loan on someone else's behalf, concealing the true buyer's identity.
A straw buyer knowingly or unknowingly serves as a front for a buyer / borrower but has no association with the property, i.e., will not actually own, possess, or control the property. That can include applying for the loan on someone else's behalf, concealing the true buyer's identity.

4.12 (c) Karl uses potential rental income to help qualify for a loan to buy a property but plans to use it as his primary residence.
In reverse occupancy fraud, a borrower uses potential rental income to help qualify for loan, making it look as if the property will be an investment when it will actually by the borrower's primary home. The stated potential rental income is used to help the borrower qualify for the loan.

4.13 (d) A lender's investors allow for a 650 credit score for loan qualification, but the lender requires a minimum credit score of 750.
While a lender's minimum credit score policy may not explicitly target minority applicants, the cumulative effect of historical discrimination, credit score disparities, and limited access to credit can result in a disproportionate impact on minority communities.

4.14 (b) Suspicious Activity Report (SAR)
Financial institutions, including banks and mortgage lenders, report potentially suspicious or unusual activities that may indicate money laundering, fraud, or other illicit financial transactions using the Suspicious Activity Report (SAR).

4.15 (b) fraud.
This is a definition of fraud.

4.16 (a) negligence.
Eric's actions are negligent. MLOs have a duty of care to accurately assess borrowers' financial qualifications and ensure that they can afford the loans they are being approved for.

4.17 (d) Borrower
Borrowers are typically the culprits in fraud for property.

4.18 (b) TILA
The Truth in Lending Act (TILA) imposes rules and requirements for lender advertising to ensure transparency and accuracy.

4.19 (d) $10,000 down
The amount or percentage of down payment is considered a trigger term in ads, requiring additional disclosures to ensure consumer protection.

4.20 (c) Fraud for property
This describes fraud for property.

4.21 (b) Predatory lending consists of unethical or abusive lending practices that exploit vulnerable borrowers, often resulting in financial harm or disadvantage.
Predatory lending involves several different types of unethical or abusive lending practices, all of which exploit vulnerable borrowers and result in financial harm or disadvantage.

4.22 (a) Asset-based lending
Asset-based lending is one example of predatory lending.

4.23 (c) maintain a level of financial integrity and responsibility.
MLOs are expected to maintain a level of personal financial integrity and responsibility.

4.24 (d) Mortgage companies reporting detected compliance violations to the applicable regulatory entity
Mortgage companies are expected to report all detected compliance violations to the applicable regulatory entity, aka self-reporting.

4.25 (a) Keep the client's private information confidential.
MLOs in a fiduciary relationship with a client must keep the client's private information confidential. However, they must also protect the company and investor(s) from misrepresentation. Sharing facts material to the transaction, for example, is crucial.

4.26 (c) A written cybersecurity program to protect consumer information
The GLBA Safeguards Rule requires financial institutions to develop a written cybersecurity program outlining how they will protect the security, confidentiality, and integrity of consumer information.

4.27 (d) Prevent deceptive advertising practices in mortgage lending
The CFPB's Reg N's main purpose is to prevent deceptive advertising practices in mortgage lending.

4.28 (a) stating or implying any affiliation with any government entity.
The MAP Rule expressly prohibits stating or implying any affiliation with any government program, benefit, or entity.

4.29 (b) Ethical consumer education considerations often take the form of personalized, professional service.
Ethical consumer education considerations often take form of personalized, professional service in helping borrowers understand their financial situation and options for mortgage financing.

4.30 (b) General business ethics
General business ethics focus on moral principles and standards that guide the conduct and decision-making of individuals and organizations in the business world.

4.31 (a) Companies' codes of ethics serve as formal guidelines and principles outlining expected standards of behavior and conduct for everyone in the organization.
Companies' codes of ethics serve as formal guidelines and principles outlining expected standards of behavior and conduct for everyone in the organization.

4.32 (c) Regular review and updates ensure that the code remains at the forefront of ethical conduct and aligned with the latest legal requirements.

Regular review and updates ensure that the code remains at forefront of ethical conduct and aligned with the latest legal requirements.

4.33 (a) Requires recordkeeping and reporting to help detect and prevent money laundering activities

The Bank Secrecy Act (aka Anti-Money Laundering [AML] law) combats money laundering and other financial crimes by imposing recordkeeping and reporting requirements on financial institutions to help detect and prevent money laundering activities, terrorist financing, illicit financial transactions, etc.

4.34 (d) Both legal obligations and ethical standards are crucial to a professional, successful loan origination practice.

Both legal obligations and ethical standards are crucial to a professional, successful loan origination practice.

4.35 (c) requiring clear and conspicuous disclosures of important terms and conditions.

Truth in Lending Act (TILA) imposes rules and requirements for lender advertising to ensure transparency and accuracy, such as including clear and conspicuous disclosures of important terms and conditions, e.g., mortgage type, interest rate details, repayment terms, etc.

Section V Quiz: Uniform State Content

5.1 (b) presenting specific interest rates, loan amounts, or repayment terms to a potential borrower

Presenting specific interest rates, loan amounts, or repayment terms to a potential borrower is considered offering or negotiating loan terms, and that requires a license.

5.2 (a) Shelly works under a licensed MLO's supervision.

Shelly works under a licensed MLO's supervision.

5.3 (c) Model state law

The CSBS and AARMR jointly developed model state law, including recommended wording.

5.4 (b) 8

MLOs must completed a minimum of 8 hours of CE during each renewal period.

5.5 (a) It covers non-depository financial services industries.

It covers non-depository financial services industries, e.g., money services businesses, mortgage lenders, securities firms, et(c)

5.6 (b) 75%

The minimum passing score is 75%.

5.7 (c) Actual nexus

The SAFE Act requires actual nexus between unlicensed processors / underwriters and licensed MLOs acting as supervisors.

5.8 (b) CFPB

The CFPB has authority to establish and maintain a state's licensing system when the CFPB determines the state's existing licensing system fails to meet the SAFE Act's minimum requirements.

5.9 (a) maintain a central database with comprehensive licensing and supervision information.

One purpose of the NMLS-R is to maintain central database with comprehensive licensing and supervision information.

5.10 (c) They do not need to be licensed but do need to be registered.

Loan originators who work for depository institutions, subsidiaries of depository institution, or Farm Credit Administration-regulated institution generally do not need licensure but do need to be registered.

5.11 (a) Two licenses are required: one for himself and one for the business.
Sole proprietor companies engaged in loan origination are required to hold two licenses: one for the business owner as an individual and one for the business itself.

5.12 (b) She has to wait 30 days before she can retake the test.
A 30-day waiting period between tests applies when an applicant initially fails and wants to retest.

5.13 (c) maintain a surety bond based on a dollar amount of originated loans
Maintaining a surety bond based on a dollar amount of originated loans is the most common approach for borderline license applicants. This is generally fulfilled at the company level.

5.14 (a) A tax lien
A tax or other government lien filed against a license applicant is grounds to deny an MLO license.

5.15 (b) take a Late CE course and apply for a new license.
Former MLOs who have not held an MLO license for fewer than 3 years and want to return to the field must take a Late CE course, which will service as their last year of licensure's CE requirement, and then apply for a new license.

5.16 (d) regularly reporting enforcement actions and licensing violations to NMLS-R.
To avoid regulatory intervention, state agencies overseeing MLO licensure are required to meet certain standards, such as regularly reporting enforcement actions and licensing violations to NMLS-R.

5.17 (b) unique identifier
An MLO's unique must appear on their advertisements and all other consumer-facing materials.

5.18 (c) A state-licensed MLO who wants to be licensed in another state as well
The temporary authority to operate (TA) provision pertains to federally-registered MLOs seeking state licensure to work in a state-licensed mortgage company and state-licensed MLOs seeking licensure in another state.

5.19 (b) Lamar's previous license revocation is grounds for his license application to be denied in his current state.
A license revocation in one state is grounds for denying a license in another state.

5.20 (c) loan originator
A loan originator is an individual or entity that initiates the process of securing a loan for a borrower in exchange for some sort of compensation. In general, loan originators work with a wide range of loan types, including mortgages, personal loans, car loans, business loans, et(c)

5.21 (a) Taking disciplinary action when a violation occurred
State agencies may take disciplinary action when an investigator determines that a licensee or licensed company is in violation of the SAFE Act.

5.22 (b) Actual nexus
Actual nexus is a connection in which a supervisor provides training, guidance, compliance review, and work assignment for processor / underwriter.

5.23 (c) 20
The MLO pre-license course comprises 20 hours of coursework.

5.24 (d) To distinguish the MLO and track their conduct
The unique identifier that NMLS-R assigns to loan originators is used to distinguish each one from the others to track their conduct, among other things.

5.25 (a) CSBS
The CSBS is a nationwide organization representing state regulators overseeing all types of banks, including those involved in mortgage lending.

5.26 (d) Retake pre-license education coursework and then retake and pass the NMLS SAFE exam
A former MLO who has not held a license for 6 years and wants to return to the profession must retake pre-license education coursework and then retake and pass the NMLS SAFE exam.

5.27 (c) Negotiating loan terms for an immediate family member
Individuals are exempt from licensing requirements when offering or negotiating loan terms / arranging credit for an immediate family member.

5.28 (b) No universal federal requirements apply.
While state licensure may be required for business loan origination activities, no universal federal requirements apply.

5.29 (c) Engaging in an activity that represents a conflict of interest in a loan transaction
Engaging in an activity that represents a conflict of interest in a loan transaction is prohibited.

5.30 (a) Grants eligible MLOs authority to originate loans before obtaining full state licensure
The TA provision grants eligible MLOs authority to originate loans before obtaining full state licensure.

5.31 (d) Gathering general borrower information to set up an appointment with an MLO
Gathering general borrower information to set up an appointment with an MLO is considered an administrative / clerical task..

5.32 (b) Providing a revised loan offer on a pending application in response to the borrower's request for a different rate
Providing a revised loan offer on a pending application in response to the borrower's request for a different rate or different fees is considered an activity that requires a license.

5.33 (a) They are almost always licensed due to their supervisory role.
Underwriting / loan processing managers are almost always licensed due to their supervisory role. However, they are not required to register with the NMLS-R because they are not loan originators.

5.34 (b) MLO license violations
States are required to report to the NMLS-R all MLO license violations and enforcement actions taken.

5.35 (c) Detail a company's mortgage activity from the previous quarter
The *Mortgage Call Report* details state-licensed mortgage companies' mortgage activity from the previous quarter, including data on loan application activity, origination, and servicing.

Comprehensive Practice Exam I Answer Key

1. (c) Hometown provides the Affiliated Business Arrangement Disclosure within three business days of the loan application.
Lenders must provide the Affiliated Business Arrangement Disclosure within 3 business days of the borrower's loan application submission when the lender requires borrowers to use a specific business affiliate.

2. (b) He calls a borrower to talk through a Loan Estimate that he emailed the day before.
Discussing the details of a Loan Estimate with a borrower requires an MLO license.

3. (b) Borrower and lender
The borrower and lender sign these documents.

4. (b) Per ECOA, equal access to credit does not equate to identical loan terms.
ECOA prohibits lenders and MLOs from discriminating against borrowers based on factors such as race, color, religion, national origin, sex, marital status, age, or receipt of public assistance. Equal access to credit does not equate to identical loan terms; individual circumstances apply.

5. (b) A numerical / character series that NMLS-R assigns to each entity and individual who has an account on the NMLS-R platform
A unique identifier is a numerical / character series that NMLS-R assigns to each entity and individual who has an account on the NMLS-R platform.

6. (b) Fine of much as $25,000 per offense
MLOs in violation may be fined as much as $25,000 per offense.

7. (b) Negative amortization
Negative amortization occurs when a borrower's monthly payments are not large enough to cover interest due on a loan, and the principal balances increases over time.

8. (c) Provides an itemized accounting of all escrow items to be paid from the account in the first year
The initial escrow statement provides an itemized accounting of all escrow items to be paid from the account in the first year.

9. (a) Lenders may only require an escrow account per government loan program requirements for a given loan.
Per RESPA, lenders may only require an escrow account according to government loan program requirements for a given loan.

10. (c) $800
The maximum permissible cushion for an escrow account is 1/6 (or about two months) of the total annual escrow amount. $4,800 ÷ 12 = $400. $400 x 2 months = $800

11. (c) financial information
A loan application submits a borrower's financial data, personal details, employment and income specifics, property information, and the like to a lender so that the lender can make an informed credit decision involving a federally related mortgage loan.

12. (d) A more lenient application process
A more lenient application process is one aspect of non-qualified mortgages.

13. (c) When the surplus is $50 or more, the surplus must be returned to the borrower within 30 days after it is discovered.
When an escrow surplus of $50 or more exists, the surplus must be returned to the borrower within 30 days after it is discovered.

14. (d) Reverse mortgages
Reverse mortgages are exempt from QM requirements.

15. (a) duplex, and she will live in one unit.
FHA loans may only be used to buy owner-occupied one- to four-unit residences.

16. (b) insured or guaranteed by the federal government.
Federally related mortgage loans include loans insured or guaranteed by the federal government, such as FHA, VA, and USDA loans.

17. (c) They typically involve two phases: a draw period and a repayment period.
HELOCs typically involve two phases: a draw period and a repayment period.

18. (b) 15 or fewer days before transfer occurs
Lenders must notify borrowers of the intent to transfer loan servicing rights to another entity within 15 or fewer days before the transfer occurs.

19. (c) Conventional fixed-rate loan
Of these for loan products, only the conventional fixed-rate loan is a conforming loan. The others are non-conforming.

20. (a) Desired loan amount
The borrower's desired loan amount is one item of basic required information on a loan application.

21. (c) Conventional loans that do not adhere to Fannie Mae or Freddie Mac rules
A non-conforming loan is a conventional loan that does not adhere to Fannie Mae or Freddie Mac rules.

22. (a) jumbo loan
A jumbo loan is useful for high-value properties, especially in markets where housing prices exceed national average.

23. (c) purchase money second mortgage
A purchase money second mortgage is a secondary loan taken out at the same time as a primary mortgage to help finance a home purchase. It is often used to cover part of the purchase that the first mortgage does not cover.

24. (d) MIP
MIP continues over the life of the loan.

25. (b) Assists borrowers in understanding mortgage loan process
The CFPB Home Loan Toolkit assists borrowers in understanding mortgage loan process.

26. (b) Borrowers and lenders work directly together to create new mortgages.
The primary mortgage market is where loans are originated, meaning borrowers and lenders work directly together to create new mortgages.

27. (a) Gramm-Leach-Billey Act
The Gramm-Leach-Billey Act addresses consumer privacy and data protection regarding their personal financial information.

28. (a) it is averaged with employment income on 2 required years of tax returns.
When a borrower uses unemployment compensation for income purposes on a loan application it is averaged with employment income on 2 required years of tax returns.

29. (b) A license revoked in another state
A license revocation in another state may cause an application denial.

30. (d) Loan-Level Price Adjustments (LLPAs)
Loan-Level Price Adjustments (LLPAs) help Fannie Mae and Freddie Mac manage the risks of buying and guaranteeing mortgages by aiming to offset potential losses from defaults.

31. (a) Uniform Residential Loan Application
The Uniform Residential Loan Application (URLA) is the industry standard form. It is also called the 1003, which is Fannie Mae's for number for the application.

32. (b) File a Suspicious Activity Report (SAR) with the appropriate compliance workers
When financial institutions discover potentially suspect or unusual activities that may indicate money laundering, fraud, or other illicit financial transactions, they file a Suspicious Activity Report (SAR) with the appropriate compliance workers.

33. (b) teaser rate
A teaser rate is an initial discount a lender provides to ARM borrowers that is lower than fully indexed rates and lasts for a specific duration.

34. (b) $976.03
The formula for prepaid interest due at closing is: (Interest Rate in Decimal Form ÷ 365) x Principal x Number of Days. (0.05 ÷ 365) x 475,000 x 15 = 0.00013699 x 475,000 x 15 days = $821.92. Do not count the day of closing.

35. (b) the MLO must be licensed and so must the business.
For MLOs working as sole proprietors, both the MLO and the business must be licensed.

36. (b) hinders a consumer's ability to comprehend a transaction, product or service.
An unfair act or practice is one that hinders a consumer's ability to comprehend a transaction, product or service.

37. (a) Subprime loans
Subprime loans are designed for borrowers with poor credit scores or other financial challenges making them a higher risk for lenders.

38. (c) A home equity line of credit
RESPA applies to federally related mortgage loans: secured by 1- to 4-unit residential property, including home purchases, home improvement loans, refinances, home equity loans and HELOCs, reverse mortgages, and approved loan assumptions.

39. (b) asset-based lending.
With asset-based lending, a lender offers a loan based on equity in a borrower's home or other assets, rather than the borrower's ability to repay the debt, putting the borrower's property at foreclosure risk. it is a type of predatory lending.

40. (d) Inquiring about the applicant's purchase timing
Inquiring about the applicant's purchase timing is one approach an MLO can take to help match borrowers with suitable loan products for their particular situations and goals

41. (c) 80%
LTV ratios exceeding 80% generally mean a borrower must purchase PMI.

42. (c) Offering similar loan terms to applicants in similar financial situations
Offering similar loan terms to applicants in similar financial situations is one aspect of ECOA.

43. (d) All Recurring Monthly Debt ÷ Gross Monthly Income
The formula for DTI is: All Recurring Monthly Debt ÷ Gross Monthly Income.

44. (b) Helen's gift may cover all costs regardless of Darren's down payment amount.
For borrowers with a credit score of 620 or greater and who are using an FHA / VA loan, the gift may cover all costs regardless of the down payment amount.

45. (a) ADA
The ADA requires that reasonable accommodations be made to serve borrowers living with a disability.

46. (a) She is protected from any legal liability.
MLOs are protected from legal liability for filing SARs in good faith, even if the reported activity does not result in criminal charges or prosecution.

47. (c) any outstanding judgments against the borrower.
The declarations section of Form 1003 includes details about any outstanding judgments against the borrower.

48. (c) the number of payments.
The number of payments is a trigger term that requires additional disclosures.

49. (c) Giving or receiving something of value in exchange for referrals of settlement service business
Giving or receiving something of value in exchange for referrals of settlement service business is a RESPA violation.

50. (c) Fees paid to third-party service providers not affiliated with the lender
Fees paid to third-party service providers not affiliated with the lender are subject to the 10% cumulative tolerance threshold.

51. (c) Fixed-rate
A fixed-rate mortgage's interest rate stays the same over the life of the loan, ensuring housing costs remain unaffected by market changes. It is a suitable choice for borrowers who plan to stay in their homes for a long time.

52. (d) Closing Disclosure
The Closing Disclosure provides a detailed breakdown of final loan terms and closing costs.

53. (c) Verifying authenticity of assets and liabilities directly with financial institutions, creditors, and other relevant sources
Verifying authenticity of assets and liabilities directly with financial institutions, creditors, and other relevant sources helps MLOs prevent fraud.

54. (c) Government-backed loans may allow for higher LTV ratios compared to conventional loans.
Government-backed loans may allow for higher LTV ratios compared to conventional loans.

55. (b) Deceiving others for personal gain or to cause harm
Fraud is the act of deceiving others for personal gain or to cause harm.

56. (b) VA loans
VA loans require that the property meet minimum property requirements (MPR) for safety, security, and soundness.

57. (a) Verifying the identity of individuals who want to open an account
Verifying the identity of individuals who want to open an account is one requirement of the Bank Secrecy Act.

58. (a) A financial service corporation that Congress created to enhance credit flow, particularly in the housing sector
A government-sponsored enterprise (GSE) is a financial service corporation Congress created to enhance credit flow, particularly in the housing sector. GSEs are privately held but supported by the federal government.

59. (a) Revised Loan Estimate
A Revised Loan Estimate may be necessary if the loan amount or interest rate changes during the transaction.

60. (c) creating a system that mandates loan originators to prioritize consumers' best interests.
Creating a system that mandates loan originators to prioritize consumers' best interests is one of the NMLS-R's purposes.

61. (b) qualified mortgages.
Limiting points and fees charged to borrowers to help prevent excessive costs is a key feature of qualified mortgages.

62. (c) To give the lender information that may determine if the borrower qualifies for a foreclosure alternative
During the pre-foreclosure period, a borrower may submit a loss mitigation application for the lender to evaluate whether the borrower qualifies for any foreclosure alternative.

63. (c) VOD
The Verification of Deposit (VOD) form confirms the availability and source of funds the borrower intends to use for the down payment and closing costs.

64. (b) It is a discriminatory practice that is prohibited by the FHA.
This is an example of redlining, a discriminatory practice that is prohibited by the FHA.

65. (a) 8
MLOs need to complete 8 hours of CE during each renewal period.

66. (a) measures the relationship between the mortgage loan amount and the property's appraised value or purchase price.
The LTV measures the relationship between the mortgage loan amount and the property's appraised value or purchase price.

67. (b) Borrower violates a due-on-sale clause
Lenders' first notice of default can only be sent when a borrower is 120 days delinquent on payments, OR the borrower violated the due-on-sale clause, OR another lienholder has begun a foreclosure action.

68. (b) Assessing borrowers' information to estimate their potential qualifying mortgage amount
Lenders assess borrowers' information to estimate their potential qualifying mortgage amount during the pre-qualification phase.

69. (a) Disparate impact
This is the definition of disparate impact.

70. (b) Because the gap is fewer than 6 months, Sabrina can qualify with her current job verification, as long as she meets other criteria.
Because the gap is fewer than 6 months, Sabrina can qualify with her current job verification, as long as she meets other criteria.

71. (b) It believes the state's existing licensing system fails to meet the SAFE Act's minimum requirements.
When the CFPB believes a state's existing licensing system fails to meet the SAFE Act's minimum requirements, it may deem it necessary to establish and maintain that state's MLO licensing system.

72. (b) MLO
The MLO is responsible for ensuring loan applications re completely accurately and thoroughly.

73. (b) FHA will not insure a mortgage when a potential buyer contracts to buy a home within 90 days of the previous sale.
When a potential buyer contracts to buy a home within 90 days of a previous sale on the home, FHA will not insure the mortgage. This is an anti-flipping provision.

74. (c) occupancy fraud.
This is an example of occupancy fraud.

75. (b) 3%
When borrowers put less than 10% down on a conforming loan, seller concessions are capped at 3% of the home's purchase price.

76. (c) A museum
The cost approach is useful when appraising properties that are not frequently bought or sold, such as unique or specialized properties, like museums or hospitals.

77. (d) negligence.
A breach in one's duty of care, such as errors, omissions, and failures to fulfill responsibilities, is a type of negligence.

78. (d) 96.5%
The maximum LTV on an FHA loan used for a home purchase is 96.5%.

79. (b) Fiduciary
MLOs have a fiduciary relationship with their clients.

80. (a) initiates the process of securing a mortgage loan for a borrower in exchange for some form of compensation.
A mortgage loan originator initiates the process of securing a mortgage loan for a borrower in exchange for compensation.

81. (d) an assessment of the borrower's likelihood of repaying the loan and the property's value as collateral.
An underwriter's credit decision is based on an assessment of the borrower's likelihood of repaying the loan and the property's value as collateral.

82. (c) Retake both the pre-license education and the NMLS SAFE exam, and then submit a new license application.
Molly will need to retake both the pre-license education and the NMLS SAFE exam, and then submit a new license application.

83. (d) Another lienholder has already begun foreclosure action against Ted, and the lender is joining that action.
Lenders' first notice of default can only be sent when a borrower is 120 days delinquent on payments, OR the borrower violated the due-on-sale clause, OR another lienholder has begun a foreclosure action.

84. (b) gather information and evidence as part of the investigation.
When a consumer files a complaint and an investigation begins, the SAFE Act permits state agencies to gather information and evidence as part of the investigation.

85. (a) No tolerance
The no tolerance threshold applies to fees that can change from Loan Estimate to final Closing Disclosure without restrictions.

86. (c) have no disqualifying issues.
One condition an MLO must satisfy before taking advantage of the TA provision is that the MLO must have no disqualifying issues.

87. (b) reverse occupancy fraud.
This is an example of reverse occupancy fraud.

88. (a) Lance's lender has agreed that the property may be sold for less than Lance's principal loan balance.
A short sale is an agreement in lieu of foreclosure between the lender and borrower in which the property is sold for less than the principal balance.

89. (a) omitting relevant details about loan terms.
All MLOs are prohibited from omitting relevant details about loan terms.

90. (a) convert the loan to a standard amortizing fixed-rate or adjustable-rate loan.
Borrowers with interest-only loans typically convert their loans to a standard amortizing loan after the interest-only period ends.

91. (a) Applying for a loan on someone else's behalf to conceal the true buyer's identity
Applying for a loan on someone else's behalf to conceal the true buyer's identity is one variety of a straw buyer scheme.

92. (c) Mortgage Servicing Disclosure Statement
The Mortgage Servicing Disclosure Statement informs the borrower of the lender's intent to service the loan or transfer it to another lender

93. (c) simple assumption
With an FHA simple assumption, the new borrower takes over the original borrower's payments, but the original borrower remains liable if new borrower defaults

94. (d) address change
An address change would require an NMLS-R profile update.

95. (c) generally non-binding
The pre-qualification phase is generally non-binding.

96. (b) Details projected interest rates, monthly payments, and total closing costs
The Loan Estimate details a borrower's estimated interest rates, monthly payments, and total closing costs for a particular loan product.

97. (d) A supervisory connection where the MLO provides training, guidance, and work oversight to the processor/underwriter by the MLO
Actual nexus is a supervisory connection where the MLO provides training, guidance, and work oversight to the processor/underwriter by the MLO.

98. (a) Mortgage interest from the day of closing until the end of the month
Borrower prepaids include property tax portion, homeowners insurance premium portion, mortgage interest from the day of closing until the end of the month, PMI premium portion, and escrow account funding to cover future property tax and insurance payments.

99. (c) an installment loans' monthly payments
Fannie Mae/Freddie Mac allow the exclusion of installment loans' monthly payments in DTI calculations when 10 or fewer payments remain.

100. (a) 72%
The formula to use is: Principal Loan Amount ÷ Purchase Price OR Appraised Value = LTV. Use the lesser of the purchase price or appraised value. So: $450,000 ÷ $625,000 = 0.72 = 72%

Comprehensive Practice Exam II Answer Key

1. (b) Unfair, Deceptive or Abusive Acts or Practices
UDAAP stands for Unfair, Deceptive or Abusive Acts or Practices.

2. (d) QMs
QMs protect lenders against borrower lawsuits, serving particularly as a "safe harbor" in proving lender compliance with ability-to-repay rules.

3. (c) originating loans as employees of non-depository institutions.
Per federal regulations, individuals who perform loan origination activities are required to be licensed when originating loans as employees of non-depository institutions.

4. (b) borrowers and lenders work directly together to create new mortgages.
In the primary mortgage market, borrowers and lenders work directly together to create new mortgages.

5. (d) The financial advantages or benefits that a borrower is expected to gain from refinancing an existing mortgage loan into a new one
The tangible net benefit is the financial advantages or benefits that a borrower is expected to gain from refinancing an existing mortgage loan into a new one.

6. (b) Vacant lot purchase loan
RESPA exemptions include loans to purchase vacant lots.

7. (c) $136,250
This scenario requires three calculations. First, calculate the loan amount: Purchase Price x LTV = $625,000 x .75 = $468,750. Then calculate the down payment needed: Purchase Price – Loan Amount = $625,000 -- $468,750 = $156,250. The subtract the earnest money already paid: Down Payment Amount – Earnest Money = $156,250 -- $20,000 = $136,250.

8. (d) written cybersecurity programs outlining how they will protect the security, confidentiality, and integrity of consumer information.
The Gramm-Leach-Bliley Act Safeguards Rule requires financial institutions to develop written cybersecurity programs outlining how they will protect the security, confidentiality, and integrity of consumer information.

9. (c) Actual nexus
Actual nexus is a connection in which a supervisor provides training, guidance, compliance review, and work assignment for processor / underwriter.

10. (d) Federal Home Loan Bank System (FHLB)
The Federal Home Loan Bank System (FHLB), created in 1932, is designed to bolster lending in local communities by providing stable, low-cost funding to financial institutions for home mortgage and economic development loans.

11. (a) After the title search, the title report notes any outstanding liens, mortgages, or encumbrances on the property.
The title report provides a detailed history of the property's ownership and any associated legal issues, including any outstanding liens, mortgages, or encumbrances on the property.

12. (a) obscuring information so a consumer takes out an unaffordable loan.
Regulators use UDAAP standards to evaluate all mortgage-related entities for practices such as obscuring information so a consumer takes out an unaffordable loan.

13. (b) is a numerical value or percentage of the loan amount that is used to calculate the annual PMI premium.
An MI factor is a numerical value or percentage of the loan amount that is used to calculate the annual PMI premium.

14. (a) discount points.
Discount points are optional fees paid upfront to lower the interest rate on a mortgage; each point typically costs 1% of the loan amount.

15. (d) Lenders must select independent appraisers with the necessary qualifications and experience to perform reliable appraisals.
Lenders must select independent appraisers with the necessary qualifications and experience to perform reliable appraisals.

16. (c) promissory note
A promissory note is a legally binding contract between a borrower and a lender outlining the borrower's promise to repay the loan amount to the lender under specific terms and conditions.

17. (c) Fraud for profit
In a fraud for profit scheme, individuals often work together to gain money for themselves via the transaction process.

18. (c) current (2023) baseline loan limit for single-unit properties of $726,200 in most areas.
Fannie Mae/Freddie Mac key conforming loan standards include a current (2023) baseline loan limit for single-unit properties of $726,200 in most areas.

19. (b) $1,458.33
The formula for period interest is: (Annual Interest Rate in Decimal Form ÷ Number of Compounding Periods) x Principal Balance. $(0.07 \div 12)$ x $250,000 = $1,458.33

20. (a) receipt of public assistance.
The ECOA prohibits lenders and MLOs from discriminating against borrowers based on factors such as receipt of public assistance.

21. (b) Loan counseling
Loan counseling is considered a mortgage brokerage service.

22. (a) alimony
Monthly debt obligations in DTI calculations includes PITI, revolving debts, installment debts, alimony and / or child support.

23. (c) The assets are liquid and have been held in the account for 60 days or more.
Liquid assets are generally considered seasoned when they have been held in an account for 60 days or more.

24. (c) misrepresents their holdings to inflate their finances to improve their chances of qualifying.
An example of asset fraud is when a mortgage loan applicant misrepresents their holdings to inflate their finances to improve their chances of qualifying.

25. (d) home purchase loans only.
The CFPB's Home Loan Toolkit booklet is required for home purchase loans only.

26. (c) $84,000
The CLTV max is 95% and the first mortgage is 80% of the purchase price, so the second mortgage has to be 15% of the purchase price. $560,000 x .15 = $84,000

27. (b) buys loans to provide local banks with federal money to finance home mortgages.
Fannie Mae, among other things, buys loans to provide local banks with federal money to finance home mortgages.

28. (a) fees for property inspections
Borrowers can shop for property inspectors, so those fees are exempt from RESPA disclosure requirements.

29. (c) non-judicial foreclosure with recording / publication requirement
This is an example of non-judicial foreclosure with recording / publication requirement.

30. (b) MLO license violations
States are required to report MLOs' license violations and enforcement actions taken to NMLS-R.

31. (a) Property taxes
Property taxes are prorated at closing between buyer and seller.

32. (d) exceed FHFA loan limits.
Non-conforming loans are conventional loans that do not follow Fannie Mae / Freddie Mac rules. They exceed FHFA loan limits, , allowing borrowers to access higher loan amounts

33. (b) 35%
The formula for DTI is: All Recurring Monthly Debt ÷ Gross Monthly Income. Gloria's monthly debt is $2,450 (PITI, car loan, student loan, and credit card bills). Her gross monthly income is $7,083.33. $2,450 ÷ $7.083.33 = 0.345 = 35%

34. (c) no more than 30 days
A SAR report must be filed no more than 30 days after initial detection of suspicious activity or thresholds that may require an investigation.

35. (c) Protect homebuyers from excessive PMI charges
The Homeowners Protection Act protects homebuyers from excessive private mortgage insurance (PMI) charges, ensuring they do not pay PMI longer than necessary.

36. (d) Home inspectors
Home inspectors are considered a settlement service provider under RESPA.

37. (c) is a centralized licensing system for individuals and companies in the non-depository financial services sector.
The Nationwide Multistate Licensing System (NMLS) is a centralized licensing system for individuals and companies in the non-depository financial services sector.

38. (b) rate lock
In a rate lock agreement, the lender promises to hold a certain interest rate and specific number of points for a borrower for a specified period while the loan application processes. It protects the borrower from rate fluctuations during the loan application process.

39. (d) Loan consummation
Loan consummation is defined as the point at which a borrower becomes contractually obligated to the lender on a loan. It refers to the borrower's agreement to the loan terms.

40. (c) 62
Reverse mortgages are specifically designed for seniors, i.e., aged 62 and older.

41. (a) within three business days of loan application
Lenders must provide the Affiliated Business Arrangement Disclosure within 3 business days of the borrower's loan application submission when the lender requires borrowers to use a specific business affiliate.

42. (c) A financial institution that primarily accepts savings deposits and makes mortgage and other loans

A thrift, aka savings and loan association, is a financial institution that primarily accepts savings deposits and makes mortgage and other loans.

43. (b) USDA

The United States Department of Agriculture (USDA) loan program offers two types: USDA guaranteed loans and USDA direct loans.

44. (d) Using the word "fixed" in advertising to describe a rate or payment unless it genuinely remains fixed for the entire loan term

The MAP Rule expressly prohibits using the word "fixed" in advertising to describe a rate or payment unless it genuinely remains fixed for the entire loan term.

45. (a) extraordinary events beyond anyone involved in the transaction's control.

Extraordinary events beyond anyone involved in the transaction's control, such as a natural disaster that necessitates another appraisal, might require a lender to issue the borrower a revised LE.

46. (a) qualified mortgage

A qualified mortgage meets certain CFPB standards, ensuring that lenders make loans that borrowers have ability to repay.

47. (a) Providing false information to obtain someone's personal or confidential information from financial institutions

Providing false information to obtain someone's personal or confidential information from financial institutions is known as pretexting.

48. (d) Construction loan

After approval, construction loan funds are typically disbursed to the builder in stages (aka "draws") as construction reaches specific milestones. Each stage requires inspection and approval.

49. (c) Borrowers who cannot afford their loan can sue creditors they feel did not properly determine their ability to repay.

They can sue creditors when they realize they cannot afford their loan *and* they feel creditor did not properly determine their ability to repay.

50. (a) A mortgage with total closing costs, points, and fees that exceed 5% of the total loan amount threshold

Total closing costs, fees, and points that exceed 5% of the total loan amount threshold adjusted annually for inflation results in a high-cost mortgage.

51. (b) agency MBS package

An agency MBS is an investment type that is issued by government-sponsored enterprises (GSEs). They typically consist of conforming loans and tend to be lower risk, lower yield.

52. (a) Servicing Transfer Statement

A Servicing Transfer Statement notifies the borrower that the lender is transferring loan servicing rights to another entity.

53. (c) Business, commercial, and agricultural loans

Business, commercial, and agricultural loans are exempt from RESPA requirements.

54. (d) Collecting required documents from borrowers and passing them along to an MLO

Unlicensed individuals can gather and distribute information to authorized parties. This includes collecting necessary documents from borrowers (like W-2s, pay stubs, bank statements) and passing them to the licensed MLO for review.

55. (b) When refinancing a first mortgage and a second mortgage exists
In a loan subordination, a lender agrees to position their loan claim below another lender's claim in terms of priority for debt repayment in event of default. It is most often relevant when refinancing a first mortgage and the holder of second mortgage allows their loan to remain in the secondary position.

56. (b) Temporary QMs were created to provide a transition period when QM rules were established under Dodd-Frank.
Temporary QMs were created to provide a transition period when QM rules were established under Dodd-Frank to help ensure continued access to credit while the mortgage industry adapted to the new QM standards.

57. (a) She works at a depository institution and is registered with the NMLS-R.
Loan originators who work at depository institutions must be registered but they do not have to be licensed.

58. (d) An MLO providing a Loan Estimate (LE) of settlement costs to borrowers no more than 3 days after receiving a loan application
A Loan Estimate must be provided to the borrower no more than 3 days after the lender receives the borrower's loan application and no fewer than 7 days prior to loan consummation.

59. (c) Redlining
The Fair Housing Act (FHA) prohibits discrimination in housing-related transactions, including redlining, which is the act of refusing loans based on neighborhood characteristics.

60.(c) A 2-1 buydown
A 2-1 buydown is a financing technique that reduces the mortgage interest rate in a stepped fashion during the loan's initial years, after which it reverts to a standard rate for the remaining loan term.

61. (a) The number of percentage points the lender adds to the index to determine the ARM interest rate after the initial rate period ends
The margin is the number of percentage points the lender adds to the index to determine the ARM interest rate after the initial rate period ends. It's generally measured in basis points in which one basis point is equal to 1/100 of 1%.

62. (a) ECOA
ECOA is primarily concerned with fairness in lending practices.

63. (c) acting with honesty, integrity, and fairness in all professional dealings.
The National Association of Mortgage Brokers' (NAMB) established comprehensive Code of Ethics includes acting with honesty, integrity, and fairness in all professional dealings.

64. (a) To ensure that the buyer and seller are responsible for their respective portions of certain costs based on the closing date
Prorations and adjustments are made to ensure that the buyer and seller are responsible for their respective portions of certain costs based on the closing date.

65. (d) prevent deceptive advertising practices in mortgage lending.
The CFPB's Reg N aims to prevent deceptive advertising practices in mortgage lending.

66. (b) Air loan
An air loan is when individuals or groups fabricate loan applications for nonexistent properties or for properties they do not own. This is a type of fraud for profit.

67. (c) no more than 80% of American median income.
To participate in *HomeReady* and *HomePossible* low down payment programs, a borrower's income must be no more than 80% of American median income.

68. (c) must wait 30 days to retake the exam.
An applicant who fails the NMLS SAFE Exam on the first two attempts must wait 30 days to retake the exam.

69. (b) Borrowers must qualify on both the housing ratio and the DTI ratio to be approved for a loan.
Borrowers must qualify on both the housing ratio and the DTI ratio to be approved for a loan.

70. (a) Consumers must give their explicit consent to use electronic records and signatures.
The E-SIGN Act requires consumers' explicit consent to use electronic records and signatures.

71. (a) Estimate its potential income and subtract its operating expenses
To calculate the building's NOI, Catherine will estimate its potential income and subtract its operating expenses.

72. (d) detected compliance violations to the applicable regulatory entity
Mortgage companies are expected to report all detected compliance violations to the applicable regulatory entity, aka *self-reporting.*

73. (c) streamlines the transition for federally-registered MLOs seeking state licensure to work at a state-licensed mortgage company.
The new temporary authority to operate (TA) provision streamlines the transition for federally-registered MLOs seeking state licensure to work at a state-licensed mortgage company, as well as state-licensed MLOs seeking licensure in another state.

74. (a) consideration amounts based on the percentage of applications that close successfully.
MLOs are permitted to receive payments based on their percentage of applications that close successfully.

75. (d) distinguishes him from other MLOs and helps track his conduct.
An MLO's unique identifier distinguishes that MLO from other MLOs and helps track their conduct.

76. (a) Donors must be related to the loan applicant by blood, marriage, adoption, or legal guardianship.
Donors must be related to the loan applicant by blood, marriage, adoption, or legal guardianship.

77. (b) The CFPB believes the state's existing licensing system fails to meet the SAFE Act's minimum requirements.
The CFPB has authority to establish and maintain a state's licensing system when the CFPB determines the state's existing licensing system fails to meet the SAFE Act's minimum requirements.

78. (a) introduced measures to enhance national security and prevent terrorist activities.
A legislative response to the terrorist attacks of September 11, 2001, the USA PATRIOT Act introduced measures to enhance national security and prevent future terrorist activities.

79. (c) Conventional loans on primary residences with less than 10% down have a limit of 3%.
Conventional loans on primary residences with less than 10% down have a seller contribution limit of 3%.

80. (c) Dodd-Frank Act
One of the many provisions of the Dodd-Frank Act is that is placed limitations on mortgage pre-payment penalties.

81. (a) expressed in the same font and type size as the interest rate.
Truth in Lending Act (TILA) imposes rules and requirements for lender advertising, such as clear and conspicuous disclosures of important terms and conditions. When used, the APR must be expressed in same font and type size as the interest rate.

82. (a) covers non-depository financial service industries.
The NMLS is a centralized licensing system for individuals and companies that covers non-depository financial service industries.

83. (b) establishing ability-to-repay conditions such as minimum underwriting requirements for residential purchase mortgages.
Dodd-Frank introduced new mortgage lending standards and processes to avoid risky lending practices that contributed to the housing crash in 2008, such as setting minimum underwriting requirements for residential purchase mortgages.

84. (d) the state can still enact stricter licensing requirements within its jurisdiction.
In these cases, the CFPB's licensing system does not entirely replace the state's regulatory authority. The state can still enact stricter licensing requirements within jurisdiction as long as those requirements meet minimum federal standards.

85. (a) Mortgage loan originator
A mortgage loan originator initiates the process of securing a home loan for a borrower in exchange for some sort of compensation.

86. (d) Company surety bond
The company surety bond is the most common method.

87. (c) sets the maximum increase for each adjustment period.
The periodic cap sets maximum increase for each adjustment period.

88. (a) details a company's mortgage activity from the previous quarter.
The *Mortgage Call Report* details a company's mortgage activity from the previous quarter.

89. (c) telemarketers are required to check the list at least once every 31 days.
Telemarketers are required to check the list at least once every 31 days.

90. (a) discrepancy between a borrower's reported income and their employment history, industry norms, or standard wage levels for occupation.
A potential red flag for income and employment fraud is a discrepancy between a borrower's reported income and their employment history, industry norms, or standard wage levels for occupation

91. (b) Attempting to reach a mutual understanding with a borrower regarding loan terms
Attempting to reach a mutual understanding with a borrower regarding loan terms is an activity that is considered "offering or negotiating loan terms."

92. (b) 30-year fixed rate loan
A 30-year fixed rate loan is a traditional mortgage.

93. (c) an unfavorable decision against an applicant based in whole or part on credit information.
An adverse action related to FCRA is an unfavorable decision against an applicant based in whole or part on credit information.

94. (d) set the criteria for licensing eligibility, education, training, continuing education, and testing.
Among other things, Regulation H set the criteria for licensing eligibility, education, training, continuing education, and testing.

95. (b) Some states may require more than the federally-required hours of CE coursework.
Some states may require more than the federally-required hours of CE coursework to renew an MLO license.

96. (b) 8
The minimum required CE coursework to renew a license is 8 hours annually of NMLS-approved CE courses.

97. (a) Counseling consumers about loan rates and terms
Activities requiring a loan originator license include offering/negotiating rates / terms, counseling consumers about loan rates / terms, and taking loan applications.

98. (c) do not need to be licensed but do need to be registered.
Loan originators who work for depository institutions generally do not need licensure but do need to be registered.

99. (b) Pleading guilty to a felony for breach of trust
An applicant who pled guilty to a felony for breach of trust is grounds for rejecting an application for an MLO license.

100. (a) 5%
The formula to use here is: Fully Indexed Rate = Margin + Index Rate. The margin is 2% and the teaser rate is 3% for the first 3 years. Added together, that's 5% for the fully indexed rate, the rate that goes into effect until the next adjustment date.

Appendix: Performance Programs Company's Test-Taking Tips

Introduction

Effective test-taking is more of an art and a practiced skill than a guarantee of success. Students preparing for the NMLS SAFE exam should take exam preparation very seriously. Since there are no guarantees to passing, it behooves students to optimize their chances of a successful outcome. Simply put, this is accomplished by purposeful, intensive study and question-taking practice. The harder you study and prepare, the better your odds become of passing.

There are a few beneficial pointers that can be made to improve your overall test-preparation effort. These are contained in the following compilation of tips assimilated by professional educators and test-prep experts. Please take the time to peruse these observations as they will serve to better your overall chances of passing. And in any case, we wish you the best of success!!

Make and use flashcards

Understanding tested MLO terminology is a large part of passing your exam. As you prepare for the license examination, study. Don't just memorize specific definitions. Memorize contexts of content as well. The more you know about "the environment" of each word, in addition to the term's specific definition, the more likely you will be able to use that information to lead you to the correct exam response.

Take notes

As you read and study, take notes. Often, just the act of writing information down helps cement it in your mind. Visualizing how your notes about a particular topic appeared on the page is helpful for students who appreciate visual cues.

Immerse yourself

Form or join a study group, review topics with friends and colleagues, chat with MLO experts, and read loan origination blogs. In other words, immerse yourself in the world of lending. To obtain a deeper understanding of a term or concept, Google it (using whatever search engine you employ with your computer or phone). This will shed light on varying perspectives or iterations of a term's meaning.

Prepare a "date and key quantity" sheet

As a memory device, students are well-advised to create a "date and key quantity sheet" to be able to efficiently refer back to in future study sessions. This particular summary sheet includes facts and data that are very commonly tested, including deadlines, dates, and quantities.

Some examples:

- CE requirement in hours
- Deadline for submitting loan estimates to applicants
- Definition and examples of qualified mortgages

- LTV calculation
- debt to income ratio calculation

Plan study time

Set a goal for yourself. Avoid the trap of just "studying until you're ready." Instead, determine the date you want to apply to take your exam and set aside enough time to finish your test preparations by that date. Try to limit how long each of your study / cram sessions will be. Study periods should not be too much in excess of one hour – after which time students begin to lose concentration and attention span.

Finally, select your study environment so as to avoid distractions and interruptions!

Reading is not studying

It may seem odd, but *reading* is not *studying*. Studying is an active process. Creating and reviewing your flashcards is studying. Develop study guides. Teach someone about difficult or complex topics. Relate what you are learning to your own experiences or the MLO topics you hear about in conversations or on the news. Create your own memory devices such as mnemonics, rhyming, acronyms, or images. These can be invaluable ways to remember cut and dry facts and figures.

Dissect exam questions

Take and review as many practice exams as you can find. Take and re-take quizzes in your textbook and any exam prep resource that you can find. Write down the topics you tend to miss questions on, then re-study those topics. When reviewing a missed question, be sure to understand the correct response and why the incorrect answers were not right.

Review the exam provider's handbook

A wealth of knowledge exists in the exam provider's test preparation resources. Review these materials thoroughly! You will learn the general topic areas covered and the relative weighting of a given subject.

Exam prep materials generally present the key content of a topic and how many questions will appear on your exam, particularly if the resource is state-specific. The testing service candidate handbook will further describe how your exam is scored. This knowledge will help you to understand how to answer questions you may not be sure about. In other words, you should know whether or not you are penalized for wrong answers.

It's almost time! Your exam is tomorrow. What do you do?

Candidate handbooks will provide full instructions about the exam day itself—what you can and can't take with you, how long you have to complete the exam, and how long you have to wait before you get your results, and so forth.

Immediately prior to the exam, you should limit how much to cram. At some point, nothing new should be introduced into your mind. In short, you either know it or you don't. Make a quick final pass-through, then leave it alone.

Okay, it's exam time. How do I avoid being a nervous wreck?

To alleviate stress, you can do a couple of things:

- Drive by the testing center so you know where it is and how long it will take to get there. On test day, allow extra time for traffic snarls, etc.
- Be sure you have an acceptable calculator (information will appear in the exam provider's handbook). Note that some providers don't allow you to bring a calculator in. Instead, you'll use one they provide or one embedded on the computer you'll use to take the exam.
- Assemble everything you need to take with you. Include test registration documents, required identification, a calculator, and a sweater or light jacket. Put everything in a bag or your car.
- Eat a well-rounded meal the evening before your exam and get a good night's sleep.
- Most exam providers give you a few minutes before you begin the exam to acquaint yourself with how the system works. You can answer a few practice questions, use the calculator, etc. Use this time not only to familiarize yourself with the environment but also to take a few deep breaths and get comfortable. You can do this!
- Budget your time. Know how many questions you must answer (more information from the provider's handbook).
- <u>Read every question carefully</u>. Be sure you understand what it's asking, in particular if the question is in the negative ("which of the following is NOT....," or "which of the following is NOT TRUE....". Then read EVERY possible response before you respond. Exam providers generally want you to select the BEST answer, not the only possible answer.

Answering questions

In most circumstances, you should answer every question. You will certainly receive a score deduction if you don't answer a question, but if you guess, you could guess right. So you come out ahead by answering every question.

This issue raises the question: "how much time should I spend on a question?" This becomes easy math. Know how much time you have for a given section and how many questions you must answer in that section. Then divide the number of questions into your time allocation to get your per-question time allowance. Do not stray too much from that estimate as you complete the section!

If you aren't sure of the answer to a question, keep these tips in mind:

- Are there responses that you know are incorrect? Eliminate them. If you eliminate two responses, you've increased your odds of correctly answering the question to 50/50!
- Dissect the remaining possible responses. Are there key words that indicate a correct or incorrect answer?
    - Terms like "always," "never," and "only" MAY indicate an incorrect response because seldom are things as definitive as these terms suggest.
    - Terms such as "usually," "generally," "typically," "most," and "some" are more likely to appear in the correct response.

- If you see a response that includes something you've never heard of, don't choose it! If you didn't see that information in your preparations, it's unlikely to be the correct response.
- Be particularly cautious about organization names. "The Department of Housing and Urban Development" sounds suspiciously like "The Division of Housing and Development."

After the exam

Depending on the exam provider and state, you may know right away if you passed. You may also receive a report from the testing center that details topic area scores.

If you're not successful on your first attempt, don't panic…and understand that you're not alone. Real exams can be notoriously difficult. As soon as you leave the testing center, write some notes to yourself about questions you recall struggling with or topics that you may need to review.

Then, dig in again. Use the textbook, your notes, and the information you remember from the exam and keep studying. Your career is far more important than not passing the test!

Appendix: MLO Licensing-Related Websites

MLO Testing Handbook
Make sure to download and read the NMLS candidate participant booklet to fully understand the entire test taking process.
https://nmlsportal.csbs.org/csm?id=kb_article_view&sysparm_article=6786&sys_kb_id=f143ff6a1b044ad0839587fce54bcb84

Key National Contacts

Nationwide Multistate Licensing System
855-665-7123
https://mortgage.nationwidelicensingsystem.org/Pages/default.aspx

Prometric Testing Service
7941 Corporate Dr.
Nottingham, MD 21236
866-776-6387
https://www.prometric.com/NMLS

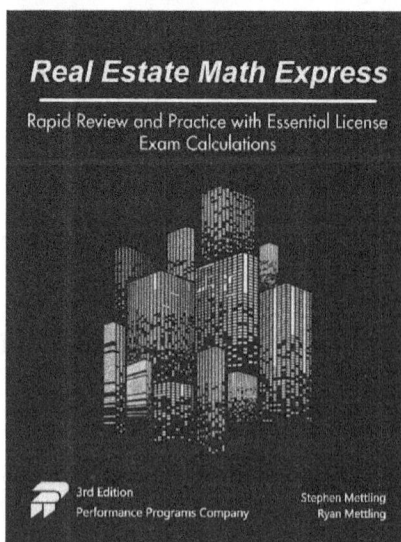

www.ingramcontent.com/pod-product-compliance
Lightning Source LLC
Chambersburg PA
CBHW080544220326
41599CB00032B/6356